# The politics of freedom of information

MANCHESTER
1824

Manchester University Press

# The politics of freedom of information

## How and why governments pass laws that threaten their power

*Ben Worthy*

Manchester University Press

Published by Manchester University Press
Altrincham Street, Manchester M1 7JA, UK
www.manchesteruniversitypress.co.uk

*British Library Cataloguing-in-Publication Data is available*

ISBN 978 0 7190 9767 6 hardback
ISBN 978 1 5261 5175 9 paperback

First published by Manchester University Press in hardback 2017

This edition published 2020

Typeset by Servis Filmsetting Ltd, Stockport, Cheshire

For Maria and Marlène

# Contents

# Tables

# Acknowledgements

This book has been more than a decade in the making. I want to start by saying a thank you to Craig Thomas, who first taught me politics in 1997 and informed me, quite rightly, that I was lazy. The original idea for the book began as a PhD long ago in 2003, and I want to thank Prof. Martin Burch for gently suggesting all those years ago that I look into the Freedom of Information Act and for being the greatest supervisor you could ever wish for. I'm grateful to all the experts, officials and politicians who helped me back then and made this study possible, some of whom have to remain nameless.

Since my PhD a whole host of people have helped me turn this into a book that, as my brother put it, 'you can read'. Prof. Robert Hazell offered me the chance to work on FOI for five years at University College London's Constitution Unit, taught me to question everything and gave me the opportunity to work with brilliant people such as Sarah Holsen, Mark Glover and Gabrielle Bourke. Prof. Alastair Roberts has given me constant encouragement and advice, and handed me the keys to writing a good article over a Starbucks in Tavistock Square. Academics and practitioners from the transparency community across the world have helped me with their thoughts, ideas and tips, including Greg Michener in Brazil, Tom Mclean, Stephan Grimmelikhaujsen, Prashant Sharma, Jenny de Fine Licht and Daniel Berliner. Lynn Wyeth, Paul Gibbons and Gavin Freeguard all offered thoughts and suggestions.

My colleagues at Birkbeck College constantly encouraged me with fine words about why so niche a topic mattered. I owe a big thank you to everyone in the Department of Politics, in particular to Deborah Mabbett, who recommended Murray Edelman, Dermot Hodson, who hinted at the institutional angle and Alex Colas and Rosie Campbell for their proofing help.

Special thanks go to Prof. Maeve McDonagh at Cork, who read over the section on Ireland, and Martin Rosenbaum, who was kind enough to cast an eagle eye over the UK case. Steven Price in New Zealand and Shekhar Singh in India both plied me with vital documents and articles. I'm grateful also for Tony Mason at Manchester University Press for his patience, enthusiasm and support.

My family supplied me with mildly perplexed encouragement. My parents updated me on FOI stories in the news, my mother-in-law Franca expressed mild amusement, while my niece, Emmy, and nephew, Salvatore, kept me joyfully distracted. The first draft of this book was written in the final stages of a pregnancy and re-drafted to the excited gurgles of a three-month-old little girl. This book is dedicated with all my love to my wife Maria and my little girl Marlène, who make it all worthwhile. I hope I'm better at writing than at changing nappies.

# 1

# FOI: hard to resist and hard to escape

Freedom of Information (FOI) laws are difficult to resist in opposition but hard to escape from once in power. A commitment to an FOI law sends out strong messages of radicalism, change and empowerment that new governments find difficult to resist. However, when politicians regret their promises, as they often quickly do, the same symbolism makes the reforms difficult to escape from.

To make the picture more complex, FOI laws bring little external advantage and generate internal unhappiness. One of the central paradoxes of FOI laws is that they are symbolically resonant but useless in electoral terms: politicians gain 'credibility' but not votes. Within government, FOI laws reach across the whole of government, running against the natural tendency of bureaucracy to be secretive (Weber 1991). Such laws carry the potential to delve deep into bureaucracies' work, triggering investigation of official decisions and procedures by those hostile to them. So how and why do governments pass them?

FOI laws are, it is argued, frequently passed out of naivety or inattention by inexperienced and new governments responding to reformist impulses from within or without or seeking to create a new 'open' approach after a scandal (Berliner 2014, Darch and Underwood 2010). Politicians have many motives for introducing FOI, from the simple politics of wrong footing or neutralising opponents to the longer-term, calculating intention of securing access to information when they are out of power (Berliner 2014). Context is also key, as laws are frequently passed amid wider change or as a response to a particular problem. As well as calculation and context there are a series of symbolic pressures. Politicians can, at least in the short term, earn a form of 'moral capital' from supporting openness (Birchall 2014; Michener 2009).

However, the conventional wisdom is that politicians rapidly fall out of love with transparency and the potential for exposure, uncertainty and unpleasant surprises it brings (Berliner 2014). Opening up equates to a loss of control and a potential empowerment of enemies and critics. So once in office, actors seek to stall, delay and water down commitments: the classic trajectory of FOI reform is one of survival through dilution.

## Symbolism versus resistance

The story of FOI is of a clash between the power of symbolism and the resistance of institutions, between abstract ideals and concrete structures. The radical, modernising and democratic symbolism of FOI helps put it onto the agenda, sometimes gradually and sometimes quickly (Fenster 2012b). The move towards FOI, particularly in the countries studied in this book, is also shaped by long-term social and political changes, as the case for secrecy gradually erodes amid institutional reform, changing societal attitudes and technological advances. Pressure builds as parties and leaders commit themselves, especially when a commitment to FOI plays into the radical self-image of reformists and modernisers.

Governments quickly regret their promise once in office. However, dropping outright a promised policy that speaks of 'freedom', 'information' or a 'right' is problematic. The symbolism, radicalism and 'moral' angle of FOI, and even its resonant name, make it difficult to get rid of it quietly. The same values it embodies make the accusation of betrayal easy and somewhat dangerous. Buoyed by an alliance of institutional and extra-institutional 'opinion formers', the symbolic power frequently cuts off any line of retreat. What happens instead is that FOI proposals are stalled, blocked and channelled away as different factions seek to submerge the radical ideals in detail and manoeuvres behind closed doors while others, inside and out, fight for it to stay in its original form. What then emerges on the statute book, after lengthy internal battles, is a compromise.

## Symbolic politics and laws

FOI laws fit with a wide range of policies and democratic activities that are laden with symbolic value, irrespective of their practical significance. Edelman (1985) likened political activity to a 'passing parade of abstract symbols' replete with 'easy objects upon which to displace … strong anxieties and hopes' (5). Even voting, the most basic of democratic actions, is a 'ritual act' intended to 'express discontents and enthusiasm' (3), and most democratic institutions are 'largely symbolic and expressive in function' (19).

While some symbolic activities serve as hermeneutic short cuts, others 'evoke emotions' more remote from reality (Edelman 1985, 5). Cobb and Elder (1973) created a broad typology of symbolic items, from the 'broadly applicable' and 'salient' objects, such as flags, down to more focused political norms or institutions. All symbols are either a 'threat or reassurance' (Edelman 1985, 7, 11). Symbolic actions frequently 'call forth a larger and more complex set of ideas than the basic meaning of the action' (Hart 1995, 386). They are 'primarily a vehicle for conveying a broader message' that 'highlight a symbolic purpose'. Such actions frequently run into difficulties when the ideal moves to policy substance, particularly as the symbolism is frequently 'decoded' or challenged by the media (386). Such symbolic acts and policies can drive new agendas and 'challenge authority relationships' as seen, for example, with the global spread of the human rights agenda (Brysk 1995, 561).

Edelman (1985) highlights laws as peculiarly symbolic objects that are often created through a mix of 'symbolic effect and rational reflection' (41). They 'suggest vigorous activity' and can cover 'noisy attacks on trivia' and represent 'prolonged, repeated, well publicised attention to a significant problem which may never be solved' (37–39). The names of laws themselves 'are important symbols' with 'subtle and potent' effects on interpretation (206). Stolz (2007) similarly argues that legislation 'in reality carries both instrumental (tangible) and expressive (symbolism)' aspects (311). Certain issues appear particularly conducive to symbolic laws, especially those that send out signals to an audience about their behaviour or concern the 'public designation of morality' (Gusfield 1967, 177). These include criminal justice issues, the war on drugs (Stolz 2007), domestic violence (Stolz 1999) and alcohol consumption (Gusfield 1967).

The importance of such symbolic laws lies not just in their enforcement or 'manifest significance' but also in 'what the action connotes for the audience that views it' (Gusfield 1967, 177; Gusfield 1968). Symbolic legislation sends signals, acting as a 'public affirmation of social ideals' or a 'statement of what is acceptable', a 'gesture important in itself' rather than a fixed end (Gusfield 1967, 177). It acts as a 'framing and signalling device' around a 'cluster of messages intended to change attitudes' based on 'narrative structuring and interpretive resonance' (Brysk 1995, 562). The idea of signalling 'effects' originates in economics, and refers to a process whereby informational asymmetry is resolved by one party 'signalling' information to induce trust or credibility (Spence 1973; Spence 2002). The signals of symbolic laws can be educative, aimed at 'simplifying complexity', or may serve to communicate a 'moral' message (Stoltz 2007, 312). Even the passage of such legislation 'persuades listeners', acts as an 'affirmation of a moral norm' and gives certain ideas 'legitimacy and public dominance' (Gusfield 1967, 177–178). Taken together, the act of creating and passing such laws constitutes a 'moral passage, a transition of behaviour from one moral status to another' (177).

The difficulty is that symbolic laws are fragile. Cobb and Elder (1973) argued that symbolic policies are often built around a 'rather shallow symbolic consensus' that may be easily exposed and frayed, and that they conflict with the 'stark realities' of power (87). Underneath the clear signal such laws can be quietly 'repealed in effect by administrative policy, budgetary starvation or other little publicised means' (37).

Matland associated symbolic policy with 'a lack of implementation'. Such policies frequently have 'substantial exposure at the adoption phase' but 'ultimately' have 'little substantive effect' and are 'almost always' a 'substantive failure' (1995, 168). In part, this is because they are, owing to their symbolism, 'conflictual' with 'actors intensely involved' (169). The 'victory or defeat' of symbolic policies is 'consequently symbolic of the status and power of the cultures opposing each other ... Legal affirmation or rejection is thus important in what it symbolizes as well or instead of what it controls' (Gusfield 1967, 179). The 'significance of prohibition in America lay less in its enforcement than in the fact it occurred' (179).

Hart (1995) later expanded on the power and dangers in symbolic policy and signals, looking at the promise of the first Clinton administration to cut presidential staff, a 'one sentence' policy in the campaign intended to symbolise the new administration's restraint and commitment to 'reduce' government (385). The media doggedly pursued the detail of the policy, and the administration found itself bogged down in a series of debates over who constituted 'staff' and how 'numbers' were calculated. This eventually resulted, rather damagingly, in a loss of staff working on drugs policy and the environment (390–391). The case highlighted a series of problems with laws as symbolic devices. First, 'symbolism is simple but the substance was complex', and the reformers had 'little grasp of the substantive problems' (397–398). Second, as consequence, the media's 'decoding' of the policy led to, sequentially, 'questions, doubts, cynicism and, eventually, disbelief' (397). While reformers believed that the symbolism would 'speak for itself', it was 'weak and riddled with detail and complexity' (398). It was exactly this 'detail and numbers' that then 'generated a hostile reception from the media and congress' (402).

## The radical roots of FOI: the most subversive idea of all?

Conceptually FOI is 'simple but revolutionary' (Wald 1984, 655). Transparency has long been championed by radicals, reformers and outsiders, and the possibility and call for greater openness punctuate history, frequently being tied to freedom of expression and the free press (Ackerman and Sandoval-Ballesteros 2006). Although 'isolated in time and space' these ideas can be traced across a lineage of very different thinkers and actors (Darch and Underwood 2010, 65). Castells (2013) sees 'free communication' as the 'most subversive practice of all' because it 'challenges the power relations embedded in institutions and society' (x).

The modern drive towards transparency has its origins in two revolutionary processes, one philosophical and one technological (Darch and Underwood 2010, 127). Though FOI may arguably have far older roots in ancient China, its modern form stems from the European Renaissance (Darch and Underwood 2010). Popper (2002) argues that the 'unparalleled epistemological optimism' of the Renaissance drove the impulse 'to discern truth and acquire knowledge' through perception and 'intellectual intuition' (6). Thus a veiled or distorted 'truth' would be revealed, driven by a 'doctrine that truth is manifest' (8). This 'ideal of emancipation modelled on lucid self-consciousness' or 'absolute self-transparency' was then completed by the Enlightenment (Vattimo 1992). Popper points out how its logical opposite co-existed with it and gave it strength: 'the conspiracy theory of ignorance' stemming from Plato, holding that man was 'blocked from knowing' by 'sin', 'prejudice' or 'powers conspiring to keep us in ignorance' (2002, 9).

The doctrine drove thinkers from Bacon to Descartes, as well as modern science and technology. Popper wholeheartedly disagreed with the premise, labelling it a 'myth' for the 'simple truth is that the truth is hard to come by and easily lost' (2002, 10). Nevertheless, it was an example of 'a bad idea inspiring many good ones', as what he labels a 'false epistemology' became 'the major inspiration of a moral and intellectual revolution without parallel in history', providing the force behind the scientific revolution, the fight against censorship and educative reform (10–11). The idea evolved in parallel with nascent conceptions of a 'free society', 'open discussion' and the 'public sphere' (Vattimo 1992, 18).

The new philosophy was powered mechanically by the 'long revolution' launched by the invention of the printing press in the 1400s (Eisenstein 2005, 335). Such a change in communication technology was inherently revolutionary:

> any new technology of communication, such as the printing press, has challenged authority because the seeds of revolt existing in individuals can grow and blossom ... breaking the barriers to social mobilisation and alternative projects of social organisation. (Castells 2013, x)

The publication of vernacular Bibles, as one example, unleashed both democratic and patriotic forces, and was used to challenge orthodoxy and established elites with an unprecedented 'intensity', while printed books of law 'democratised', or at least potentially popularised, knowledge of laws, the legal system and rights (Eisenstein 2005, 189). The Protestant movement was one of the first groups to recognise the power of the new technology, using the press as 'mass media' to persue 'overt propaganda and agitation against established institutions'. Even attempts to clamp down backfired as the Catholic index of censored works gave free publicity to dissenters and provided detailed guidance as to where to find subversive ideas (Eisenstein 2005, 164–165).

The printing press was not simply an instrument of liberation as 'open books in some instances led to closed minds' (Eisenstein 2005, 189). Eisenstein points out how it led, paradoxically, to both religious schisms alongside orthodoxy and uniformity: Some governments became adept at using the new technology for political propaganda. Nevertheless, the combination of technology and intellectual push created a new conception of knowledge and, as a corollary, information. The revolutionary effects of this combination can be seen in the new names given to the abstract entities created: the 'Republic of Letters' or 'Commonwealth of Learning' (Eisenstein 2005). It was out of this milieu that FOI was born.

*A weapon of radicals and reformers*

Like many radical ideas, FOI emerged from different revolutionary 'outbursts' as it moved from the realm of philosophy into politics. Accessing information is a modern offshoot of an 'age old struggle' over freedom of opinion and the press (Ackerman and Sandoval-Ballesteros 2006, 90).

Although its first appearance in law was in Sweden, the idea of opening government up appeared in bursts of 'pamphlet warfare' in England, America and France as revolutionaries seized the 'opportunity to shape the new polity in the cold light of reason' (Eisenstein 2005, 331–332). One starting point was the English Revolution. In the 1640s and 1650s, as a series of civil wars devastated Britain, there was an almost unique 'liberty of the press' with a 'continuous flow of pamphlets on every subject under the sun' (Hill 1991, 361). Framing this as a struggle between biblical 'dark' ignorance and 'light' illumination, Milton argued in *Areopagitica* of 1644, his famous defence of press freedom, that 'a flowery crop of knowledge' meant that a 'new light sprung up' (1979: 230–231). He pointed out that 'truth is compared in scripture to a streaming fountain: if her water flow not in perpetual progression, they sick into a muddy pool of conformity and tradition' (see discussion in Stiglitz 1999).

Nor was Milton alone. The 'Diggers' or 'True Levellers' of Gerrard Winstanley, an offshoot of the radical English Levellers who called for equal voting in the 1640s, proposed that two postmasters 'elected in each Parish' should be responsible for 'collecting and reporting statistical information about the health and welfare of communities and other important information' and distributing it to the populace (Hill 1991, 137). Winstanley also called for the end of 'trade secrets and patents', a call that still has distinct echoes today (Hill 1991, 138). Like Milton's, these calls were framed in biblical language, contrasting the 'blindness' of ignorance with the 'god given power of reason' or 'light' (Hill 1991, 138–139, 117).

Just over a century later, the world's first FOI Act, correctly a Freedom of the Printing Press Act, appeared in 1766, underpinned by the *fentlighetsprincipen* or 'principle of publicity' (Manninen 2006, 18). The origins of the first ever piece of FOI legislation are somewhat murky. A Finnish cleric and member of the Swedish Diet, Anders Chydenius, distilled (possibly wrongly) from ancient Chinese texts a principle of government openness, which he then championed as part of his vision of an anti-mercantilist, inclusive society (see Darch and Underwood 2010; Erkkilä 2012). Chydenius united with a Swedish pamphleteer, Peter Forsskål, to push this new or 're-discovered' idea. The suggestion played to a rather unusual context in Sweden at the time when a radical new reformist government was seeking to limit the power of the Swedish monarchy and prevent a coup after a long period out of power, during a brief 'age of liberty' (1719–1772) (see Robertson 1982) that also involved an 'early experiment in parliamentarism' (Manninen 2006, 20). No one is certain why the Act, intended to ensure liberty of the press, contained a provision on public access, and the law survived only for six years (Darch and Underwood 2010).

The next outburst of openness was in the political and intellectual ferment of the American Revolution, where it was linked to free speech and education. The institution of 'open meetings' and public decision-making in American towns, as practised in New England, echoed Leveller ideas (Hood 2006). In one of the most famous quotations on the virtues of openness, James Madison spoke of the importance of 'popular information' in the US:

> A popular Government without popular information or the means of acquiring it, is but a Prologue to a Farce or a Tragedy or perhaps both. Knowledge will forever govern ignorance, and a people who mean to be their own Governors, must arm themselves with the power knowledge give. (Emerson 1976, 1)

Although Madison was referring only to education in Kentucky schools, rather than FOI, the speech is now 'endlessly' quoted (Darch and Underwood 2010, 49), and is the reason why international Right To Know Day now falls on his birthday (Schudson 2015). Thomas Jefferson also spoke of how information could act as a 'self-correcting' mechanism: 'whenever the people are well-informed, they can be trusted with their own government; whenever things get so far wrong as to attract their notice, they may be relied on to set them to rights' (Darch and Underwood 2010, 50). It is unclear to what extent the revolutionaries would have supported any FOI law, and many scholars have their doubts, as they were keen to keep some discussion private, but their comments have been used ever since for political leverage (Schudson 2015; Chambers 2004). The French Revolution offered a similar burst of free speech and expression (Eisenstein 2005).

The belief in the virtues of transparency continued to then run like a thread through eighteenth- and nineteenth-century thought. Kant famously criticised secret treaties and the culture and morality behind secrecy (Chambers 2004). Rousseau extolled the power of the 'eye of the public' to prevent cabals (Hood 2006, 6–7). Tom Paine attacked the secrecy of the monarchy and argued that its exposure to the public gaze would de-legitimise it, characterising the institution as 'something kept behind a curtain, about which there is a great deal of fuss and a wonderful air of seeming solemnity … but when, by any accident, the curtain happens to be open, and the company see what is, they burst into laughter' (Keane 1995, xii). Jeremy Bentham then offered the 'strongest challenge to administrative secrecy in print', arguing that 'without publicity no good is permanent: under the auspices of publicity, no evil can continue' (Bok 1986, 174). Bentham's *On Publicity* discussed at length how openness would allow the government to know public wishes, and the governed to increase their knowledge and trust. He dismissed fears of the adverse consequences as spurious (see Hood 2006). The power of publicity and any consequent 'anticipatory reactions' would help create a 'system of distrust' to hold government power in check (Chambers 2004). Later J. S. Mill stated that the 'liberty of the press' was as important as the 'liberty of thought itself', and Karl Marx argued that to 'make public the mind and the disposition of the state appears

... to the bureaucracy as a betrayal of its mystery' (Darch and Underwood 2010, 96).

Despite this intellectual heritage, the idea remained on the political fringes. As Roberts (2015) argues, transparency as a policy began to appear only as 'a reaction to some other transformation that had already occurred ... usually the expansion of bureaucratic capabilities and the concentration of executive power' (6). This formed part of a 'broad pattern of ... Polanyi-style frameworks of movements and counter-movements' as concern over growing state and bureaucratic fed greater demands for openness (Roberts 2015b, 9). By the early twentieth century two very different radicals pushed transparency as a rhetorical and political weapon, and these were among the earliest examples of politicians using their stance to position themselves and connote radicalism and difference (Moe 2015). In the US Woodrow Wilson's 1912 presidential campaign made the moral case for openness, arguing that 'government ought to be all outside and no inside', though in a now familiar pattern he did little in office to give effect to his words, rejecting press conferences and then passing the draconian Espionage Act of 1917 (Bok 1986, 170–171). His later 'Fourteen Points' made one of the first attempts at international openness when he committed himself to 'open covenants openly arrived at' (Hood 2006, 11). In 1918, in a very different environment, Leon Trotsky, Commissar for Foreign Affairs in the new Bolshevik government in Russia, published the previously secret treaties of the Allied powers. In an odd pre-echo of WikiLeaks, he announced that publication would eliminate 'secret diplomacy' and bring about 'honest, popular, truly demo-cratic foreign policy' (Deutscher 1979, 349–350).

From this point onwards, the idea of opening government up slowly moved into the mainstream, flowing from debates on freedom of the press after the Second World War, where the term 'freedom of information' was coined (Fenster 2012b). Mentions of the virtues of transparency and vices of secrecy spread across political and geographical divides. Radical outsiders of very different hues made the case for greater transparency, including Mohandas Gandhi's urge for government to be truthful (Fischer 1991), Deng Xiaoping's admonition to 'seek truth from facts' (Gaddis 2005, 195) and Sartre's attempt to create 'human life with transparency and totality' (Bok 1991, 52). In the democratic world, FOI began to be adopted slowly in the 1960s and 1970s (Bennett 1997; Darch and Underwood 2010). Even in authoritarian regimes, there were attempts at illicitly increasing information access: in the post-Stalinist USSR the creation and circulation of so-called *samizdat* (self-publishing) works began in the 1960s with a mixture of banned literature, news and poetry that gave way to regularly published underground journals (Applebaum 2003). The collapse of Communism, the information revolution and contagion and imitation have led to successive waves of information laws across the world, with estimates of more than 100 countries, democratic, authoritarian and some in between, having some form of openness law (Bennett 1997; Darch and Underwood 2010; Berliner 2014).

## FOI and secrecy: signalling and symbols

So what is it that FOI symbolises and signals? The symbolic resonance of FOI is both wide and deep, an interlocking bundle of ideals, principles and effects. FOI laws still carry the aura of new relationships and a new moral tone while promising a series of instrumental benefits. For a politician, a call for transparency 'tells a transformative narrative' as it 'enables – and, indeed forces [a] virtuous chain of events' towards more accountable and democratic government (Fenster 2015, 151). The symbolic power is frequently magnified by the fact that FOI is often part of a wider set of legal, constitutional or political reforms and is given renewed force and momentum by a wider policy overspill (Evans 2008).

FOI offers a narrative about morals, rights and new relations. FOI is a 'moral idea', stemming from the idea that a government *should* be 'accountable' and 'open to scrutiny' (Darch and Underwood 2010, 49, 7). As seen above, it draws on a deep well of philosophical and political thought over the virtues of publicity and moral imperatives behind reasoned deliberative debate (Chambers 2004). In its more modern form, the argument runs through the 'market place of ideas', whereby the 'best test of truth is the power of the thought to get itself accepted in the competition of the market' (Moon 1984, 1171).

For a politician, FOI symbolises a decisive break with the past. While it brings little direct electoral advantage, 'transparency bestows cultural and moral capital on those who promote and implement it' (Birchall 2014, 77). In its 'moral passage' it offers to bind government to better behaviour and a new 'moral status' of openness rather than closure (Gusfield 1967). The arrival of a new government, often ideologically different from its predecessor, is frequently accompanied by a promise of FOI (Robertson 1982). Self-consciously 'reforming' administrations in the UK in 1997 and 2010, the US in 2009 and Italy in 2013 all made transparency a priority. Democratic transitions offer an even more powerful opportunity, as seen from Mexico to South Africa (Berliner 2014).

A promise of greater openness 'signals' a whole set of messages: that a government is somehow more 'democratic' in providing the raw material for rational, public deliberation, and is prepared to be monitored or overseen by the public. It also gives citizens the 'capacity to penetrate ... defences and strategies' built up over centuries to preserve secrecy and offers them the chance to create Bentham's 'system of distrust' for monitoring their rulers (Bok 1986, 9). It also represents an 'apparently simple solution to complex problems – such as how to fight corruption, promote trust in government, support corporate social responsibility, and foster state accountability' and is an acceptable response to problems 'at moments of crisis or moral failure', a 'visible response to public disquiet [with] attractive, palliative qualities for politicians and CEOs who want to be seen to be doing rather than reflecting' (Birchall 2014, 77). On a symbolic level FOI 'allows an incumbent to make credible promises of greater transparency and anti-corruption efforts to a wary public' (Berliner 2014, 479).

Alongside this, FOI represents the 'giving' of a powerful new right. Its origins are as a negative right or as a bulwark to 'prevent the manipulation of information'. However, FOI has gradually become recognised as a positive, if not a human, right (Birkinshaw 2006; McDonagh 2013). It is bound up in a proprietorial or economic right to information in the sense that citizens 'paid for the government and abuse is theft of their goods' (Robertson 1982, 12). It can also be a 'leverage right' and tool for furthering proprietary rights, social justice or a political mobilisation (Darch and Underwood 2010, 43).

FOI also symbolises how government views its own citizens, as empowered partners in government with an active role to play, signalling the 'creation of a new mind-set, one which sees government as an agent of the citizens for whom they work' (Stiglitz 2002, 12). Ralph Nader, and it appears not Thomas Jefferson, famously spoke of how 'information is the currency of democracy' and how 'the good society requires the maximum free movements of ideas and knowledge' (Robertson 1982, 12; Schudson 2015). Stiglitz argues that this is

> the most compelling argument for openness ... the positive Madisonian one: mean-
> ingful participation in democratic processes requires informed participants ... if effec-
> tive democratic oversight is to be achieved, then the voters have to be informed: they
> have to know what alternative actions were available, and what the results might have
> been. (Stiglitz 1999, 15–16)

Although knowledge is not necessarily power, it opens up the possibility: 'without knowledge ... there is no chance to exercise power' (Bok 1986, 9).

It is hoped that FOI will also have powerful instrumental effects. These may be more or less tangible, but vital for democratic health: an FOI Act may increase public involvement and participation in decisions and, through a reduction in secrecy, public trust in government. The very existence of an Act may prevent corruption via anticipated reactions, while use and exposure will highlight and further deter maladministration and abuse.

Taking all these possible effects together, for a leader and a party, FOI offers the potential to create a 'distinctive position' that give those supporting it a 'purpose and recognition' (Carter and Jacobs 2014, 138). FOI represents a 'badge of progressive politics' and offers a powerful 'narrative identity' to politicians (138).

The symbolism of FOI contrasts sharply with that of secrecy, an ancient 'social control mechanism ... signalling what behaviour is acceptable and unacceptable', bound up in 'beliefs, norms and values' and defined against 'threats and assaults' (Keane 2008, 111, 108). The idea of secrecy and the dangers in becoming enlightened or opening up secret matters resonate across mythology, from Pandora's Box to Faust (Bok 1986). The most 'primordial sense of government secrecy emphasises distance and sacredness', with absolute monarchy in the seventeenth century borrowing the mysterious 'aura' of religion (172–173). Its more modern variant has evolved into the need for concealment and protection of security and decision-making, bound up in an 'aura' designed to 'elicit awe' (Costas and Grey 2014, 1425). It is also a social and culture process, embedded in group and organisational identity and often buried in a 'rich array of ritualistic and symbolic practices' (1426). Secrecy can take the form of formal rules and regulations, as a formal boundary or marker, or can be informal as a result of unofficial concealment, taboos and socialisation. Against the positive instrumental effects of openness, secrecy breeds suspicion and distrust (Keane 2008). Bok quotes Woodrow Wilson's aphorism that 'secrecy means impropriety' (Bok 1986, 8).

The clash between the two symbolisms equates, rather too simply, to one between good and bad, and between democratic and undemocratic. Georges Simmel (1906) wrote of how 'enlightenment aimed at the elimination of deception in social life is always of a democratic character' (447). It is rooted in a moral sense that secrecy, or too much concealment, is 'incompatible with democracy' (Bok 1986, 8). By contrast, secrecy continues to be associated with evil, with 'stealth and furtiveness, lying and denial' (8). This dichotomy over-simplifies a more nuanced reality, as secrecy is closely entwined with the more positive notion of privacy, while publicity can be associated with manipulation and distortion (Bok 1986). There are also broad swathes of social and political activity where confidentiality is deemed necessary, from juries to peace negotiations, and even Bentham qualified the power of publicity with the need to prevent injustice (Chambers 2004). Nevertheless, it is the stark symbolism between the two competing ideals that frames the debate as FOI laws develop. At its heart was the conflict 'over power: the power that comes through controlling the flow of information' (Bok 1986, 19).

### Contested transparency

A further problem lies in the ambiguous nature of transparency and FOI. There is a 'general, widespread agreement that public sector transparency means access to government-held information', but its 'realization in terms of what, why and how information should be accessible is highly contested, and perhaps essentially contested' (Stubbs and Snell 2014, 160). FOI sits across various bureaucratic, legal and political dimensions that can make its operation problematic (Terrill 2000; Snell 2001). It resembles democracy itself, with a general consensus on the broad meaning of the concept, but with its detailed interpretation 'open to complexity, contradiction and numerous varieties'. It is in some senses an 'empty signifier' that can be 'filled' by very different interpretations or emphasis (Stubbs and Snell 2014, 160).

As explained in Chapter 7, FOI laws represent a legal framing or staking out of permissible access, amid a shifting landscape or information ecosystem where the borders are constantly moving. FOI serves as the legal 'backbone' of ever expanding and evolving transparency regimes, made up of diverse 'arrangements and policies' as well as 'practices, symbols, and discourses' (Ruijer and Meijer 2016). FOI disclosures sit alongside other laws, innovations such as Open Data and 'radical' actions like leaks and mega-leaks in an evolving system where the demarcation between 'open' and 'closed' or between 'legal' and 'illegal' is constantly shifting (Pozen 2013). Meaning is greatly complicated by the closing off of certain issues, such as the transparency of citizens through government surveillance, a rarely mentioned aspect of the wider transparency debate that is frequently disconnected or separated from the broader discussion (Birchall 2014).

As well as the meaning of openness, the implicit assumptions within such reforms are contestable and contested. Darch and Underwood describe them as an 'ideologically determined political initiative that can be deployed to achieve a range of different agendas' (2010, 49, 7). Classic arguments for FOI, rooted in rational choice assumptions of behaviour change, are bound up with neo-liberalism (Darch and Underwood 2010; Birchall 2014). FOI can have numerous different aims and purposes, from public monitoring to hierarchical control of lesser bodies (Heald 2012). More challenging approaches address the reversal of assumptions around who is being open to whom and debating the size of the political spaces opened (or closed) by its arrival (Birchall 2014). Transparency remains a 'contested political issue that masquerades as an administrative tool' (Fenster 2012b, 449).

### Symbolism meets institutions

The instuitionalist approach to policy development focuses on historical time and processes within political institutions (see Thelen 1999; Peters et al. 2005; Pierson 1994 and 2000). Institutions are marked by 'path dependence' and increasing returns that create 'self-reinforcing feedback and support for the status quo', with institutions populated with 'vested interests' determined to resist change (Moe 2015). Such path dependency appears partly technical but is also rooted in values, cultures and the existence of a 'shared script' (Thelen 1999, 387). This reinforcing 'stability' means that even politicians and reformers with radical intent and the political will may find change difficult (see, for example, Pierson 1996). Nevertheless, slow-moving changes erupt onto agendas, pushed by organised and multiply situated actors when bereft of popular attention. Symbolism plays a powerful role in any change, as 'ideas are crucial elements in the battle to place issues on the agenda' (Peters et al. 2005, 1295).

What could be seen as simply the 'clash' of radical policy and resisting body has been shown to be more nuanced. Even 'sudden' change is often preceded by the gradual erosion or de-legitimisation of previous policy or ideas, a process of erosion then used by advocates to lever change (Thelen 1999). Policy can also be altered by changing social circumstances and 'drift' as alterations in context make the policy different or by 'contagion' as established rules are manipulated to change their effect (Hacker and Pierson 2014). Moreover, certain radical periods of change encourage policy experimentation and lead to a 'co-evolution' as policies feed off other and change breeds change elsewhere (John 1999, 45). Political systems are rarely coherent, and change can also be bought about by 'friction' between institutions (between government, courts and legislatures, for example) and even from within bureaucracies themselves (Moe 2015). As arrangements fail, politicians may sometimes seek to artificially sustain existing institutions 'politically' (Thelen 1999, 396). Within institutions political actors may shift and change according to their views on the 'feasibility, possibility or desirability' of a policy (Hay and Wincott 1998, 956). Battles are often many-sided 'conflicts' whereby the 'victorious side does not win a single encounter' but a 'more complex process unfolding over time' (Pierson 2015, 133). Moreover, the passing of policy is the beginning, not the end, as after this battle begins over the practical implementation and symbolic meaning of a law that can profoundly shape its success (Patashnik and Zelizer 2013; Moe 2015). As well as positive feedback, policies can generate negative returns, becoming self-undermining (Jacobs and Weaver 2015).

### FOI and institutionalism

What happens when the symbolism of FOI meets concrete political institutions? At its root, the struggle for access to information is a 'political struggle' (Ackerman and Sandoval-Ballesteros 2006, 90). The exact dynamics and divisions vary from country to country. Transparency is 'not a sudden conversion' but one created by the 'specific conditions of competition for political power' (Blanton, quoted in Darch and Underwood 2010, 64). A number of studies of transparency have drawn on institutionalism, and its emphasis on time, to explain the growth and development of national transparency systems, including comparisons of the rules-based versus principles-based approaches in the US and Netherlands (Ruijer and Meijer 2016), the stalemate over openness in the European Union (Hillebrandt et al. 2014) and the shifting trajectory of the publicity principal in Finland (Erkkilä 2012).

As Michener (2011) argues, the 'primary dilemma is political. The symbolic qualities of FOI laws attract political support but the ideal effects – to expose the actions of politicians and bureaucrats to public scrutiny – weaken the will to enact strong laws' (146). This is further complicated by a host 'technical and legal issues' that confront what can be a complex change (146).

The interaction of the symbolism of FOI with the 'path dependence' of institutions goes to the heart of explaining why and how governments pass FOI laws. FOI offers the chance to remake politics, redistributing power and ending informational asymmetries and 'closed' cultures. This symbolism is powerful enough to place it on the agenda and to mobilise and, to an extent, cut off lines of retreat for governments wishing to renege. But it is not enough to overcome the entropy, opposition and problems of turning symbol into law.

Political institutions and organisations traditionally use secrecy to preserve their power, in a path-dependent and self-confirming process (Weber 1991). Pierson (2015) likens power to an 'iceberg' where the majority of influence 'lies below the waterline, built into institutions and organisational structures' (124). Secrecy is a powerful exemplar of just such a 'hidden', iceberg-like structure, enmeshed within a complex interplay of laws norms, organisational cultures and ideas (Keane 2008). Weber argued that the 'concept of the official secret is the specific invention of bureaucracy and nothing is so fanatically defended ... out of a sure power instinct' (Weber 1991, 233). This secrecy habit becomes self-perpetuating and expansive as secrecy then goes 'far beyond purely functional interests' (233). Such deep secrecy can express itself through either formal rules or regulations or more informal conventions and cultures (Costas and Grey 2014).

FOI emerges slowly over time, gathering force over decades, in part through its own symbolic value, as a beacon of democracy and as a 'right'. It can also be reinforced by failures of secrecy through scandals or very obvious attempts at oppression or suppression (Michener 2015). Government reactions then create 'gaps and lags' and openings. As this momentum gathers pace, FOI then appears to punctuate agendas, taking its place in manifestos and frequently co-evolving within wider reform programmes (John 1999). FOI thus exists within what Kingdon (1984) termed a 'policy window', when the arrival of a new government or event converges with a ready-made policy solutions to create opportunities (Worthy 2007; Michener 2011). Yet for all its symbolic power and appeal it attracts very little direct public support. FOI is a supreme example of a policy where voters are 'typically only dimly aware of the policy positions' (Hacker and Pierson 2014, 21).

The 'window of opportunity' is brief (Michener 2011). Once a government is in power, FOI is almost always a story of various small groups battling and shifting over 'feasibility, possibility or desirability' (Hay and Wincott 1998, 956). While the conventional portrait is of wholesale 'counter-mobilisation' across bureaucracy, there is more often conflict between supportive, hostile and less interested bodies. Though key departments frequently resist others fight, rethink and manoeuvre. Nevertheless, the process is frequently one of gradual weakening. It is a battle over the detail and meaning of the policy far away from public gaze: as with other changes, 'a tremendous amount of conflict is controlled by keeping it so private that it is almost invisible' (Schattschneider in Hacker and Pierson 2004, 17).

### Passage of FOI: Trojan horses and hidden influences
The first attempt to map the process of passing FOI was Snell's (2000) exploration of two early developers, Australia and New Zealand, which was followed by an examination of Australian Federal state laws (Snell 2001). Snell explains how laws are 'formulated on the fringes' from a mix of 'political hopes and democratic motives' by small groups of reformers and political opposition, and how context is key, as proposals frequently use 'windows of opportunity such as new governments and elections'. In a process likened by Snell to a 'Trojan horse' within government, reformers are frequently met with support from a 'limited cohort of Ministers', with a wider group making only 'tokenistic public pledges' and 'bureaucratic responses [vary] from the lukewarm to the hostile' (345–347). The proposals are

then subjected to a 'refinement process' that will frequently 'produce a significantly lower quantity and quality of information than the original proposals' and leads to 'heavily compromised laws'. To survive, laws require 'white knights' and are often a story of 'lone crusaders and reluctant stewards' pushing against growing resistance (347, 349). Snell found state-level FOI passage to be generally a similar story of an 'external reformist movement ... battling an entrenched and, with a few notable exceptions, non-receptive bureaucracy' (Snell 2000, 578). The movements were often 'narrowly based' groups of academics and lawyers, seizing opportunities to push a reform that was then 'guided by often hostile ministers and a foot dragging bureaucracy' (Gillis in Snell 2000, 579). One of the frequent difficulties is that FOI legislation faces not outright resistance but apathy or disinterest: rather than being persuaded to change their minds, many have to be persuaded to pay any attention at all (Snell 2000 and 2001).

Since Snell's work, other research has explored more deeply the hidden influences and motives behind FOI. Berliner (2014) challenges the conventional idea that political leaders cannot always gain from openness laws. It is true that most political leaders (privately) 'prefer secrecy to openness and oppose constraints on their actions' and that FOI laws create substantial costs, including 'increased monitoring' and 'increasing risks of exposure', risks that 'bind' not just present but also future governments (479, 480–481). It is for this reason that 'many newly elected leaders who promised to pass FOI laws fail to do so or are delayed for long periods' (481).

Yet in certain circumstances 'the benefits outweigh the costs'. On a practical level, by 'institutionalising transparency', FOI laws 'allow incumbents to ensure that groups out of power in the future will not be shut out', and the binding can work both ways (Berliner 2014, 479). Transparency can have further uses for a central or federal government, as a tool to monitor local government or remote agencies (Heald 2012). This explanation is frequently given for China's passage of transparency legislation (Weibing 2010). The People's Republic of China's seeming tolerance of netizens' exposure of corruption follows a similar logic (King et al. 2014).

Michener (2015b) also challenges the idea that 'political leaders uncontrollably shy away from strong transparency policies' and argues that the 'how' and 'when' of the legal or political events that underlie enactment are 'pivotal' (17, 15). Politicians require a 'justifying narrative', whether real or created, often a corruption case or legal ruling. This justification, combined with the control of agendas, means that a determined leader can 'enact strong transparency laws in spite of tacit or explicit resistance' (14, 18). In a study of Brazil, Michener found that politicians, particularly in broad multi-party coalitions, pass laws as a means of controlling information and enabling monitoring of their allies. Agency plays a vital part, and in the case of Brazil strong presidential support and the interest of the Chief of Staff and influential senators were crucial (13–14). Partisanship also plays a role. Cases across South America displayed a similar variety, with the nature of party and legislature control a crucial variable (Michener 2015a). Research at state level in the US also found partisanship to be an important factor (Wood 2012).

The importance of partisanship also points to a further key influence. In the absence of electoral support, pressure for openness frequently comes from within political parties, through the grassroots or supportive groups in the legislature, which are linked to external campaign groups and which can then grow into cross-party support (Birchall 2014). Parties thus generate a 'competitive consensus' in an area relatively insulated from voters (Wood 2012). Such tensions between parties help to keep windows open for longer (Carter and Jacobs 2014). While competition between parties rarely ignites public interest, 'serious political challenges' from other groups create a positive momentum and 'reduces the risk of punishment in media and public debate' (Carter and Jacobs 2014, 138). Parties and backbench members frequently push for openness from below out of principle, while leaders recognise the branding power of FOI as a means to create a 'policy image' (Carter and Jacobs 2014, 138). Given its symbolism, FOI offers a 'radical' way of displaying 'political identity' (138).

Further support comes from the veto players who often choose inactivity. Berliner (2010) examined the various veto players within a political system with the power to stop FOI, from branches of government to political parties. He concluded that, rather than stopping a law, the presence of more veto players increased the likelihood of its passage. For the many veto players, FOI legislation allowed access to information for deals and the capacity to 'expose wrongdoing' (7–8). Like politicians, veto players feared also the risk of 'reputational or electoral harm' by opposition, either from the 'voting public' or from the increasingly powerful international transparency lobby (8, 10).

A final significant but often overlooked driver is reform-minded officials within government. As seen in the cases throughout this book, FOI generates internal battles rather than wholesale opposition. Certain departments and ministers do champion openness to reinforce their own power, gain credit or 'lock' government into wider reform processes. This internal push can be seen in other openness reforms, such as the international push towards extractives industries transparency (David-Barrett and Okamura 2016). Across governments, officials react in varying ways, with a mixture of support, hostility and acquiescence and, for reformers, can be a source of support as well as opposition (Moe 2015).

## The UK: a most difficult case?

As a case study, the UK represents one of the most challenging environments for FOI in a developed democracy, and one of the least conducive to success. UK governments resisted reform throughout the 1970s, 1980s and 1990s, just as other Westminster countries and the UK's neighbours passed FOI laws.

For much of the twentieth century, the UK carried a reputation as the developed world's most secretive democracy. 'Secrecy' according to Hennessy 'is the glue that holds the rambling structure of British central government together' (2003b, 346). A potent mixture of executive dominance, 'political tradition' and institutions created a formidable set of obstacles to opening up (Evans 2003). The Official Secrets Acts, passed in 1889 and 1911 and updated in 1989, were 'a prime illustration of the culture of secrecy which [has] dominated British public life' and 'symptomatic of the secretive nature of the state' (Bogdanor 2003, 413). Such legislation remains a symptom of a wider and deeper problem, with the 'law ... only one part of a broad constellation of forces which impede the flow of information' (Vincent 1998, 11). On top of this were layered more 'than a hundred pieces of legislation that curb the flow of information from central government to populace' (10).

Secrecy was a historical, cultural and institutional phenomenon, with instruments built up since 1250, when the Privy Councillor's Oath swore all members to secrecy (Hennessy 2003b). A bundle of restrictive conventions and rules, from Collective Responsibility to the Royal Prerogative, created a constitution in which, as Leigh described it in 1980, 'secretive components are heaped one on top of the other' (20). The result was what Rowat described as a 'principle of discretionary secrecy' whereby 'all administrative information is to be considered secret unless the government decides to release it' (Rowat 1979, 19). Secrecy became 'the very essence of the establishment view of good government' and was 'built in to the calcium of a policy makers bones' (Hennessy 2003b, 346). It was partly instinctive and partly cultural, rooted in the 'idea that there existed a natural ruling class. Secrecy as a part of this rule was as natural as breathing' (Rogers 1997, 14). Hennessy, reflecting on Orwell's observation on the 'privacy of English life', pointed to 'obsessive secrecy' as its 'regrettable obverse' (2003b, 347). He argued that 'it is as natural for the secretary of a village cricket club to stamp the minutes of its committee meetings confidential' as it is for a Cabinet Secretary to keep Cabinet notes secret (347). By the 1980s, despite social and technological change, secrecy remained firmly in place with, it is said, even the brand of tea drunk by ministers technically an official secret (Hennessy 2003b).

The inherent secrecy of British government went deeper than individual laws or discretionary practice. Although it was an 'inheritance from the past, from earlier undemocratic times ... later Executive government ... preserved the tradition of discretionary secrecy for their own convenience' (Rowat 1979, 20). The Westminster system, with its executive dominance, one-party government and strict lines of control, made both for power hoarding and, as a corollary, information hoarding (King 2015). One 1980s study concluded that 'levels of secrecy [are] a direct consequence of the foundations of British democracy [in particular] the Sovereignty of Parliament and the oppositional nature of politics' (Robertson 1982, 22). It was not just culture and laws but systematic and institutional design that made for information control:

> All government information will be seen as having consequences for their ability to
> exercise the degree of control the structure of responsibility implies and for their
> political survival since any information may affect their reputation and popularity.
> (Robertson 1982, 2)

The 'minimal conception of liberal democracy' meant that information access and
availability 'is not taken to be an important measure of democratic life' (Evans 2003,
189).

According to Diamond (2011) 'the structures and processes of central British
government have endured historically because they appeared to offer very substantial power to the incumbent administration', and this 'power paradox' presented to
reform-minded governments, 'which has provided a formidable obstacle to radical
political change in Britain' (68). To pass an FOI law required not only overcoming
'secrecy' laws and layers of culture and practice, but potentially challenging and
upending the UK's political system itself.

## Methodology

The question that drove this book began as a relatively simple one: 'why did Labour
pass FOI?' This then led to an equally interesting follow-up, 'why did it not drop it?'
The Duke of Wellington famously warned against writing the history of a battle or a
ball, and the same challenges of partiality, recall and revision face anyone wishing to
trace the history of any policy. The process is also hidden, in that the very symbolism of FOI means that fighting is (mostly) done behind closed doors while in public
there are palliatives and reassurances (Kennedy 1978).

Tracing the separate parts of FOI involved piecing together very different
sources, reports and views from inside and outside government. The primary means
of accessing the story was a series of interviews with twenty people with knowledge
of the process from different perspectives, including ministers such as Jack Straw
and David Clark as well as MPs, experts, campaigners and academics. A series of
interviews were conducted between 2003 and 2005 with additional work in 2014 and
2015. Some of the interviewees wished to remain anonymous.

The interviews were supported by a number of primary sources. These included
White Papers, draft bills, a series of Select Committee reports and minutes and
Hansard. The hearings in 1998 and 1999 by the Public Administration Select
Committee (PASC) and the ad hoc Lords committee HL 97 provided some
enlightening testimony. The minutes from the Cabinet sub-committees are not
yet available: the Cabinet committee documents for the Constitutional Reform
Programme-Freedom of Information (CRP (FOI)) committee will remain closed
for twenty years. However, in 2014 I put in an FOI request to the Home Office
and the Ministry of Justice for any background documents relating to the process.
The documents were, at the time, being used by the Independent Commission on

Freedom of Information and could not be obtained. FOI requests were also sent in 2016 to selected government departments and other bodies in order to measure to what extent senior politicians came into contact with requests; the results of which can be seen in Chapter 8.

Beyond the official record, the Campaign for Freedom of Information (CFOI) provided the most detailed commentary. Robert Hazell and the Constitution Unit followed the process with a series of practical, comparative and ultimately prescient analyses that correctly guessed what had been happening behind the scenes (see Hazell 1998 and 1999). In the media, the *Guardian* and *Independent* also followed what was happening in some detail from the outset, as did *The Times* to a lesser extent and some regional and local newspapers. A series of searches in the Lexis newspaper archive were used to trace media coverage, and the University of Glasgow's excellent Hansard Corpus was used to trace the history of the phrase 'freedom of information'.

In political memoirs FOI is generally mentioned only in passing, if at all, though the glimpses offered are fascinating. In 2011 Tony Blair rather surprised the world by devoting two pages to FOI in his memoirs, memorably describing himself as a 'nincompoop' for passing it and characterising FOI as an 'abused' law that served to 'undermine' sensible government and hand power to the media. In an interview with the *Guardian* he spoke of it as one of his biggest regrets. Blair claimed the law was developed 'with care but without foresight' (Blair 2011, 127) and wove a picture of a new, inexperienced government blundering naively into passing a radical law:

> At that time the consequences were still taking shape and it didn't impact much in 2005. It was only later, far too late in the day, when the full folly of the legislation became apparent, that I realised we had crossed a series of what should have been red lines. (Blair 2011, 417)

The Home Secretary Jack Straw devoted a more detailed and thoughtful chapter of his own memoirs comparing the creation, passage and impact of FOI with that of the Human Rights Act. FOI policy was also mentioned, again in passing, across other sources including diaries by New Labour's communications director Alastair Campbell (2011), the Liberal Democrat leader Paddy Ashdown (2002) and the Labour backbencher Chris Mullin (2011), as well as in the memoirs of Blair's Chief of Staff Jonathan Powell (2010).

A number of academics have discussed FOI. Robertson in 1982 and Chapman and Hunt's collection of 1987 were two of the of the first; they were followed by Vincent's fascinating 1998 work on Britain's culture of secrecy, which stopped on a rather hopeful note with the 1997 White Paper, and Robertson's updated portrait of Britain's move to open government, published in 1999. Flinders used FOI as a case study in 2000 in a neatly argued piece on the changing attitudes of the government from 'Whig' to 'Peelite'. Two rigorous analyses of Labour's wider reform agenda by Evans (2003) and Dorey (2008) had excellent chapters devoted to FOI. Patrick

Birkinshaw followed the twists and turns with some very clear-eyed legal analyses (Birkinshaw and Parkin 1999; Birkinshaw and Parry 1999; Birkinshaw 2001), as did Rodney Austin (2000, 2004 and 2007). There was also an overview of the whole process by CFOI (Gundersen 2008). The sheer extent of Labour's constitutional reform programme overshadowed FOI, but the latter was also mentioned as part of a number of other works (see for example King 2009 and Bogdanor 2009).

Since 2005, when it came into force, the Act has been the subject of academic analysis, some of which I undertook with Robert Hazell and others at the Constitution Unit, in terms of its impact on central government (Hazell et al. 2010; Worthy 2010; Worthy and Hazell 2016), local government (Chapman and Hunt 2010; Worthy 2013; Richter and Wilson 2013) and Parliament (Hazell et al. 2012) as well as the separate regime in Scotland (John 2014, Dunion 2011; Cherry and McMenemy 2013; Taylor and Burt 2010). There was also investigation of particular requester groups such as journalists (Hayes 2009) and non-governmental organisations (NGOs) (Spence 2010). Since its passage and implementation FOI has been the subject of two inquiries into its operation in 2006 and 2007 by what was then the Constitutional Affairs Select Committee. It was then the subject of detailed post-legislative scrutiny by the Justice Committee in 2012 as well as the Ministry of Justice in 2011, and by the Independent Commission on Freedom of information in 2016. The Justice Committee hearings proved to be a rich trove of material on the development of the Act (Justice Committee 2012d).

Care has been to taken to critically analyse sources and match them up. However, the picture presented here is necessarily incomplete. One of the reasons the law took the path it did was that it was created in a rather confused process, at a hugely disorientating time.

FOI has remained controversial. The sharp divisions between supporters and sceptics during its creation carried over into its operation. While those outside government see it as symbolic tool of anti-corruption and popular power, to some senior politicians and officials it is representative of a tendency for too much openness, something that damages trust and ties up government. The Act has perhaps come to symbolise something that is 'wrong' or 'right' about contemporary British politics.

For all these reasons, certain facts, events and timings crucial to the story have been lost or distorted. For example, few media reports or memoirs mentioned Lord Irvine's central role in the early stages of the policy. Blair, rather than realising 'too late' what his generous promises had wrought, had been alerted to FOI in 1998 and gave the green light to reversing the early radical proposals soon afterwards, specifically instructing Jack Straw to cut them back and even attempting to introduce a blanket protection for 10 Downing Street (Justice Committee 2012c). Straw himself played a dual role in FOI, acting as opponent in its White Paper incarnation and then, albeit grudgingly, pushing the Bill through Parliament with a high degree of skill and expertise. As policy lead, Straw was responsible for the Act and was blamed for later reversals; he casts himself as 'the villain' of FOI in his memoirs. However, it was the government as a whole that rowed back on the law, weakening it through a mixture of fear and indifference. While relatively minor details, when rearranged, they combine to tell a rather different story.

The book then turns to a selection of other brief comparators to pull out commonalities and threads. It examines in turn three other important cases: the creation of the first modern FOI legislation in the US, one of the first pieces of legislation in a Westminster system in Australia in 1983 and India's powerfully symbolic Right to Information Act of 2005. It then takes a look at two rather different examples: the radical legacy and retrenchment of Ireland's 1997 FOI law, rebooted in 2014, and New Zealand's Official Information Act, driven almost wholly by the very insiders who normally oppose such change. Each case draws on detailed academic studies, as well as selected primary documents where available, to show that FOI is easy to promise and difficult to duck.

# 2

# From radical to inevitable: the development of FOI in Britain

The road to FOI in Britain was one strewn with successive failures or half-measures, all 'neutered by the realities of executive office' (Matthews 2015, 330). The fundamental difficulty was that real openness reform required 'supreme altruism', 'but altruism has not been a notable characteristic of UK governments' (Judge 1993, 213). Between the 1960s and 1990s the forces of change seemed too weak, and resistance of government institutions too strong, for any chance of legislation. FOI was simply too radical for a succession of governments 'wedded' to the orthodoxies of information control and Parliamentary and executive sovereignty, who foresaw only negative outcomes from reform (Dorey 2008; Matthews 2015). Instead, there were decades of half-hearted and belated moves designed to head off statutory access to information legislation with lesser change. The story of openness reform mirrored that of constitutional reform more generally as a series of 'missed opportunities, executive intransigence and institutional stickiness' (Matthews 2015, 310). UK governments appeared locked into a 'path-dependent' process of information control and secrecy, a self-reinforcing pathology of law, culture and behaviour embedded deep within the Westminster model.

Change began not with a demand for FOI but with pressure to reform the Official Secrets Act of 1911. By the 1970s debate shifted to FOI legislation, when the promise of FOI first appeared in a Labour Party manifesto. Reform was pushed by an ad hoc group of radical outsiders, internal party advocates, lobbyists and campaigners, and given leverage by a series of secrecy scandals and exposes. This growing network of openness advocates then waged their campaign through a succession of Private Members' Bills, media campaigns and policy documents. In the next decade there was a notable 'drift' towards openness as secrecy scandals, minor reform and new technology gradually eroded the case for information control. Away from central government, there were moves in local government towards opening up meetings and greater access to health and personal information. The 'frictions', 'gaps' and 'lags' created opportunities for the many groups arguing for reform (Thelen 1999, 382).

The story is of gradual movement, a tale of 'modest incrementalism' (Matthews 2015, 310). What began as too radical in the 1960s was becoming seemingly inevitable by the 1990s. Each 'jump' or reform moved FOI closer and entrenched its place on the agenda. Even the Thatcher governments, the most resolutely pro-secrecy, passed a series of access-to-information laws across local government and policy sectors. The chapter examines the frequent reform attempts through case studies of the Wilson governments (1964–70) and the Labour governments of Wilson and Callaghan (1974–79) and finally Major's attempt to pass an 'FOI light' via his Code of Access. It ends by looking at the concurrent 'locking in' of transparency across local government in the UK.

## Central government

At central government level, pressure for change focused initially on reform of the draconian Official Secrets Act of 1911. The successive Official Secrets Acts had become 'a prime illustration of the culture of secrecy which [has] dominated British public life' and 'symptomatic of the secretive nature of the state' (Bogdanor 2003, 413). They were viewed as one part of a wider culture of secrecy with deep attitudinal roots (Vincent 1998; Hennessy 2001).

As early as 1899 the future Prime Minister Lord Roseberry had compared the UK government to a 'Vatican council' in its attitude to secrecy (Vincent 1998, 5). In the early part of the twentieth century, the only sustained pressure for openness in government came from a very small group of radical Labour MPs, including the future Prime Minister Ramsay MacDonald, who had opposed the passage of the Official Secrets Act of 1911 (Dorey 2008, 184). The first mention of Open Government was made in the 1880s over the government of Ireland, and the first reference to 'Freedom of Information' was mentioned by the Liberal MP Richard Holt in July 1916:

> if there is one matter on which I feel more strongly than another it is that in a democratic community the foundation of good government lies in freedom of information, freedom of thought, and freedom of speech: You cannot have a country, which is governed by its people, wisely and well governed, unless those people are permitted access to accurate information, and are permitted the free exchange of their views and their opinions: That is essential to good government. (Hansard Corpus; Informationrightsandwrongs 8/112015)

However, as Table 2.1 shows, there was little interest or mention of either FOI or Open Government until the 1960s.

Table 2.1 Mentions of 'freedom of information' and 'open government' in the UK
Parliament, 1880–2000

| Year | Mentions of 'freedom of information' | Mentions of 'open government' |
| --- | --- | --- |
| 1880 | 0 | 2 |
| 1910 | 1 | 0 |
| 1920 | 0 | 1 |
| 1940 | 12 | 0 |
| 1950 | 8 | 0 |
| 1960 | 2 | 4 |
| 1970 | 256 | 746 |
| 1980 | 630 | 512 |
| 1990 | 2021 | 980 |
| 2000 | 1415 | 173 |

*Source*: Hansard Corpus 2015.

Even though the Labour radicals achieved power in the 1920s, there were only minor adjustments to press releases of Cabinet meetings by the first Labour government of 1924 (Dorey 2008). Aside from local government reform, little happened apart from a brief and poorly timed examination of official secrecy in 1939 (Vincent 1998).

### 1960s: false start

The first signs of pressure emerged in 1957 when a committee looking into the administration of tribunals recommended open inquiries and the regular publication of inspectors' reports – an 'illustration that, at least in specific areas, pressure short of a law can lead to slightly less secrecy' (Michael 1982, 193–194). The issue of information access rose as part of a 'general mood of self-questioning' and wider 'discontent' concerning Britain's perceived decline, symbolised by the Suez crisis (Cornford 1982, 38). Prime Minister Anthony Eden's attempts to obscure and destroy the paper trail around the Suez intervention and infamous 'colluding' with France and Israel highlighted the dangers of secrecy in high places (Thorpe 2003).

The first concrete reforms began in 1968 when the Fulton Report into reform of the Civil Service concluded with twenty-two recommendations, one of which proposed analysis of 'ways and means of getting rid of unnecessary secrecy' (Hennessy 2003a, 5). As a by-product, Prime Minister Harold Wilson then pushed for a change to the Public Records Act 1958 to reduce the time limit on closed documents from fifty to thirty years and for a review of the Official Secrets Act (Hennessy 2003b; Theakston 2006). Wilson, however, was an unreliable champion for openness. He 'combined in a bizarre fashion an opener's temperament and paranoia about leaks'

(Hennessy 2003b, 29) and a 'basic institutional conservatism' (Theakston 2006, 165). A memorandum of late 1968 describes Wilson as being 'not in any particular hurry to reach conclusions' on reform until stirred into action by the opposition (Theakston 2006, 164). Even against a Prime Minister, the 'path dependency' of information control was revealed to be easily capable of counter-mobilising. Both the Foreign Office and the Ministry of Defence sought to 'delay for as long as possible' an official secrecy review and attempted to turn the changes inside out and use them to 'hold back more material' (Theakston 2006, 163). An official briefing for the Prime Minister pointed to the 'cost' of any reform and described the review as neither 'practical or expedient' (Theakston 2006, 164). Another briefing paper 'mocked the fashionable myth that the quality of current public business would be improved if it were carried out in a kind of goldfish bowl' (Theakston 2006, 165). The Cabinet Secretary informed Wilson that the appointment of outsiders to examine cases would mean the involvement of someone 'probably ... naturally biased against secrecy' and warned that the particular candidate Wilson recommended 'might come out with a far too liberally minded report – almost Swedish' (Theakston 2006, 164).

Consequently, the first attempt at opening up government was diverted and resisted in a classic case of policy inaction (McConnell and 't Hart 2014). In an illustration of the strength of resistance, Prime Ministerial 'pressure' had to be brought to bear upon both the Foreign Office and the Lord Chancellor's Department to push even these relatively minor changes, while Wilson's hoped-for review of the Official Secrets Act never took place (Theakston 2006, 163). The energy resulted only in a change to the Public Records Act and a White Paper. The latter revealed the full extent of Wilson's failure. Entitled 'Information and the Public Interest', it asserted that secrecy 'ought to be limited', immediately qualified this by saying that 'there would however be the greatest difficulty in defining what categories of information should qualify' and concluded 'a sanction is needed to ensure the protection of official information and the Official Secrets Acts provide it' (Cabinet Office 1969, 11). By the end of the 1960s, openness remained a 'minority interest' even within the Parliamentary Labour Party (Dorey 2008, 186). Nevertheless, the very fact of movement represented the beginnings of change.

### 1970–74: radicalism diverted

In 1969 openness became an electoral issue when Edward Heath, then leader of the Conservative opposition, committed himself to reforming the Official Secrets Act at a press awards ceremony and Wilson, a week later, followed suit (Hennessy 2003b). In the early 1970s, events gave the issue added urgency. A series of inquiries early in the decade constituted a potential 'turning point' that became a 'missed opportunity' (Vincent 1998, 252, 254). Heath's narrow electoral win in 1970 led to a far-reaching examination of secrecy. The Franks Inquiry looked at the retention, removal or replacement of section 2 of the Officials Secrets Act and concluded that it should be replaced with an Official Information Act with narrower limits on document protection (Robertson 1982). The inquiry was used as the basis for Labour's repeated pushes over the next eight years. It did not, however, recommend an FOI Act (Vincent 1998).

A succession of secrecy scandals in the 1970s then added momentum and began a slow erosion of the case for information control and a 'drift' towards openness. In 1971 a controversial secrecy trial of journalists led to an embarrassing defeat for the government when the judge advised that section 2 of the Official Secrets Act be 'pensioned off' (Wraith 1979, 206). The following year a bizarre secrecy case concerning the *Railway Gazette* 'petered out' despite a police raid (207). There was growing pressure from within political parties, particularly the Labour Party. In 1972 the senior Labour politician Richard Crossman famously wrote that 'one problem we face [is] the English addiction to secrecy' (Crossman 1972, 99). In 1973, the ex-minister Tony Benn argued in a *Times* article that 'secrecy has at last become a major political issue ... There is a growing public recognition that democracy itself cannot function unless the people are allowed to know a great deal more about what goes on inside government' (Benn 1974, 232). Benn and a small group of Labour MPs then urged a commitment to FOI in a future Labour administration; this entered the manifesto for the October 1974 election (Dorey 2008). The conjoined pressures around secrecy met with a wider crisis of government and legitimacy in the early 1970s. Secrecy 'symbolised and concealed and concealed the declining efficiency of government' and cast government against the 'modernising forces' that openness represented (Vincent 1998, 254).

## 1974–79: a veto through indifference

However, attempts at reform met more powerful forces of institutional inertia. The Labour administration of 1974 entered power with a clear pledge to reform the Official Secrets Act and introduce an FOI Act. In a recurring theme seen again in the 1990s, the commitment was 'not the subject of any debate or perhaps even discussion ... if it had been partly understood it would almost certainly been toned down or dropped' (Michael 1982, 197). There then began a further five years of inertia, inaction and institutional and political resistance, as politicians and officials united to defend the secrecy status quo (McConnell and 't Hart 2014).

For the first time reformers had a powerful claim through a manifesto pledge and an influential advocate in the form of the pro-openness Home Secretary Roy Jenkins (Campbell 2014). Jenkins visited the US to study the benefits and costs of the newly implemented FOI Act, an improved and revised version of the original 1966 legislation (Kellner and Crowther-Hunt 1981, 267; see Chapter 8 below). The US 1974 Act was 'not well drafted and contained serious loopholes', and the visitors 'picked up a lot of opposition and concern in the federal administration' (interview with James Cornford 2005). Jenkins returned 'unimpressed' by openness through legislation (Burch and Holliday 1996, 165), describing the proposal as 'too costly, cumbersome and legalistic' (Kellner and Crowther-Hunt 1981, 267).

Nevertheless, Jenkins 'pressed for changes' and was, according to Bernard Donoughue, the only major political actor to take a 'radical stand' (Michael 1982, 198; Theakston 1992, 187). Fellow ministers greeted the proposals with disinterest and dislike. Benn, back in Cabinet, claimed there was 'deep hostility' from ministers and, again, attempts by the Home Office to strengthen, rather than weaken, the Official Secrets Act (Dorey 2008). The Attorney General and Chancellor were both against any reform, and the Cabinet Secretary Sir John Hunt 'sent in an enormously long brief' that argued against the 'dangerously liberal' pro-openness conclusions of the Franks Committee (Donoughue 2005, 474). Donoughue describes a meeting of Misc 89, the Wilson-chaired Cabinet sub-committee looking into reform:

> it was quite clear that the majority of the Committee – led by H[arold] W[ilson] [and] Callaghan – were for tightening things up. Roy Jenkins would not have that and lost his temper several times ... the meeting was chaotic at times with half a dozen people talking at the same time. What the machine wants is a more repressive measure under a liberalising gloss. (Donoughue 2005, 683-684)

The 'choice of one moment' in a policy can then 'eliminate a whole range of possibilities' (Hay and Wincott 1998, 955). Openness reached just such a juncture when Misc 89 rejected an FOI Act at an early stage and instead sought a 'simpler', and lesser, means of reforming information control (Burch and Holliday 1996, 166). The new policy was split into two policy tasks, with Wilson appointing the Civil Service department to suggest methods of 'liberalising' government information while the Home Office examined reform of the Official Secrets Act (Michael 1982, 206; Burch and Holliday 1996, 165; Kellner and Crowther-Hunt 1981, 267). The Queen's speech of 1975 revealed the scaled-down commitment to 'amend the Official Secrets Act and to liberalise practices relating to official information', less precise and less far-reaching than the manifesto pledge (267).

After this, the Wilson government's approach was 'spasmodic' (Kellner and Crowther-Hunt 1981, 267–268) and characterised by 'prevarication', a 'blatant lack of progress' and 'attempts to deflect pressure' (Burch and Holliday 1996, 168–169). Jenkins later spoke of the difficulties of making any change:

> there were certain departments where secrecy had become a way of life. I found the war of resistance so strong that I decided ... if you cannot be fairly confident that you will improve matters and not make them worse, it is better to leave them as they are. (Ewing and Gearty 1990, 208)

Although Misc 89 continued to 'spasmodically' review the Official Secrets Act neither the Home Office nor the Civil Service department had presented its proposals when Wilson resigned and was replaced by Callaghan (Kellner and Crowther-Hunt 1981, 267). The new Prime Minister was 'unsympathetic' to openness, having told the Franks committee, 'we are not going to tell you anything more than we have to about what is going to discredit us' (in Judge 1993, 213). The new Home Secretary Merlyn Rees was equally unenthused (Theakston 1992; Michael 1982). Callaghan ordered all investigation into reform to stop (Burch and Holliday 1996, 166).

Despite the overt resistance 1977 'was the year open government legislation ideas reached adolescence' as legislative pressure and controversy forced openness back on the agenda once more (Michael 1982, 201). Backbench pressure manifested itself in the formation in 1975 of an all-party Committee for a Freedom of Information and Privacy Act, which marked the beginning of 'a process of serious attention on the issue' within Parliament (Michael 1982, 198). Two Private Members' Bills and a draft Bill were drawn up on the subject, and a new lobbying coalition, the Outer Circle Policy Unit, began lobbying for change (Michael 1982). At the same time, Labour's National Executive Committee also published a draft FOI Bill, and another controversial Official Secrets Act Trial involving two *Guardian* journalists led once more to the failure of the section 2 charges (Wraith 1979; Wilson 1984).

The government response was two-fold, offering two lesser policy alternatives that would, in essence, preserve existing information structures. The first, the so-called 'Croham Directive', was a non-statutory order separating policy advice from 'factual background', and the second was a commitment in the Queen's speech to reform of the Official Secrets Act (Wraith 1979). Callaghan sold the Croham Directive as a kind of voluntary disclosure scheme:

> When the government makes major policy studies, it will be our policy to publish as much as possible of the factual and analytical material which is used as background ... unless there is some good reason, of which I fear we must be the judge, to the contrary. (Kellner and Crowther-Hunt 1981, 327)

There was less progress on the second part. Following the 'hostile reception' of the Home Secretary Rees at a meeting of Labour backbenchers, the White Paper on Official Secrecy was finally released, though Callaghan warned prior to its publication that 'the Cabinet was now unable to take the position held in the 1974 manifesto' (Burch and Holliday 1996, 169). After investigating the possibilities of implementing Swedish- or American-style FOI legislation, the White Paper stated ambiguously that 'this is a matter on which the government has come to no conclusion and has an open mind' (Home Office 1978, 19–20). The paper then pointed out the problems associated with FOI, including 'unexpectedly high ... resource costs' that might mean that FOI was 'neither necessary nor desirable' and suggested that perhaps 'a declared obligation to make more information available, operating on a voluntary and discretionary basis' would be better (20). Taken together, the government's actions were what Edelman called a 'palliative', whereby political language was used to mask inaction and regime defence (McConnell and 't Hart 2014, 4).

As a measure of the party's unhappiness, the White Paper 'caused uproar in Parliament and disappointment in the press', and its hesitation was thrown into stark contrast by the publication on the same day of the Labour Party Machinery of Government Study Group's draft FOI Bill, later carried at the 1978 conference and approved by Labour's National Executive Committee (Robertson 1982, 90; Theakston 1992). The combined effects of this opposition were 'enough to convince the government that it should do its best to forget the whole subject' (Michael 1982, 208).

However, FOI was proving hard to stop as the multiple groups now pressing for change began to press harder. The issue was forced once more onto the government's agenda when, in early 1979, the Liberal member Clement Freud MP won the ballot for a Private Member's Bill and was persuaded to exchange his legislation decriminalising cannabis for a draft FOI Bill drawn up by the new openness lobbying organisation the Outer Circle Policy Unit (interview with James Cornford 2005). Private Members' Bills stand a very small chance of success at Westminster but can, whether successful or not, provide a powerful signal for change (Norton 2013). Freud 'spoke skilfully' and 'organised support' for the Bill, which aimed at achieving what the Labour government had so far failed to do: a positive assertion of a right of public access to information and the abolition of section 2 of the Official Secrets Act (Michael 1982). According to Benn, the proposed Bill 'galvanised the whole of Whitehall against it … officials are panicking … attacking all the proposals and listing the difficulties' (1990, 445–446). Freud used the opportunity to embarrass the government and mobilise widespread support across Parliament and the press (Wilson 1984). The combination of hostility, ambivalence and disinterest from ministers was reflected in Tony Benn's description of a later meeting of the committee looking into it, Gen 29, following the appearance of the Bill:

> Only the active and articulate minority wanted it but they were a minority and the rest didn't care … Callaghan said he found the subject utterly boring … Foot was lukewarm [but] wanted to repeal section 2 … Shore argued passionately against the Bill calling it 'a charter for paranoids [that] showed a lack of faith in Parliament. (Benn 1990, 472–473)

In a further response, the government published a Green Paper on Open Government, and the Civil Service department carried out a 'thorough, if sceptical, survey' of FOI legislation across the world (Michael 1982, 214). The Green Paper concluded that 'reform of section two is an essential step', proposing it be amended to cover only 'a strictly limited range of information' (Hooper 1988, 295). It then qualified its endorsement by saying, like the White Paper, that any reform should be slow: 'greater openness must be fully in accord with our constitutional tradition and practice [and] the government believes that the objectives will be best achieved by gradual development, which build on existing arrangements' (Robertson 1982, 90).

Meanwhile, Freud's Bill was steered through the committee stage by members of the Outer Circle Policy Unit following a 'tense encounter' with Home Office civil servants (Michael 1982, 213). The government promised not to oppose Freud's Bill on its second reading, although this was 'more a question of other pressures on the government' (interview with James Cornford 2005). However, the Callaghan government lost a vote of confidence before Freud's Bill or the government's proposals could be taken further.

### Avoiding FOI, 1974–1979

Despite a decade of pressure, scandal and campaigning, the most concrete policy was the Croham Directive. Lord Croham later claimed that the directive represented a kind of 'short-cut', a 'radical yet practical and inexpensive policy' (Vincent 1998, 260), and Home Secretary Rees described it as 'the best we could do at the time' (Chapman and Hunt 1987, 34). It was greeted with 'tepid enthusiasm' by officials and was deflected in an artfully worded circular by Permanent Secretary to the Treasury Sir Douglas Wass (Ponting 1986, 285). The circular concluded with a revealing paragraph that urged minimal and temporary compliance:

> many want the government to go much further (on the lines of the formidably burdensome Freedom of Information Act in the USA). Our prospects of being able to avoid such an expensive development here could well depend upon on whether we show that the PM's statement has reality and results. (Quoted in Kellner and Crowther-Hunt 1981, 325)

Theakston describes the flow of documents as 'rather ... uneven' with some departments, notably Benn's, releasing a 'great deal' whereas for others 'the exercise simply became part of the normal government public relations machine' (1992, 184). Between May and October 1978 twenty-eight different departments released a total of 200 documents, but this flow soon 'slowed to a trickle' and by 1979 the initiative was 'dead' (Vincent 1998, 261). A leading article in the *Times* stated that 'the government demonstrated blatantly it cannot be relied upon for the voluntary disclosure of official information' (Leigh 1980, 270).

Despite the external pressure, the 'lack of policy drive is an outstanding feature' across the reforms of the 1970s, with a series of 'non-decisions' at numerous levels (Burch and Holliday 1996, 171). Labour's time in office was a seeming text-book example of how reform could be delayed, resisted and compromised through a 'campaign of outflanking and sabotage' (Leigh 1980, 251). Opposition to openness encompassed the majority of senior ministers who 'didn't want to do anything ... at the most they were willing to do something about the Official Secrets Act but not about a statutory right of access' (interview with James Cornford 2005). Bernard Donoughue, then head of the Number Ten policy unit, was disappointed by 'how many Ministers took a reactionary position'. Moreover, the two key actors from 1976 to 1979, Prime Minister Callaghan and Home Secretary Rees, were sceptical of reform, and their 'lack of enthusiasm was critical ... these two Ministers exercised a veto through indifference' (Burch and Holliday 1996, 171). Both consistently stuck to the 'minimalist line' of reform and their qualified support out of 'tactics [rather] than of principle', giving the appearance of action only when the issue was repeatedly forced upon the agenda (Vincent 1998, 300). Elements of the Civil Service were also opposed, and there was a 'general mood of scepticism' (interview with James Cornford 2005). The opposition of senior civil servants was clearly set out upon Wilson's arrival in 1974. The Cabinet Secretary Sir Burke Trend and the head of the Home Civil Service Sir William Armstrong presented the Prime Minister with a 'beautifully crafted brief' against information reform 'which moved from one classic fallback position to another' (Hennessy 2003a, 26).

The resistance to change had numerous sources that would reappear in the 1990s. First, politicians and officials were firmly wedded to the highly centralised Westminster system and the information control embedded within it (Evans 2003, 187). Donoughue wrote of how 'most people in government saw only embarrassment in revealing to the electorate more about their activities' and he was 'shocked by the elitism and reactionary assumptions behind many of the arguments made against change' (Theakston 1992, 182).

Second, the policy carried little electoral benefit. Callaghan's opposition was partly grounded in his view that the policy was electorally valueless (Vincent 1998). Home Secretary Rees made this explicit: 'the *Guardian* can go on for as long as it likes about open government and reform of the Official Secrets Act but I can tell you that in my own constituency of 75, 000 electors I would be hard pressed to find many who would be interested' (Rees 1987, 32). To most ministers open government had 'no votes in it' and so 'could wait' (Michael 1982, 204).

Third, for the reformers there was a problem of policy focus. As Rees later observed, 'the individuals who supported reform were their own worst enemies. They all had brilliant ideas but could not agree what they wanted to get through … the individuals who support open government … could not agree on what was the lowest common denominator they wanted to get through' (Rees 1987, 32). Competing ideas led to a lack of clarity as 'refocusing the Official Secrets Act was not interchangeable with open government … and neither were necessarily the same as Freedom of Information' (Vincent 1998, 302).

Fourth, Theakston describes the failure as a 'failure of political management' rooted in the government's 'precarious position' (Theakston 1992, 186). On one level Parliamentary arithmetic was against reform. Wilson's 1974 government had a tiny majority, and on the day Callaghan took office it became a de facto minority administration, then governing through a supply-and-confidence arrangement with the Liberals in 1976–78 and finally through uneasy agreements with minority nationalist parties until 1979 (Clarke 2004). In later stages the legislative timetable was filled with other constitutional reforms that took 'vast amounts of Parliamentary time', particularly attempts to grant devolution to Scotland and Wales (Clarke 2004, 354). Rees, reflecting in the 1980s, claimed that legislation of any complexity simply could not have passed, as the 'nature of the subject' meant that

It is very complicated … the subject is such that it raises issues outside the control of the whips [and also] outside the confines of the political parties [thus] in my view the government will have a very difficult time getting a majority. (Rees 1987, 32)

At the 1979 Labour conference, Callaghan similarly argued that the government was unable to enact FOI legislation because it 'lacked a Parliamentary majority', a claim that was apparently treated with derision from members (Leigh 1980, 259). Whatever the difficulties of political management, the Callaghan government faced a series of 'almost intractable problems' (Morgan 2001, 382), from the International Monetary Fund crisis to Northern Ireland and the ending of its fragile contract with the trade unions (Clarke 2004). These problems 'taxed' the minority government's 'ingenuity' and appeared to leave it, at times, in 'near paralysis' (Morgan 2001, 420).

There was, however, a drift towards transparency. During the course of the 1970s a number of pieces of legislation were passed containing minor provisions for public access to information, notably the Control of Pollution and Health and Safety Acts of 1974 (Michael 1982, 202). These represented piecemeal movements, each of which eroded slightly the monopoly of information control. Alongside this, secrecy scandals had eroded the 'moral' case for closed government. Perhaps most importantly, there was a growing advocacy group stretching from the media to lobbying organisations and with a powerful and vocal group within Parliament who could lever change. The process was a 'neat illustration of how far the issue progressed from a cranks' charter to a respectable proposal' (Michael 1982, 192).

## 1980s: the clampdown?

The 1980s is traditionally seen as the decade of secrecy in the UK. Prime Minister Margaret Thatcher was generally in favour of information control and had an intense dislike of leaks, restricting the circulation of documents and, occasionally, warning officials and politicians against expressing views on paper (Moore 2015). When asked whether Britain would benefit from an American-style FOI Act, Thatcher replied, 'not at all, our system is much more open than the American one' and advocated reform of the Official Secrets Act 'only to make some of its provisions against the disclosure of information stronger not weaker' (Cockerell, Hennessy and Walker, 1984, 14–15). In 1984, Thatcher described proposals for an FOI Act as 'inappropriate and unnecessary' (Wilson 1984, 34).

Consequently, the Thatcher governments were 'resolute in their defence of secrecy in high politics' (Evans 2003, 201) and prosecuted someone under the Official Secrets Act once every eighteen weeks, compared with once every two years under previous administrations (Vincent 1998). A succession of high-profile secrecy prosecutions punctuated the 1980s, from Clive Pointing's attempted prosecution for leaking information over the Falklands war to the 'spy catcher' scandal over a former intelligence officer's memoir. In 1989 the Official Secrets Act was also reformed, though, as Thatcher promised, this was to enhance its effectiveness rather than liberalise it.

However, the drift towards FOI continued. The very strength of Thatcher's opposition helped frame the debate (Wilson 2011). The 'gaps' and 'lags' within the government information control regime grew larger as frictions emerged (Thelen 1999, 382). Using Orwell's famous date as a jumping-off point, in 1984 the Outer Circle Policy Unit, newly renamed the Campaign for Freedom of Information (CFOI), began a sustained lobbying effort that gained widespread attention (Wilson 2011). It led to supportive editorials from the *Guardian*, the *Times*, and regional and local papers up and down the country and expressions of public support from more than 20 peers, 100 MPs and 50 local councils (Wilson 1984; Wilson 2011; CFOI 1984b). The new 'impressive coalition' expanded to new areas such as consumer rights or sector-specific problems such as health (Vincent 1998; Wilson 2011, 165). Crucially, as part of a deliberate strategy to elicit public promises from politicians, the leader of the Labour Party Neil Kinnock, as well as David Steel of the Liberals and David Owen of the new breakaway centrist Social Democratic Party, all committed themselves to FOI (CFOI 1984a; Wilson 2011).

Support for FOI also extended to parts of the Civil Service. Though frequently a force for inertia, officials can also provide impetus for reform (Moe 2015). In March 1983 the former Permanent Secretary to the Treasury Douglas Wass came out in favour of openness legislation in a BBC Reith lecture. He argued that there was now 'a need for governments on a systematic basis to publish the information they possess which will contribute to public understanding of policy issues'. He pointed out that 'so far, all British governments have resisted a Freedom of Information Act' and concluded that he was 'profoundly sceptical about the arguments for secrecy':

> The reasons for deciding against publication have often been nothing more weighty than political embarrassment. Publication has caused very little, if indeed any, damage. The onus, I now believe, ought to lie heavily on those who oppose publication to justify their opposition ... An alternative approach would be to give the public the right of access to official files, subject to certain limited safeguards. (BBC 1983)

Lord Croham, author of the directive, also expressed support for a full FOI law, as did the First Division Association and affiliated Civil Service trade unions (Wilson 2011).

Given central government opposition, CFOI opted for a 'guerrilla strategy' focusing on smaller-scale legislative change, targeting local government with gradual and piecemeal information access reforms (Wilson 2011). The 1984 Data Protection Act, originating from the then European Economic Community, gave subject access rights allowing citizens access to their personal data (Robertson 1999). A series of Private Members' Bills supported by CFOI became the 1985 Local Government Act extending public access to meetings, the Access to Personal Files Act 1987 and the Access to Health Records Act 1990 (Vincent 1998). Although these were often 'forced upon a reluctant and unwilling government' they nevertheless meant that the UK drifted, often unwillingly, towards forms of statutory access (Robertson 1999, 141). Moreover, Thatcher's time in power was bookended by two symbolically significant events. In 1979 St John Stevas, the Leader of the House of Commons, persuaded, or possibly hoodwinked, Margaret Thatcher into greatly enhancing the power of Parliamentary Select Committees, a step that made 'an important contribution to greater openness' through Parliament's power to call witnesses, access documents and publicly scrutinise (Vincent 1998, 268; Norton 2013). In November 1989 the UK House of Commons was televised, initially on an experimental and then on a permanent basis, later, as some pointed out, than the USSR televised its proceedings (Franks and Vandermark 1995).

By the end of the 1980s there was a clear campaign for FOI, led by CFOI but with supporters in Parliament and the media, at national and local level – exactly the sort of 'multiply situated actors' best able to push for policy change (Hacker and Pierson 2014, 23). Thatcher's action in pressing hard had created secrecy scandals that further delegitimised secrecy and, as Chapter 3 below shows, energised the Labour Party's support for FOI. All these pressures pushed the symbolism of FOI, which now sat on two major parties' manifestos, centre stage.

### 1990s: FOI-lite

John Major's government was the last to initiate non-statutory access, following a commitment in the 1992 Conservative manifesto to be 'less secretive about the workings of government' (Judge 1993, 213). Major himself was a supporter of open government and was pressured by the Labour Party's championing of FOI in the late 1980s and early 1990s (see Chapter 3 below).

The Conservative government's proposals, however, fell short of a full FOI Act. In its 1993 White Paper, the Major government explicitly rejected an FOI Act, calling it 'costly and cumbersome', and instead created a voluntary Code of Access. The Code offered 'practical steps' that would 'meet the principal objectives of those who have sought a full statutory Freedom of Information regime ... without the legal complexities' (Cabinet Office 1993, 2). Major himself argued that it was part of a wider citizen's charter project to give consumers established rights and benchmarks that constituted 'true radicalism ... a patient piling up of bricks ... the launch of a long slow process of change' (Major 2000, 260, 262).

The 1994 Code of Access extended across government unless statutory authority or established convention argued 'to the contrary' (Cabinet Office 1997a, 1). It provided access, within twenty days and at a cost left to departmental discretion, to 'copies, compressed short hand notes' or summaries of documents pertaining to them (Cabinet Office 1997a, 42). As the White Paper pointed out, the Code 'does not constitute a right of access to documents or records [but instead] a digest of the relevant information will be available' (Cabinet Office 1993, 3). The Ombudsman could be used as an appeal route in the event of problem or controversy. The information available was limited by fifteen exemptions including tax, the monarchy, the Cabinet, internal discussion and advice, internal advice, recommendation, consultation and deliberation (Cabinet Office 1997a, 3).

In parallel the government declassified documents early on a range of controversial topics from Rudolf Hess and Churchill's wartime correspondence with Roosevelt to the Derrick Bentley case. By 1995, under what became known as the 'Waldegrave initiative', over 100,000 'highly sensitive' documents had been released (Hennessy 2003b, 35). Further symbols of the new more 'open' political climate occurred in 1995 with the publication of previously secret details of Cabinet sub-committees and the holding of press conferences by the heads of both MI5 and MI6 (Willman 1994, 71).

### John Major's information revolution?

Major claims that the Code was part of 'my desire for nothing less than an information revolution' (2003, 73). Peter Hennessy praised Major for creating 'the first properly institutionalised openness regime on a codified basis' and his 'sense of delayed open government' (2003a, 34). Others were less impressed. Robertson argued that 'the measures reflected the little boy with his thumb in the dyke trying to resist the flood of liberal democratic opinion' (1999, 142). Vincent characterised the policy as a 'revived and extended version of the failed Croham directive [the] last in a long line of reform attempts designed to prevent reform' (Vincent 1998, 323). Major's policy was reminiscent of early attempts to initiate some sort of reform that fell short of a full FOI Act.

As in the past, one of the weaknesses lay in policy drive and support. Major himself was the prime mover but he received the support of only two Cabinet colleagues (Seldon 1997, 399). Most of Major's Cabinet were against any change 'on the grounds of realpolitik' and greeted it with 'open scepticism' (Seldon 1997, 399). The policy also created 'division and conflict' within the Civil Service, leading to virtual 'war within' (Vincent 1998, 303). The opposition within the Cabinet and Civil Service consistently 'continued to dismiss the cry for open government [regarding it as an issue] confined to the chattering classes of north London' (Seldon 1997, 400).

Disinterest was compounded by political problems. After 1992 the Conservative government was beset by Parliamentary rebellion and economic crisis as well as a dwindling parliamentary majority (Clarke 2004). Major's premiership was also undermined by a continuous wave of secrecy scandals, exposés and a drip of 'sleaze' allegations (see Chapter 3 below). He was widely seen as weak, and so his championing of the cause may not have been helpful, particularly as it was associated with his widely derided personal charter initiative (Hennessy 2001).

Judge concluded that the Major government was simply 'not serious' about openness (Judge 1993, 214). The opening up of Cabinet committees and the intelligence services was 'more symbolic than real', offering little that was new (Judge 1993, 214). The Code was further undermined by government disinterest:

> it could be argued that the Code failed to take off because there was insufficient enthusiasm from those who created in fostering the climate that would allow them to succeed ... not only did virtually nobody know the Code existed but that suited the government perfectly well. (PCA 2005, 32)

Nevertheless, as the closest reform yet to a full FOI Act, CFOI gave the initiative a qualified welcome, calling it a 'significant advance, though one that has substantial weaknesses' (CFOI 1995, 1). The new Code 'limits the ground for withholding information, provides a mechanism for independent review [and] introduces the important principle that even exempt information may be disclosed if there is an overriding public interest in doing so' (1). Reviewing the Code a decade later, the Ombudsman argued that although the Code's success 'is mixed ... during the decade or so of its existence [it] resulted in a significant enlargement in the kind of information that has routinely released into the public domain' (PCA 2005, 20). The Code had pulled out information from government, 'educated' departments and instituted a 'massive change' in expectations (PCA 2005, 31, 38, 37).

There were, however, serious limitations. The fundamental problem lay with the Code's lack of statutory force. Unlike an FOI Act, the Code had no 'legal basis' and could not override statutory or constitutional conventions relating to information control (CFOI 1995). This was essentially 'a signal to Whitehall not to bother about it' and meant that 'nobody paid attention to it' (interview with James Cornford 2005). Major admitted that 'predictably, institutions were rarely enthusiastic ... there was a widespread reluctance to publish information' (Major 2003, 73). Even a decade later, with an FOI Act soon to be in force, there were still 'notable pockets of resistance' with departments 'clearly determined to play the "exemptions game"', as 'although the Ombudsman frequently dragged departments to water, departments often showed a marked reluctance to drink' (PCA 2005, 20).

Second, the wider reception among those supposed to use it was decidedly tepid. As a symbol of 'Open Government', the policy, Seldon asserts, had 'depressingly little impact upon the public' (Seldon 1997, 309). The lack of seriousness was exemplified in the launch of the Code. The policy was 'launched very quietly without much encouragement for anyone to use it' and 'without any obvious enthusiasm' or 'clear champions' (PCA 2005, 36). It had an 'inconspicuous start', being launched on a bank holiday during a Parliamentary recess, and journalists were given little opportunity to scrutinise or publicise the document beforehand (CFOI 1995, 5). The government spent £51,527 on the project compared with £2,000,000 on the Parent's Charter of 1991 (CFOI 1995, 4). According to Robertson, the initiative was 'welcomed by few and described as inadequate by many' (1999, 141). Major himself admitted that the charter 'failed to catch the public imagination ... we were so quiet about our revolution that few noticed the wall being scaled' (Major 2000, 261). On a more practical level the 'low level of casework' indicated that, until the issue was given publicity through Labour's arrival in power, few people were using the Code (PCA 2005, 14, 31, 32). There were 6,000 requests under the Code between 1994 and 1996 (Wilkinson 1998, 17). While individuals made up 49% and NGOs 9%, journalists appeared to make up only 3% of the total (Wilkinson 1998, 17). Ironically, the 'key catalyst in this changing position' was the announcement of FOI legislation 'that helped publicise the existence' and led to 'greater use' of the Code (PCA 2005, 14). Robertson concluded that 'the government remains as hidden as ever' (1999, 143–144).

This lack of political enthusiasm was further compounded by confusion as to what exactly the Code was. The priority was to support public service improvement rather than provide an entrenched public right to access information. The 'main purpose' of the initiative was to 'supply factual information' in order to help consumers make judgements and 'pursue grievances' (Robertson 1999, 146). Consequently 'the kind of information revealed by the Charter process is about the delivery of services and not about policy-making or decision making [and so] only enables one to see the tip of the iceberg ... visible outcomes' (Robertson 1999, 143–144). The Code was about, as Hugo Young put it, 'opening up government to consumers' (Judge 1993, 214).

## Local government, 1960–2000

While preserving their own secrecy, both Labour and Conservative administrations in the period had a noted enthusiasm for 'other people's openness' at local government level (Wilkinson 1998, 13). Long subject to rigorous political and financial control, local councils were jolted towards openness through a series of significant pieces of access legislation from 1960 onwards (John 2014; Wilson 2011).

As Wraith points out, the two tiers of government developed different approaches towards information access. Local government had a consistently more liberal regime thanks to centrally created legislation (Wraith 1979, 189). The triggers for changes were frequently to do with press, rather than public, access rights and were driven by political controversy and party politics. Local authorities had granted informal access to the media to some of its meetings since the turn of the twentieth century. However, in 1908, a court ruling in *Tenby Corporation v Mason* affirmed the common-law right of councils to meet in secret (Chandler 2010). The Liberal government, in the same year as it sought and failed to pass a strengthened Official Secrets Act, gave the press a legal right to be admitted to meetings (Chandler 2010). Despite model standing orders asserting that 'all proceedings of Committees and Sub-Committees be treated as confidential', elements of access were introduced through the Local Government Act of 1933 and successive Town and Country Planning Acts, all of which carried statutory duties to provide certain information (Wraith 1979, 195).

Press access to meetings again drove the second major access law in 1959, when Labour councils refused access to local journalists involved in a strike (Chandler 2010, 106; Moore 2013). This controversy led the newly elected MP Margaret Thatcher to push a Private Member's Bill granting journalists and the public access to council and committee meetings (Thatcher 1995, 111). What she viewed as a 'socialist connivance with trade union power' rapidly became an issue of 'civil liberties' and access to information (111–112). Thatcher was supported by the Newspapers Editors' Guild and other parts of the press. However, her Bill met substantial opposition from what she claimed were officials 'echoing the fierce opposition in local authorities' (112). Thatcher's own party leadership, wary of stirring up 'unnecessary conflict' and seeking legislation that would do as little as possible, inclined to a code rather than a statute (Moore 2013). The result was a compromise that gave statutory access to full meetings for both the press and public but not to local authority sub-committees. It was greeted by both left and right as a victory (Moore 2013). Thatcher's victory was followed between 1960 and 1970 by a series of reviews of local government that all called for greater openness (Chandler 2010, 107). The Heath government passed the Local Government Act of 1972, which gave further access to sub-committees within authorities as a succession of local government corruption scandals kept the issue of 'town hall' secrecy in the headlines (Chandler 2010).

By the middle of the 1980s, local and central government were locked into a 'bitter conflict' over finance with 'new left' councils in Sheffield, London and Liverpool engaged in 'open revolt' and a 'bitter struggle' with the Thatcher government (Chandler 2010, 108). Openness laws, especially over finance, offered a means of central government curbing local government excess. In 1985 further legislation, again beginning as a Private Member's Bill, meant that 'all documents, agendas and minutes' were open unless there was good reason not to be (108). At the same time there were experiments in openness in councils such as Bradford and widespread support for FOI (Wilson 1984; CFOI 1984a). By the end of the 1980s a series of small pieces of access legislation on data protection and access to files had opened up various spheres of local government (Robertson 1999). The final piece of local government reform came with the arrival of New Labour. In the same year as FOI received royal assent, the Local Government Act 2000 authorised local authorities to proactively publish a range of information on its decisions as part of a wider structural reform (Chandler 2010).

## Conclusion

Between 1960 and 1990 the power of secrecy outweighed the persuasive symbolism of openness. The pre-FOI history of openness in the UK is of a series of compromise reforms forced upon uninterested, if not hostile, politicians and officials seeking to do as little as possible to 'head off' Parliamentary and media criticism. The

Select Committee looking into Major's Code in the 1990s concluded that openness reforms over the previous decades had been 'ignored, avoided, quietly forgotten or otherwise rendered ineffective' (quoted in Robertson 1999, 150).

Each reform followed a similar pattern as pressure was diluted or diverted through indecision or lesser compromises (Snell 2000). The few White Knights were half-committed (Wilson), weakened (Major) or simply isolated (Jenkins), while those against could choose to resist outright or smother change with indifference and delay. There was also the lack of a supporting context: successive governments were beleaguered, weak and coping with far more pressing crises and problems. Open government reform appeared to them voteless, with no pressing reason *for* it and many arguments *against*, especially in a system that was politically and culturally wedded to information control. The 'executive mentality' that 'permeated' government succeeded in repeatedly halting reform (Judge 1993, 143). Despite growing pressure and embarrassing scandals, politicians and officials resisted change, becoming locked into a series of delaying tactics and lesser policy options.

However, each half-hearted reform moved government a step closer to statutory access. The alliance of pro-FOI advocates grew, and the prevailing secrecy regime was undermined by exposure, gradual, limited policy change and altering contexts. By the 1990s politicians were 'politically' seeking to cover what was an eroding and outmoded culture of secrecy. The process and the failures also helped create a growing network of supporters across Parliament and the media, making future legislation more likely. As governments struggled with inaction, an array of institutional and extra-institutional forces strengthened the case. By 1997 FOI was an idea whose time had come.

# 3

## New Labour, new openness?

Transparency laws are frequently introduced by a combination of external and internal changes (Michener 2015d). New Labour's support for FOI was partially through willing embrace and partially through having it forced upon them. By the 1990s party backing, policy shifts and pragmatic opportunism had pushed the law centre stage. Despite its lack of electoral salience, for New Labour there was 'no question of backing away from it in 1997' (interview with Mark Fisher MP 2005).

FOI was partly thrust upon the Labour Party leadership. In the legislature, FOI's long support in the Labour Party had built into a powerful current of cross-party support, seen through a series of Private Members' Bills in the 1980s and early 1990s and bolstered by support from a varied alliance of extra-institutional forces. It was also powered by the spread of FOI around the world and, perhaps mostly importantly, by rapidly shifting technology and changing public expectations in the area of information provision.

FOI was embraced by the leadership as very much a product of Labour's eighteen years of out of power. On a narrow, partisan level, FOI was an opportunistic policy that served to embarrass the secretive and 'sleaze'-ridden Conservative government. It also chimed, after the experience of Thatcherism, with a current of Labour Party thought on breaking up power, and locked into a wide-ranging programme of constitutional reforms aimed at redesigning politics. More than this, the idea itself had obtained a powerful magnetic force. It was bound up with Labour's sense of self and appealed as a policy that symbolised Labour's radicalism and its new approach towards government and the people.

Taken together, these factors offered New Labour a powerful 'justifying narrative'. A defining moment came in 1996, when the leader of the opposition Tony

Blair spoke at the annual Freedom of Information Awards organised by CFOI. Blair's speech covered the symbolism behind the promised legislation. FOI was given a prominence, centrality and urgency never before accorded to it. However, underneath the apparent inevitably of a strong FOI law, doubts persisted as to the leadership's understanding and commitment.

### The push towards FOI: Parliament, lobbying and the changing world

A series of pressures helped thrust FOI as a policy upon the New Labour leadership, from within and outside the political system.

#### *Parliament, Labour and cross-party support*

For those policies shorn of public support, parties are crucial (Hacker and Pierson 2014). By the middle of the 1990s FOI attracted support from across the Labour Party. From the left, it had been long championed by the radical 'Bennite' wing led by the ex-minister and openness champion Tony Benn, where it was tied with the reduction of secrecy and increased scrutiny of the intelligence services (Dorey 2008). From the political centre, FOI was also a key part of the wide-ranging constitutional reforms of the breakaway centrist Labour group that became the Social Democratic Party in the 1980s (Crewe and King 1995).

By the 1980s and 1990s support for FOI had begun to build across party divisions. Between 1979 and 1992, six FOI Private Members' Bills were launched by Liberal Democrat or Labour backbenchers, culminating in Mark Fisher's Right to Know Bill (CFOI 1993). Fisher's Bill, introduced in 1993, gave a right of access to government information (and some private company information), with an independent commissioner able to order disclosure, and it proposed a parallel reform of the 1989 Official Secrets Act (CFOI 1992). It won an unopposed second reading and survived the committee stage only to be blocked by the government (CFOI 1993). Support stretched from the Labour front and backbenches and the Liberal Democrats (long supporters of it) to a 'libertarian current of Conservative backbench opinion' backed by senior MPs such as Richard Shepherd and Teddy Taylor (Evans 2003, 207). By 1997 the passing of an FOI Act was part of a broad formal constitutional reform programme agreed between the Liberal Democrats and Labour under the Cook-MacLennan agreement: one Liberal Democrat member of the committee described it as the 'jewel in the crown of successful constitutional reform' (Flinders 2009a; Hansard, House of Lords, 20/4/2000, col. 836).

Parliamentary committees also began to champion an FOI law. In 1996 the Select Committee on the Parliamentary Commissioner for Administration, looking into the operation of Major's Code of Access, called for a full FOI Act. After looking at other Westminster-style Commonwealth jurisdictions it concluded that 'on balance the advantage lies in favour of legislation. We recommend that the Government introduce a Freedom of Information Act' (House of Commons Library 1997, 50). By the mid-1990s FOI was an all-party, pan-political issue.

### Extra-parliamentary pressure

As Chapter 2 shows, since the late 1970s CFOI had lobbied for openness and by the 1980s had been the motive force behind a series of 'targeted' transparency legislation (McClean 2011, 202; Wilson 2011). By the 1990s CFOI had successfully won the high-level 'war of ideas' over an FOI law, through a sustained lobbying effort championing a 'right to know' as a principal and pragmatic instrument of change (Evans 2003, 199). It had successfully pushed for openness in various areas from school access to local government corruption, emphasising the 'asymmetries of power' and threat to 'self-determination' that secrecy represented (McClean 2011, 202). As well as lobbying, combined with academic bodies such as the Constitution Unit, CFOI also provided information regarding the practicalities and 'methodology of change' (Brazier 1998). Straw (2012) paid tribute to their influence in placing FOI on the Labour agenda.

CFOI was at the centre of a growing 'umbrella group' aimed at 'cognitive' and 'elite' mobilisation (Evans 2008, 199). New groups like Charter 88, Liberty and Democratic Audit all advocated for FOI as part of a wider process of constitutional change. Charter 88, as one example, supported 'holistic change' and a coherent agenda towards 'explicit limits on executive powers [that] aimed to replace Britain's power-hoarding constitution with a more pluralistic and consensual system' (Flinders 2009a, 647). The discourse and arguments had a powerful influence on the Labour leader John Smith's support for wholesale constitutional reform (see below). Alongside these groups CFOI had sought to build the 'broadest possible coalition' to bring 'different constituencies together as one', as Maurice Frankel explained:

> when we were campaigning for the Act, we had about a hundred national organizations supporting us including the leading press bodies, campaign organizations, animal welfare organizations, organizations that wanted to see less animal testing, safety organizations [as well as] religious churches, other religious organizations [and] professional bodies. It turned out to be a wide constituency. Although most of them preferred somebody else to be doing the campaigning and the lobbying, they did put their voices behind it. (Muck Rock 2016)

### The global spread of FOI

International pressure was also growing. By 1996 there was 'a continuous worldwide movement towards FOI' and a danger that Britain would be left behind. Tony Blair pointed to the growing acceptance of FOI across the world, which was driven by a complex interplay of legitimation and regional contagion effects, with sudden 'jumps' of countries in the 1960s and then 1980s with the end of the Cold War (Blair 1996; Bennett 1997; Berliner 2013). A cluster of important countries had

FOI, from Scandinavian countries such as Sweden in 1766 and Finland in 1951 to the Netherlands in 1970 and Denmark and France in 1978. Three Westminster-style democracies had also passed FOI legislation in the 1980s: Australia and New Zealand in 1982 and Canada in 1985 (Bennett 1997). In the seven years between 1990 and 1997, thirteen more countries passed different forms of openness laws, from Italy to Belize, with another eighteen following between 1997 and 2000 in what amounted to the beginnings of a 'global explosion' (Ackerman and Sandoval-Ballesteros 2006). Countries as diverse as South Africa and, closer to home, Ireland were also planning or implementing legislation while the European Union was also moving forward in promoting access to documents. This global movement could, in Mark Fisher's words, make Britain 'look foolish' (interview with Mark Fisher MP 2005).

As seen in Chapter 2, arguments against open government had frequently been framed by the need to protect the existing system. The presence of FOI in similar Westminster-style systems like New Zealand, Australia and Canada gave the UK the opportunity to 'look at the strengths and weaknesses and learn from them' but also undermined traditional arguments that FOI was not suited to the British system (interview with Mark Fisher MP 2005). Hazell (1997b) argued that 'these Commonwealth countries ... show that FOI can readily fit into a Westminster system' (2). Many of the claims made against FOI were eroded: their presence demonstrated that 'Collective responsibility is protected by the exemption for Cabinet and Cabinet Committee papers; civil service neutrality is protected by the exemption for opinion and advice; and Ministerial accountability to Parliament is strengthened through the greater flow of information' (2).

### Technical change

The push across the world to FOI was also driven by policy 'drift'. The shift from mass communication to mass self-communication, begun in the 1980s, began to take shape in the 1990s as new hybrid networks of information emerged and the communication sphere increasingly became a 'driver of social change' (Castells 2013). Although mainframe computers had been used since the 1960s and e-government was only beginning in the 1990s, in a pre-search-engine age, it marked the beginning of a decade of radical change to both the 'front end' of government interaction and the 'back end' of internal systems: Blair's 1998 promise to make 25% of government-public interaction 'electronic' now looks positively quaint (Margetts 2006, 261). There were emerging signs of greater information sharing and open cultures (via the philosophy of software itself) as well as the growing influence of data-driven 'audit, rating and ranking' (Margetts 2011, 519). As Keane (2011) argued, this new 'communicative abundance' led in turn to a 'democratisation of information': 'thanks to cheap and easy methods of digital reproduction, we live in times of a sudden widening of access to published materials previously unavailable to publics, or once available only to restricted circles of users' (6). This meant the 'dismantling of elite privileges' and an end to information monopolies (6). As a result, even by the 1990s, as Blair put it, 'citizens' expectations had changed'. By the time Blair spoke in 1996, 'more and more people became more accustomed to finding information on the internet' and 'it became less acceptable for government not to provide it' (Blair 1996).

### The embrace: New Labour, new openness

While external pressures grew stronger, there was a parallel internal embrace of FOI from within the party after 1992. Central to this, as Tony Blair and Jack Straw both acknowledged, was the experience of opposition (Blair 2011; Straw 2012). Blair later explained, somewhat ambiguously, that it was a 'commitment given in opposition … before the experience of government' (Justice Committee 2012a).

#### *Opportunism: a stick to beat the government*

There was a heavy dose of political opportunism in advocating FOI. Put simply, FOI was 'a good stick to beat the government with' (interview with James Cornford 2005). Major's Conservative government suffered a continual series of scandals and exposés between 1992 and 1997 and became a byword for impropriety (Dunleavy, Weir and Subrahmanyam 1995). Under the catch-all term 'sleaze', the media revealed a stream of 'corruption, semi-corruption or near corruption' covering sexual 'misconduct', lobbying and financial mis-dealings (603). No fewer than nine members of the government stepped down over sex scandals alone (Denver 1998). The effect was heightened by Major's 1995 'Back-to-Basics' campaign, presented as a renewal of Conservative ideology, which the media portrayed as a hypocriti-cal claim to a new morality (Turner 2013). The continued exposure was justified as a 'right to know' issue, whereby the public were entitled to know how, and by whom, they were governed (Turner 2013). The 'drip' of scandals helped make Major's administration 'the government that could do no right' and meant that it 'plumbed depths of unpopularity never before experienced by a modern govern-ment' (Denver 1998, 15–16).

The scandals also covered government-wide policy mistakes, cover-ups and secrecy. Foremost was the long running 'arms to Iraq scandal', which stemmed from a collapsed trial in 1992. In 1996 the Scott Inquiry revealed ministerial complic-ity in illegally selling arms to Iraq against its own stated policy and recommended greater government openness, though it stopped short of calling for an FOI Act (Turner 2013; House of Commons Library 1997). Although the rather 'technical and obscure' inquiry was 'unlikely to command the attention of the average voter' it exposed a continued 'endemic culture of Whitehall secrecy' (Hennessy 1995, 80) and 'confirmed what the opposition had long claimed' (Denver 1998, 35–36). At the same time, the BSE health scare, concerning the spread of so-called 'Mad Cow Disease' into the human food chain, further exposed government secrecy and inconsistency in dealing with a major public health crisis.

Major's attempts to counter the allegations of sleaze and secrecy through reform stimulated rather than dampened the pressure for change. In 1994 Major appointed an independent committee, the Nolan committee, to 'clear the air' and suggest political reform. Its recommendations were 'far more radical than anyone expected', with fifty-five wide-ranging proposals, most controversially over disclosure of MPs' financial dealings and a new code of conduct for members (Denver 1998, 30). This then resulted in an embarrassing attempt by the government to block publication, which was then defeated in the House of Commons (Denver 1998).

As leader of the Labour Party, Blair hammered at Conservative sleaze and secrecy in justifying FOI. In a speech he gave in 1996 the Scott Inquiry was a 'devastating indictment' proving that 'the culture of secrecy permeates almost every single aspect of government activity … Information was treated as a precious resource to be given out only when absolutely necessary and even then not in full'. He added, 'I believe, if the case was not unanswerable before, Scott has made the case for a Freedom of Information Act absolutely unanswerable now' (Blair 1996). The BSE crisis was also evidence of a government 'wishing to manage even nation-wide health scares from behind closed doors [giving] information only when absolutely necessary and even then not in full' (Blair 1996). Blair did acknowledge Major's reform attempts but argued that their main legacy was to 'underline the need for action on a far greater scale' (Blair 1996).

John Major complained that the barrage of sleaze exposures made Labour appear 'above reproach and Conservatives beyond redemption' (Turner 2013). Between 1994 and 1996 Gallup recorded a clear majority of voters agreeing with the view that the Conservative government was 'sleazy and disreputable', a proportion that rose to 75% by 1995 (Denver 1998, 37). Although it appeared to have little direct effect on voting in the 1997 general election, sleaze contributed to the scale of the Conservatives' defeat (King 1998). It clearly influenced the election campaign, taking up 18% of overall media coverage and constituting the most popular issue for newspaper editorials (Norris 1998). Blair himself spoke of how 'it was a media game and as Opposition we played it' and how, despite his later regrets, it was 'just too easy to score' (Blair 2011, 127). Labour famously used the stream of scandals to appear 'not just better at governing but more moral, more upright' (126).

### Labour thought and FOI

A commitment to openness stemmed from a particular, often suppressed, stream of Labour thought, 'an anti-bureaucratic strain of opinion … at variance with the tacit assumptions of the democratic-collectivist tradition' (Marquand 1999b, 241). The stream can be traced through a series of outsiders and radical thinkers, from G. D. H. Cole to the Webbs and George Lansbury. The Webbs were 'early champions of the public right to know', calling for the 'disease' of official secrecy to be ended by the 'searchlight' of publicity in their *Socialist Commonwealth of Great Britain* (Theakston 1992, 177).

This stream of Labour philosophy was frequently lost amid the statist impulse to 'capture' and use the state rather than reform it (Dorey 2008). However, 'in the 1980s and early 1990s it began to come in from the cold' (Marquand 1999b, 245). Labour, out of power between 1979 and 1997, witnessed the full force of 'power-hoarding' constitutional power (King 2015) and was on the receiving end of the 'ferocious centralism' of successive Conservative governments (Marquand 1999b, 245). A Labour policy document in 1990 described the Thatcher government's actions as a 'sustained assault on both individual liberty and democracy' (Judge 1993, 195) and its use of Official Secrecy and state power left a series of marks on Labour, who were given what Tony Wright called a 'crash course of constitutional education' (Straw 2010, 359). FOI was part of an 'anti-conservative mantra' concerned with breaking up power and had a 'big emotional steam behind it' (Straw 2012) and part of a 'drumbeat' of change (interview with Jack Straw 2015).

Like FOI reforms elsewhere, the promise drew strength and momentum from a wider set of changes and were subject to 'co-evolution' as they fed and interacted with other proposed reforms (John 1999). Labour's 'rediscovered' ideas flowed into a broader reformulation of policy. Commitment to FOI remained a manifesto pledge during Labour's years of internal division in the early 1980s. In 1984 the new leader Neil Kinnock had promised to make FOI a 'priority' for any future Labour administration (CFOI 1984a). As the Labour Party began to modernise its policy platform, it developed a 'shopping list' of constitutional reforms including FOI, albeit still within the confines of executive power (Flinders 2009b, 39). FOI was given 'a strong and renewed commitment reiterated on public occasions and major policy speeches' (interview with Mark Fisher MP 2005). Kinnock's late 1980s policy review 'Meet the Challenge: Make the Change' criticised the new 1989 Official Secrets Act as 'reinforcing' rather than diminishing secrecy, and promised 'a FOI Act covering information held by national, regional and local government' with exemptions 'clearly specified and highly drawn' and an appeals procedure to an independent tribunal (Labour Party 1989, 59).

By the time of the 1992 election, FOI had become a priority constitutional issue. In 1991 the Shadow Home Secretary Roy Hattersley drafted a FOI Bill which was intended to be the first Bill the incoming Labour government of 1992 would introduce (interview with Mark Fisher MP 2005). As a measure of the seriousness of Labour's commitment, before the 1992 general election that it was widely predicted to win, the Shadow Home Secretary announced that:

> Anyone who looks at our detailed plans for a Freedom of Information Act must know that it is not only suitable for early enactment. It is ready for early enactment. If a Labour government was elected on Thursday I would be able to send the headings of a Bill to parliamentary draughtsman on the following day. (Gundersen 2008, 226)

The closeness of Labour's defeat in 1992 led to preparatory analysis by the Civil Service on an FOI law, including a series of advisory notes that would have been presented to Prime Minister Kinnock. One document, released under FOI to the BBC journalist Martin Rosenbaum in 2014, argued that Labour's draft was a 'lobby group's opening bid' and that even campaigners would be 'astonished' if it was 'accepted'. Its 'faults were likely to defeat its purposes', including its potential to have a 'damaging effect' on policy advice and Cabinet collectively as well as potentially large 'costs'. The briefing recommended that a 'fresh draft' would 'more closely follow' Commonwealth models and the 'particular circumstances of the UK'. An FOI law would have to be made 'more manageable and practicable' (BBC 1/11/2014).

Following Labour's shock fourth election defeat, the new leader John Smith turned Kinnock's constitutional 'shopping list' into a radical reform programme at the centre of Labour's pledge (Flinders 2009b, 39). In a speech to Charter 88 in 1993, Smith spoke of how he 'wanted to see a fundamental shift in the balance of power between citizens and the state – a shift away from an overpowering state to a citizens' democracy where people have rights and powers and where they are served by accountable and responsive government' (Flinders 2009a, 649).

By 1994, Labour's programme had become increasingly radical, proposing strengthening the legislature, introducing electoral reform and giving away power to subnational government, apparently offering the 'supreme altruism' that so many previous governments lacked (Judge 1993). When unwrapped, the platform was seen to contain a huge range of 'massive and radical constitutional changes' that were 'almost certainly, irreversible, and which have permanently altered the way that Britain is governed' (Bogdanor 2010, S54). Looking back on the process, Bogdanor argues, '1997–2007 can be regarded as an era of constitutional reform comparable to that of the years of the Great Reform Act of 1832 or the years before 1914' (S54). Hazell (1997a) spoke at the time of how the changes 'will fundamentally alter the relationship between the different parts of the United Kingdom, between parliament and the judges, between government and the citizens' (10). The key parts were:

- Devolution to Scotland and Wales, providing for a directly elected Scottish Parliament, and with a Scottish Executive responsible to it on devolved matters and a directly elected National Assembly in Wales.
- The establishment (following the successful outcome of a referendum) of a directly elected Assembly in Northern Ireland.
- A directly elected mayor and assembly for London.
- The introduction of proportional representation for the elections to the devolved bodies in Scotland, Wales, Northern Ireland and the London Assembly and the introduction of proportional representation for elections to the European Parliament.

- A Local Government Act requiring local authorities to abandon the committee system and providing for directly elected mayors, following referendums.
- The Human Rights Act 1998, requiring government and all other public bodies to comply with the provisions of the European Convention of Human Rights.
- The removal of all but ninety-two of the hereditary peers from the House of Lords, intended as the first phase of a wider reform of the Lords.
- Provision for a statutory right of access to government information.
- Reform of party funding, requiring the registration of political parties, controlling donations to political parties and national campaign expenditure and providing for the establishment of an Electoral Commission to oversee elections and to advise on improvements in electoral procedure. (Adapted from Bogdanor 2010)

The sheer size and weight of the programme appeared to increase the chances of FOI. In terms of policy momentum, the component parts would benefit from 'overspill' from other parts of the programme (Evans 2003; John 1999).

FOI fitted with several different parts of the reform programme. Establishing a right to access information fitted the rights agenda of the Human Rights Act and with the democratic innovations promised across local and central government, from referendums to citizens' juries. Compared with previous reform attempts, FOI was 'locked' into a range of other commitments, rather than added as a 'side-product' of a process or an isolated promise: it was part of a 'form of coevolution [whereby] the momentum of evolutionary change … had a knock on effect on the evolution of the proposal' (John 1999, 58). The 'radical policy choices' on offer by the mid-1990s appeared to promise a rare period of far-reaching and transformative policy-making. The 'reformulation of social democracy in the 1990s' presaged what John (1999) terms 'a culture of policy experimentation which relied on rejecting conventional wisdom and reaping the possible rewards of risk' (57).

The proposed changes, while far-reaching, were not coherent. They were simultaneously 'confused and ambiguous' while also 'dynamic and open-ended' (Marquand 1999a, 1). They represented an amalgam of commitments with diverse, if not contradictory, aims: some gave away power and others reshaped existing institutions. The sources of the reforms were similarly diverse: some were responding to pressure for change or perceived electoral threats, such as those in Wales or Scotland, while other, less popular reforms emanated from limited, primarily elite, groups (Bogdanor 2009; Flinders 2009b). While the overall plans were criticised for their 'piecemeal' approach and lack of a 'grand design', the overall result would be to 'limit the power of government' and 'cut power into pieces' in a historic move away from the Westminster model (Bogdanor 2010, 56–57). The reforms made Tony Blair, somewhat reluctantly, the 'most far reaching, radical reformer of the formal edifice of the constitution since Oliver Cromwell' (in Matthews 2015, 312).

## New Labour and the symbolism of FOI

FOI is frequently rooted and justified by tying it to varied political norms and wider values (Fenster 2012b). For the Labour Party, FOI exhibited 'congruence' and 'symbolised Labour's core values', reflecting its self-image (Scammell 2001, 530). Alongside the Human Rights Act, FOI had become a cause championed by progressive legal and political actors. It was part of a number of reforms driven by 'radical lawyers' and by the 1990s was a 'very fashionable idea' (interview with David Clark 2015). FOI was perhaps a classic case of policy developed via the 'transmission of ideas and argument in elite circles and in the media' (John 1999, 39).

New Labour's leading figures were vocal in their support. Between 1992 and 1997, Blair repeated the commitment and its importance in at least eight major interviews, four ministerial statements and one major speech (CFOI 2000b, 4–5). Blair's commitment to FOI appeared to go a long way back. In 1984, as a newly elected MP, he called on Margaret Thatcher to pass an FOI law in the wake of the prosecution of the civil servant Sarah Tisdall under Official Secrets Act prosecution for leaking information on US cruise missiles: 'Does the Right Honourable Lady agree that there is an urgent need for legislation so that … the government cannot conceal the scale of what they are doing?' (Rentoul 2001, 126). Fellow Labour politicians who would soon become central policy actors, such as the Shadow Home Secretary Jack Straw, Gordon Brown, Robin Cook, Derry Irvine and Peter Mandelson, further emphasised the importance of the policy on numerous occasions (CFOI 2000b, 6–11).

The key event came with Blair's 1996 speech to the CFOI Awards in 1996. The organisers of the event hoped to obtain a definite commitment from the Labour leadership to legislate for FOI (interview with James Cornford 2005; Wilson 2011). As Chapter 2 above shows, throughout the 1980s CFOI had sought specific public promises. Wilson explains how the 'opposition leaders or Home Secretaries' would be asked to 'present prizes and make speeches at our annual freedom of information awards', which were 'attended by newspaper editors and senior politicians'. The promises were then 'recorded and heavily publicised' and so CFOI were 'pinning them down, committing them to a policy' (2011, 184–185). Blair's speech, written by Pat McFadden, perhaps exceeded expectations. Blair outlined the centrality of FOI to New Labour's agenda and philosophy in a rich symbolic 'justifying narrative', explaining why FOI was needed (Michener 2011). In Blair's speech, FOI formed a crucial part of New Labour's vision of how Britain was to be modernised and its government was to function. It also sent a series of signals about Labour's radicalism, its vision of modernisation, a new government morality and its intent to change citizen-government relations.

As Chapter 1 above shows, FOI had long carried an aura of 'radicalism' in its principle and image. Blair later described FOI, somewhat ruefully, as a 'revolutionary offer' (2011, 127). In his speech Blair spoke of how FOI 'is not some isolated constitutional reform … It is a change that is absolutely fundamental to how we see politics developing in this country over the next few years'. He explained how it was also bound up in Labour's self-image, as 'information is power and any government's attitude about sharing information with the people actually says a great deal about how it views power itself and ... the people who elected it' (1996). FOI fitted with what Blair elsewhere described as the need to 'construct a new and radical politics to serve the people in the new century ahead ... where power is pushed down to the people instead of being hoarded centrally' (quoted in Flinders 2009b, 41). Increased openness flowed into a growing 'demand for democratic self-government ... fed by better educated citizens and the free flow of information provided by new technology' that could create an 'open, vibrant, diverse [and] democratic debate' and 'laboratory of ideas' (Blair 1998). By 1997 the policy was being driven by politicians who were 'outsiders from power' from within a party that was, and viewed itself as, distinctly 'non-establishment' (interview with David Clark 2015). FOI thus fitted with a wider, if vague, process of 'democratisation and reconnecting government with the people': in symbolic terms it represented part of a radical break with past practices and an 'anti-establishment' tool of political empowerment (Dorey 2008, 201).

In this form, the policy fitted neatly with the Third Way idea of the 'radical centre' and New Labour's 'radical yet simple' approach to reform. Foley characterises FOI as 'captivating in its radical simplicity [although] it may appear nothing more than connecting a disjunction between theory and practice ... in reality it would represent a profound change in the sources and usage of power within the British government system' (Foley 1999, 69). If constitutional reform was about promoting accountability and 'breaking up centres of power', then the ruction of information hierarchies offered a simple yet radical way to do it (Straw 2010, 360). FOI formed a 'core tenet' of a process of change which involved 'participation, openness, transparency, diluted executive power' as well as creating new forms of democracy 'other than the orthodox voting process' (Flinders 2009a, 649).

From another perspective, Jack Straw spoke of how FOI was part of the diagnosis that Britain 'wasn't democratic enough' (interview with Jack Straw 2015). Professor Peter Hennessy later reflected that FOI was a completion of democratic reforms began with the arrival of the popular vote:

> the Freedom of Information Act ... was the completion of the circle that began with the extension of the franchise. It took from 1832 to 1948 to get to one person one vote, but the remaining ... test [is whether] an elector could cast an informed vote. The answer was that until the Freedom of Information Act very probably not. It has to be seen as part of completing the virtues of the franchise in an open society. (Justice Committee 2012b)

FOI was also a symbol of a 'modern society' (interview with David Clark 2015). To Blair it was a practical step in modernising democracy:

> A Freedom of Information Act is not just important in itself. It is part of bringing our politics up to date, of letting politics catch up with the aspirations of people and deliv-

ering not just more open government but more effective, more efficient, government for the future. (Blair 1996)

It formed part of New Labour's 'cure' for government, part of its attempt to restructure political institutions to promote 'greater transparency', while developing a strong civil society and promoting 'partnership' with its citizens. The particular emphasis was on technological change. Tony Blair outlined the effect of this change upon information related policy in 1996: 'There has been a huge explosion in communications...in recent years. The internet has made instantaneous electronic communication a fact of life for millions of people.' This created a growing pressure for openness as people 'demand more information from their government' (Blair 1996). Consequently 'knowledge is everywhere and people demand more information from their government, from their local councils, from their health service, from their quangos, from other organisations, from private sector organisations' (Blair 1996).

FOI would meet the demand to empower citizens, offering a new means to challenge and a new right. New Labour's emphasis on individual rights was a new innovation, that distinguished it from the rather 'old Labour' emphasis on securing collective rights secured through state action (Klug 2010). Blair asserted that 'the first right of any citizen in a mature democracy should be the right to information' while Jack Straw argued the more radical case, that FOI would 'move us away from the notion of the 'ruler and ruled ... the end of the citizen as "subject"' (CFOI 2000b, 5–6). It was 'the best way to give citizens new rights' (interview with David Clark 2015).

FOI was also a concrete offering and a symbol of how a government could be 'not just better at governing but more moral, more upright' (Blair 2011, 126). Blair pointed to the effects of secrecy as part of the 'disaffection from politics' and the 'disillusion' and argued that FOI was an 'essential' part of the constitutional reform programme, because it was about 'genuinely changing the relationship in politics today' (Blair 1996). Elsewhere Blair offered a false choice: 'we can continue with the over-centralised, secretive and discredited system of government. Or we can change and trust the people to take more control over their own lives' (Dunleavy et al. 2001, 405). Restoring lost trust in the political system was a central aim of the constitutional reform programme (Curtice 2010), and entrusting citizens with information previously held secret would be a way of 'restoring lost trust in government [and] will bring greater confidence to our system' so damaged by the Thatcher and Major governments (CFOI 2000b, 5). Here FOI was linked to a series of changes designed to promote a more ethical approach to governing such as mandating the public declaration of all donations to political parties and also, as Blair mentioned in his speech, reforming whistle-blowing laws (House of Commons Library 2015).

Finally, FOI was intended as part of a recalibration of relations between citizen and government: 'if a government is genuine about wanting a partnership with the people who it is governing, then the act of government itself must be seen in some sense as a shared responsibility and the government has to empower the people and give them a say in how politics is conducted' (Blair 1996). FOI also came to symbolise both personal empowerment against government and the limitations of government, with a re-calibrated 'partnership' as the cornerstone of modern government. FOI would benefit government instrumentally:

> I believe that there is a limit to what government can do, and the power of society or community to act and to influence the lives of the individuals within it depends on a far more diverse and diffuse set of relationships. I don't believe it is possible for government to govern effectively now, unless it governs in some sense in a relationship of partnership with the people whom it is governing. It is one of the reasons why decentralisation of power is actually in the interests of government. (Blair 1996)

Blair ended the speech by reaffirming New Labour's commitment to FOI legislation:

> We want to end the obsessive and unnecessary secrecy which surrounds government activity and make government information available to the public unless there are good reasons not to do so. So the presumption is that information should be, rather than should not be, released. (Blair 1996)

Blair joked that people may cynically see his promise as a media ploy, to be quietly changed once Labour were in office: 'people often say to me today: everyone says this before they get into power, then, after they get into power you start to read the words of the government on the screen and they don't seem so silly after all' (Blair 1996).

## The doubts

FOI sat high on the Labour Party's agenda as the 1997 general election approached. For a voteless policy, derided and ignored two decades before, it had undergone a remarkable transformation. There was, however, concern over how committed the party was and how such a decidedly complex and electorally unappealing policy would fare.

### How committed was the Labour leadership?

As seen before with Labour governments, some feared that there would be a gap between 'principle' and 'practice' under Blair (Flinders 2009b, 38). Throughout its history, after its radical beginnings, Labour had focused on socio-political rather than constitutional reform, and leaders throughout the party's history had lacked 'sustained interest in constitutional change' (Morgan 2013, 77).

This concern was in part about design of the reforms. The party's plans 'deliberately eschewed any engagement with first principles, with grand plans and templates' (Flinders 2009b, 46–47). Lord Irvine spoke of how 'the strands do not spring from a single master plan, however much that concept might appeal to purists. We prefer the empirical genius of our nation: to go, pragmatically, step by step, for change through continuing consent' (in Flinders 2009b, 46). Evans (2003) pointed out the competing intentions and contradictory effects. The programme was part electoral strategy, drawing in a 'cross-class coalition', part 'radical liberal agenda', based on creating stronger rights, and also a 'policy instrument for securing popular approval and legitimacy' (328). So what, it could be asked, would keep it on track and moving?

The programme was also a 'curious and contradictory amalgam of radicalism and conservatism' (Dorey 2008, 2). While some parts were radical, others were 'highly conservative', and the totality of commitments were studded with 'ad hoc' and 'ambiguous' areas (1). Reflecting in 2011 Lipsey, termed it a 'very peculiar revolution' where the changes 'represent no coherent modernisation plan but are rather a ragbag of bits-and-pieces bearing little relationship to each other and with decidedly variable amounts of thought and merit attached to them' (342). In 2002 Lord Irvine's explanation of the philosophy revealed rather than resolved these contradictions. New Labour sought to maintain the 'the supremacy of Parliament and the Executive', while undertaking far-reaching change:

- To remain a parliamentary democracy with the Westminster Parliament supreme and within that the Commons the dominant chamber.
- To encourage greater public participation by developing a maturer democracy with different centres of power, where individuals enjoy greater rights and where government is carried out closer to the people.
- To devise a solution to each problem on its own terms. (Flinders 2009b, 46)

Revolutionary alteration existed alongside the preservation of the Westminster (executive) model. How, for example, could a clear support for Parliamentary (or executive) supremacy be squared with the creation of other centres of power? What precisely were 'individual responses' to problems? The confusion was reflected in very different academic analyses: Bogdanor described the proposals as 'nothing less than a revolution in our constitutional affairs' and a 'radical discontinuity' (2009, 276) while Theakston (2006) viewed the changes as simply a 'modernised and updated Westminster model' (33). Flinders argued that it was simultaneously both 'radical' and 'conservative' at different levels (2009b, 56). Flinders later called this 'bi-constitutionality' (2009) with 'significant change but only in relation to the federal–unitary dimension' but 'no dramatic shift from a majoritarian to a consensual model of democracy at the national level. The Westminster model continues to be the default option in terms of democracy in Britain' (63). The problem for supporters of FOI was that the Westminster model and the numerous secretive constitutional conventions that accompanied it had blocked reform and acted as a clear disincentive in the past (Robertson 1982). The Westminster model was 'power hoarding' and secretive, and support for it also implied opposition to a populist, popular and power redistributing instrument like FOI (King 2015). Was it possible to support both simultaneously?

As well as ambiguity in design, there was uncertainty around the extent to which the upper reaches of the party supported FOI. Those at the top of the Labour Party were less enamoured with change in private, and Blair himself, in particular, 'was always ambivalent about the merits of constitutional reform'. Blair was said to have a curious 'box ticking mentality' and to be pushed by a 'moral and political duty to see it through' as an inheritance of John Smith, rather than any deep belief (Flinders 2009b, 42, 44, 38). The doubts were rooted partly in principle and partly in practicalities. First, the Labour leadership retained support for the traditional model of UK government: Labour too wished to 'hoard power' (King 2015). At the senior level, there was no 'deeper ideological shift ... away from its traditional acquiescence with majoritarianism ... New Labour's bi-constitutional statecraft reflected [only] a partial ideological conversion to the constitutional model promoted by Charter 88' (Flinders 2009a, 646).

Second, there was a fear that reform would bring no electoral advantage and fill up parliamentary time. Former Labour Party heavyweights such as Callaghan and Healey expressed scepticism towards New Labour's constitutional reform agenda and publicly voiced their concerns (Hennessy 1995, 152). In the second Wilson government of the late 1960s, abortive House of Lords reform had taken up large amounts of the legislative timetable, while in the 1970s devolution legislation had log-jammed parts of the Callaghan government. There was a deep fear that the potential 'disruption and trench warfare' could re-emerge around Labour's many far-reaching pledges (Theakston 2006, 33). A number of the shadow Cabinet pressed Blair not to 'waste time', particularly 'valuable parliamentary time', on unimportant issues (Flinders 2009b, 42).

To the doubts was added ignorance. For FOI in particular there was a wholesale lack of awareness at the top of the party. It was an issue that was 'good for a handclap at conference' but nothing more (private information). Blair hinted at this when he said that FOI was 'agreed by most at the time' (Justice Committee 2012a). Straw (2012) claimed that the 'few words' of the manifesto commitment were 'about all the serious intellectual consideration that the PLP or the Shadow Cabinet had given to this inherently complex issue' and that there was a 'collective naivety' at senior levels about the implications (275–276). Straw later compared the preparation of FOI unfavourably with the careful, detailed planning of the legislation that became the Human Rights Act 1998 and regretted that there had not been 'more careful thought in opposition' to what was an 'inherently complex issue' (2012, 287). He claimed, 'FOI was not thought about with any seriousness' before government (275). Blair more generally spoke of how any opposition is 'woefully short on what is required to step into government and govern' and explained that 'above all, it is about knowing the complexity of policy-making [as] what may seem easy enough stated in the manifesto ... when looked at in the cold light of day can be horrendously difficult to do'. 'In the details', he argued, 'we were lacking' (Blair 2011, 105).

## The politics of voteless change

As well as the politicians' doubts, there was a lack of real popular electoral pressure. Superficially, there was demand for broad political change and, within this, openness. A Democratic Audit survey in the spring of 1995 pointed to a broad decline in faith in Britain's governing institutions, with 'the public ... rejecting established practice'; 'important cannons of faith at Westminster and Whitehall have effectively lost all legitimacy' (Hennessy 1995, 205). Democratic Audit expressed its surprise not only at the 'degree of dissatisfaction with Britain's governing process and institutions [but at] the degree of support for their radical refashioning' (20).

This appeared to filter directly into a demand for FOI. Blair claimed in his 1996 speech that four out of five voters supported the policy. This figure came from two 'state of the nation' surveys by Democratic Audit in 1991 and 1995. In 1991 77% tended to agree or strongly agreed with having a statutory right of access to information, a figure that rose by 1995 to 81%. It was a policy, at least, that few disagreed with (see Table 3.1).

However, the interest in FOI was not deep. As a nation the UK has been 'notoriously uninterested' in the constitution and reform. Only rarely have constitutional issues become electoral: the 'Great Reform Act of 1832 and the Parliament Act 1911' stand out as topics of 'intense political and public debate' (Flinders 2009b, 37). Since Gallup began recording issue salience with voters in the 1950s, constitutional issues have excited very little interest (Sanders 1998, 241). The debate on constitutional reform since the 1970s had been 'primarily conducted amongst the elite – politicians, academics, lawyers and journalists' (Bogdanor 2009, 6). There has been 'no external pressure for change', with devolution policy in Scotland being the only partial exception (Flinders 2009b, 38; Bogdanor 2009). In the 1997 election cam-

**Table 3.1** Responses to Democratic Audit (1991) and (1995) 'There should be a freedom of information act, giving the right of access to information collected by public authorities, subject to adequate safeguards on national security, crime prevention and personal privacy'

| Response | 1991 (%) | 1995 (%) |
| --- | --- | --- |
| Strongly agree | 37 | 42 |
| Tend to agree | 40 | 39 |
| Neither agree nor disagree | 8 | 8 |
| Tend to disagree | 6 | 4 |
| Strongly disagree | 3 | 2 |
| No opinion | 5 | 4 |

*Note:* Numbers appear to be rounded.
*Source:* IPSOS Mori 1991 and 1995.

paign the issue of constitutional change came fourteenth out of fourteen potential influences on voting in a MORI survey (Bogdanor 2009). Bogdanor (2009) later concluded that the public had been 'little interested' or 'perhaps even unaware' of the programme (6). The 'nation shrugged' at what 'might have been hailed as a democratic revolution', and so Blair was poised in a vacuum to deliver 'a historic set of changes to the British constitution in the unheroic posture of a technocrat fixing a basically sound machine' (Rentoul 2001, 459). This lack of interest could spell danger ahead for FOI: without the sheet anchor of electoral support, what would happen if the government lost its enthusiasm, as so many others before it had done?

## Conclusion

FOI had a made a remarkable journey to the centre of New Labour's constitutional reform agenda. This was partly opportunistic and partly came about through 'fit', but by 1997 FOI also had a powerful symbolic purchase. It signalled radicalism, morality and recalibration and, within this, ideas about trust, change and democratic reform.

Labour's 1997 election victory created a further momentum for change. As Seldon explained, 'no Labour government in history had come to power with so many initial advantages', as it was 'united' with 'a huge Parliamentary majority, a friendly media, three years of solid work preparing for power, ... and a weak and divided opposition' (Seldon 2001, 593). FOI itself also seemed ready. In 1997 a Constitution Unit study of the feasibility of FOI concluded that:

> Of all the possible constitutional reforms proposed by the political parties, Freedom of Information (FOI) is the one in the most advanced state of readiness. Good draft Bills exist, including Mark Fisher MP's Right to Know Bill 1993; Government departments have the experience of the Code of Practice on Open Government, introduced in April 1994; and civil servants have conducted detailed studies of the operation of FOI overseas. As a result Whitehall is well prepared to introduce early legislation. (Hazell 1997b, 2)

The New Labour government had an unparalleled chance to implement the law it promised. After three decades, FOI had arrived. However, doubts remained over senior actor's commitment or even awareness. Labour was being 'asked to jettison its traditional ambivalence' to change 'at precisely the time it was poised to become the chief beneficiary' of the system (Foley 1999, 242).

# 4

## The 1997 White Paper: a symbolic victory?

The story of FOI from the radical White Paper of December 1997 to the draft Bill of May 1999 is that of a 'closed door' institutional struggle isolated from electoral pressure (Hacker and Pierson 2014). Once in power FOI entered what was described in the US as a time of 'backstage in-fighting and front stage dissembling' (Kennedy 1978, 115). It is the story of mobilisation and counter-mobilisation as factions supporting first a radical and then a lesser policy gained the upper hand in different contexts. It was conducted by small groups of insiders assessing and reassessing the feasibility and desirability of the policy (Hay and Wincott 1998). Both were motivated by the symbolism of FOI, the first group regarding FOI as a signal of radical power reallocation and the second fearing its effects.

In the UK FOI policy developed in a series of phases. The first stage of the development covered the first eight months, from Labour entering power in May 1997 to the publication of the White Paper *Your Right to Know* in December 1997. At this point, FOI appeared to avoid the 'symbolic' trap and overt conflict so frequently seen elsewhere. A small, well-connected group of crusaders inside government took advantage of their own power and used a favourable context to neutralise opposition, with a rapid process lending momentum to a far-reaching policy.

Their efforts resulted in a hugely symbolic White Paper, rapidly formulated, that offered one of the most radical FOI regimes yet seen in the world. The vision was of a political redistribution of power opening up even the very centre of government decision-making (Terrill 2000). Its radicalism was based on a series of key components: a high-level 'harm test', the lack of a government veto, strong powers for the independent regulator and no clear 'class' exclusion for Cabinet. Each was symbolic of its own accord and also a means to opening up the entirety of government. The process of formulation had 'short-circuited' the often long struggle for FOI. However, rather than securing consensus, the internal supporters leveraged a mix of authority and force to override temporarily distracted opponents. The White Paper was neither fully developed nor fully supported, and the proposed policy contained large gaps: what details it gave were perceived as threatening and radical.

## The symbolic politics of FOI

FOI proposals are traditionally supported by few and feared by many, frequently emerging 'enfeebled' from drawn-out processes of discussion and institutional resistance (Darch and Underwood 2005, 78). Yet in this phase, the UK process departed from the pattern of compromise and long time scales. Although it was pushed by only a few, the crusaders were particularly powerful individuals *within* government. FOI was also developed quickly, emerging as a White Paper in eight months. While it involved compromise in a key area, it was not the product of slow negotiation or wider agreement and understanding but the result was a series of radical proposals for FOI, which were probably the closest to the 'symbolic' ideal of FOI yet seen in the world.

## May 1997: FOI imminent?

In May 1997, the chances in the UK seemed good for a strong, far-reaching FOI law. Supporters were buoyed by the promise in 1996 that legislation would be in place within the first twelve months of a Labour government (Birkinshaw and Parry 1999). A series of favourable factors and signs convinced many that an FOI law was 'imminent' (Dorey 2008, 194).

As Chapter 3 above shows, the commitment was locked into broader aims and a wider reform agenda, lending it further power and impetus. Moreover, the new government appeared highly committed to its agenda, with Blair apparently more passionate than previous leaders (Dorey 2008, 194). It was also unusually well prepared. In order to prevent the legislative gridlock that had derailed the constitutional reforms of previous Labour governments, there had been a great deal of preparation and planning, particularly for devolution and human rights (Dorey 2008; Straw 2012).

The context of Labour's victory raised expectations even higher. Labour won the 1997 with a majority of 179 seats, the second largest parliamentary majority in history. Thus FOI in the UK had both a powerful commitment and a favourable political environment where a powerful new government could easily override, if not brush away, the sources of past opposition.

## The mechanics of the policy process

Once in power, the Cabinet established a ministerial sub-committee on FOI called CRP (FOI), chaired by the Lord Chancellor Lord Irvine, with members representing every Whitehall department (Constitution Unit 2001). This was shadowed by a Civil Service committee. Parallel to this, the Chancellor of the Duchy of Lancaster, David Clark, located within the Cabinet Office, was charged with overall responsibility for developing the policy and created a FOI unit (PASC 1998c, 1). The FOI unit was a seven-member team linked to the group that had overseen the Code of Access under John Major. The unit's original brief was to produce a White Paper by the summer of 1997, a deadline that was later moved to the end of the year.

The committee CRP (FOI) was part of a 'constellation of Cabinet Committees' dealing with constitutional reform and examining separately devolution, reform of the House of Lords, FOI and the Human Rights Bill (Hennessy 1998a, 8). Lord Chancellor Derry Irvine had 'chairmanship without responsibility'. Irvine explained, 'I do not have Ministerial Responsibility for any of these: devolution lies with the Secretaries of State for Scotland and Wales, human rights lies with the Home Secretary and Freedom of Information with David Clark. [Thus Irvine's role] was to get basic policy to bed through the Committees' (PASC 1998b, 5). In this first phase, Irvine's position would be pivotal.

## The key figures

As elsewhere, FOI in this period was dependent on a small group of key figures, 'lone crusaders' pushing FOI from 'within' (Snell 2001, 347). Given its relative insulation from electoral pressure, and the apparent lack of awareness from many senior party members, it was reliant on the interplay within a small group (see Dunleavy 2009). In the case of the UK, the minister officially charged was supported by a far more powerful crusader, who was supported in turn by the Prime Minister.

The first 'crusader', David Clark, was formally appointed to oversee FOI policy. Clark was rather an 'old' Labour figure compared with the dominant group of modernisers in Cabinet, and had been appointed to the lowest Cabinet rank as Chancellor of the Duchy of Lancaster. Blair agonised over Clark's appointment, and 'there was some awkwardness' (Rawnsley 2001, 23). Clark has been variously described as 'crucial' to the process and as more of a side player. The diaries of Press Secretary Alastair Campbell complain repeatedly of his performance and concern about leaks (Campbell 2011). However, he certainly had some influence according to Straw, who speaks of how Clark 'became an evangelist for the cause' and 'went for broke' in pushing FOI (Straw 2012, 276).

Given Clark's position, it was unlikely that FOI would be pushed by him alone. The second crucial figure was Derry Irvine, Lord Irvine of Lairg, who held the post of Lord Chancellor and chaired CRP (FOI). Irvine had the 'special confidence of the Prime Minister', who had delegated the constitutional reform programme to him, a measure of his trust (Hennessy 1998a, 8). Blair was 'in awe of Irvine', having been his pupil as a barrister (Seldon 2004). Lord Irvine went through a radical learning process in overseeing the committees and began to feel he 'had a mission with the John Smith legacy' (Seldon 2004, 207). As a 'radical lawyer', Lord Irvine was persuaded 'very early on' and 'completely bought in for the need for FOI' as 'essential to a modern society' (interview with David Clark 2015). Irvine was reported to Chris Mullin MP by an unnamed minister as being 'surprisingly radical' (Mullin 2011, 317). His sense of purpose, combined with his 'knowing he carried the full support of the Prime Minister', made him a formidable reformer. This was reinforced by Irvine's 'notorious' style of debating (Seldon 2004, 207), drawing parallels with Thatcher in the way that he 'coaxed or bludgeoned' items 'through the agenda' (Hennessy 1998a, 9). Blair described him as 'tyrannical but a genius' (Blair 2011, 32). Irvine was centrally positioned 'in the right place at the right to time' to push FOI; his role was described as 'absolutely crucial', as he 'went faster and further than anyone before or since' in pursuing a robust FOI policy (private information). The FOI committee was run as Irvine's personal fiefdom.

The third and final key 'crusader' was the Prime Minister, Tony Blair. He was keen to push FOI, asking David Clark two days into the administration to legislate quickly (BBC 11/3/2011). Blair appears to have had little direct involvement in the process. However, his delegated authority was potent. Hennessy described Blair's power as the 'Tony wants' phenomenon, a phrase described as 'the two most powerful words in Whitehall' (Hennessy 2001, 486). These words, via Irvine, were put at the disposal of FOI.

As in other parts of the constitutional reform programme, key figures sat within shifting groups of senior supporters and other interested factions stretching from MPs to lobby groups (Dunleavy 2009). While these groups maintained 'stable' opinions, the political logic and availability of solutions shifted over time (Dunleavy 2009, 620). In the case of FOI, there were clear opponents and 'doubters' (who could be described as FOI minimalists), those in the middle supporting some change and the FOI radicals seeking the strongest possible FOI legislation. All were believers, but believers in very different levels of openness. The FOI minimalists were made up of Jack Straw and certain departments and key advisors such as the press secretary Alastair Campbell. In the middle were FOI moderates, including parts of the Civil Service, who supported some change. The FOI radicals seeking the strongest possible FOI legislation included Lord Irvine, David Clark and other junior ministers, as well as large parts of the Parliamentary Labour Party with (it appeared) the support of Tony Blair.

Interestingly, a large group of senior figures appeared uninterested or unengaged, from the Chancellor, Gordon Brown, to even those interested in constitutional reform, such as Foreign Secretary Robin Cook, who had been instrumental in creating the constitutional reform agreements in Parliament. As a measure of their disinterest they sent junior ministers along to meetings of CRP (FOI) (interview with David Clark 2015).

### The key moments

The process between May and December 1997 led to a highly radical policy. Two key shaping points were crucial when policy decisions were made that excluded other options: first, Irvine's decision in the summer to reject any lesser policy alternatives and, second, and his apparent victory within the committee over those sceptics.

The policy process began with disappointment for advocates of FOI, as the pledge to legislate for an FOI Act was scaled down to a commitment to a White Paper and draft Bill in the Queen's speech of May 1997 (Birkinshaw and Parkin 1999). Alastair Campbell's diaries record how the '*Indy* went big on FOI being delayed and the *Guardian* on the idea it was because Peter [Mandelson] and I were basically against it' (2011, 11). This continued during the summer, when *The Independent* ran an opinion piece calling for increased openness over the security services following revelations of surveillance by an MI5 whistle-blower but also referred to FOI: 'Ministers have hinted that the Bill was shelved for a year because the proposals before them were too limited. If so, we are prepared to wait a year. A good Bill in 1998–99 would be better than a bad one in 1997–98' (*Independent* 31/8/1997). As McDonald and Hazell explained:

> As early as May 1997 there was press criticism that freedom of information was not to come at the start of the programme. Some feared that the government would not stay the course; others (especially among the Liberal Democrats) wondered whether Labour was genuinely committed to delivering a more pluralist democracy. (McDonald and Hazell 2007, 7)

However, the delay was not the result of second thoughts but of a heavily overloaded legislative timetable. The Queen's speech setting out the legislative agenda had seven constitutional Bills including referendums, Scottish and Welsh devolution and the incorporation of the European Convention on Human Rights into British Law. As Hazell explained, it was 'confusion, not conspiracy' that prompted discussion of 'whether freedom of information was going to be in or out', and 'ministerial over-load, not Whitehall sabotage, was behind the news last week that the Freedom of Information White Paper will not now appear until the autumn' (1997a, 5–6).

According to Clark, 'what had seemed so simple in opposition, in government became very much more difficult'. His Permanent Secretary informed him on his first day in his new position that 'very little work had gone on in preparation' (PASC 1998c, 5). Irvine later confirmed, 'though our aims were clear, real work remained to be done on the detail' (CFOI 1998b). According to Straw there had been no staff or resources dedicated to FOI and the policy had been largely reliant on external work (interview with Jack Straw 2015).

As the government sought to develop the policy, the first key shaping point comprised a series of decisions and rejections of alternatives that took place at the end of June, which closed down any policy options short of a robust, if not radical, document. An initial proposal was to put Major's 1994 Code of Access on a statutory basis (see Chapter 3 above). This was seen as a 'good first step' and one, moreover, supported by Whitehall. However, Clark turned it down (private information). The FOI unit then produced what was described as a 'standard Civil Service, post-Tory draft' version of an FOI White Paper. The draft was rejected by Irvine for being insufficiently radical (private information). According to Derek Draper, 'David Clark had the weaknesses of his draft ruthlessly exposed by Irvine. One Minister described Irvine's performance as the "biggest humiliation of a colleague I have ever seen"' (1997, 168).

Clark's and Irvine's rejection of all but a radical option, and their investment of political time and energy, put the policy on a new course. Irvine ordered a new White Paper, and the FOI unit began work again on a document described as 'the thoughts of chairman Irvine' (private information). As part of this process, the unit began to look at FOI elsewhere in a process involving 'a good deal of research and travel', with a series of overseas visits by Clark and the policy unit to New Zealand, Australia and the US (PASC 1998c, 5). However, during July, Clark complained to Alastair Campbell about leaks of the costs involved: Campbell dissuaded him from holding a press conference to go public on what Clark felt were orchestrated 'smears' (Campbell 2011, 442).

The document that became the White Paper *Your Right to Know* was then 'drafted very quickly', being drawn up in around one week under the pressure to meet the end-of-year deadline and the threat that Irvine would reject the paper if it was not sufficiently radical. The FOI radicals recognised, as Clark put it, that they needed to 'strike while the iron was hot' (BBC 11/3/2011). Crucially, at no point was it intended to be a 'detailed blueprint'; it was far more of a 'radical statement of intent', based upon Irvine's views and established on 'quasi-legal' grounds (private information).

The second key shaping point then occurred with Irvine's victory over those in the committee who were opposed to a radical policy in late 1997. Long and detailed committee discussions often appeared fatal to the chances of radical FOI policy elsewhere (see Chapter 8 below). The 'trapping' of FOI policy within committees composed of the 'lukewarm or hostile' is a common occurrence (Michener 2011). Support within the committee for FOI was limited. Irvine constituted one powerful 'lone crusader', with a minority of five other FOI 'radicals', all of whom were relatively junior ministers (*Guardian* 21/6/1999a). Most of the committee were described as being 'against' FOI, though numerous key ministers never attended (interview with Mark Fisher MP 2005; *Guardian* 21/6/1999a). There was some opposition within the Civil Service and allegedly within Blair's inner circle, so much so that Hennessy claimed that 'the chances of a 'minimal' FOI policy looked like a winner at first' (1998b, 16). Opposition was 'stronger in some departments than others', with the Home Office led by Jack Straw 'very hostile' and the Ministry of

Defence under John Reid 'very worried' while Downing Street maintained a 'wary acceptance' (private information). There was a general 'muttering' but no sustained resistance (interview with Jack Straw 2015).

The debate within the committee centred upon the 'strength' or 'radicalism' of the proposals, covering how and what information would be disclosed and the power of the independent regulator. The strength of the debate was encapsulated in the decision over the level at which to set the 'harm test', the criterion by which the government could or could not refuse to release information. The minimalists, such as Straw and his Permanent Secretary Richard Wilson, argued that, as happened in other FOI regimes, if information released could potentially simply cause 'harm' then it would not have to be released. The radicals, led by Irvine and Clark, argued that the information exclusion 'bar' should be set as high as possible, to the level of 'substantial harm', and that no information should be automatically excluded but that it should be assessed on a subjective 'contents basis'. Clark admitted that there was 'a great deal of debate among Ministers' and it was 'very complicated [and] members had to argue out the issues' (PASC 1998a, 5). Irvine also admitted to 'serious arguments about whether you had a simple harm test or a substantial harm test' (PASC 1998a). Irvine's radical ideas emerged from this process almost, though crucially not quite, intact. This was achieved through a mixture of force and compromise. Irvine was described as having 'bullied' those opposed to his ideas and as 'taking apart like a good QC' any opposition (private information). As against the frequent negotiation, compromise and manoeuvre seen in FOI development, the policy was literally 'forced' through.

The White Paper was finally accepted with two compromises. First, following Home Secretary Straw's fight against it, an opt-out was agreed for the Home Office that covered justice, policing and immigration (Straw 2012, 278). Straw (2012) later explained that he 'managed to protect most of the Home Office business' with 'one blanket exemption' that 'stuck out like a sore thumb' (278). Straw did this through intransigence, explaining that he simply 'dug in at the cabinet committee' (Justice Committee 2012c). Second, a 'tortuous position' was arranged whereby all information would be subject to a substantial harm test except that relating to the sensitive area of policy formulation, where the test would be the simpler, pre-existing, one of 'harm'. The narrowness of Irvine's victory was demonstrated in the days leading up to the publication date of the White Paper, with a 'cliff-hanger' of uncertainty concerning whether the paper would be published or not.

## Symbolic victory: the White Paper

The White Paper *Your Right to Know* was released in December 1997, a mere eight months after New Labour came to power, with a preface by the Prime Minister, testament to his continued support. The initial rapidity compared well with the long processes seen elsewhere.

It was powerfully symbolic. Blair's preface explained how the paper marked a 'watershed' in government relations, giving a 'right central to a mature democracy'. The policy was linked to the wider reform agenda, with Blair listing the other constitutional reforms undertaken and emphasising how 'Labour is committed to the democratic renewal of our country through decentralisation and the elimination of excessive government secrecy'. The paper reinforced this symbolic importance, repeating that the government viewed 'Freedom of Information as central to our programme of modernising government' (Cabinet Office 1997b, 1, 3). FOI was part of a wider openness drive covering public meetings for the Foods Standards Agency and National Health Service (NHS) trusts and increased transparency over public appointments (1, 4).

The paper began by explaining its decision not to choose lesser alternatives:

> We could have scored an early legislative achievement by simply enacting the existing Code [of the Major government] into statute but ... such an approach would not have done justice to our firm commitments. We have taken longer in order to complete a root and branch examination of this whole area in order to produce a better and more lasting scheme. (Cabinet Office 1997b, 1, 6)

Clark described *Your Right to Know* as a 'very, very radical White Paper' (CFOI 1998a, 39). It contained a number of features that made it radical in practice as well as 'symbolically': its scope, its approach to judging information release and the power it gave to the commissioner who regulated it.

First, the scope of the Act was wide. The Act covered literally 'thousands' of public bodies, from central government departments and agencies to local authorities, the NHS and even privatised industries and any other private bodies 'that carry out statutory functions' (Cabinet Office 1997b, 1, 7). It was also, unlike many FOI regimes, retrospective, covering past information. Following patterns elsewhere, Parliament was excluded to ensure that the executive was the focus (Hazell et al. 2012).

Second, technically, the Act would assess disclosure based upon the particular contents of each document. This meant that anything could be released with 'necessary deletions ... rather than being completely withheld' (Cabinet Office 1997b, 3, 8). The decision to disclose would thus operate on a 'case by case' basis (3, 19). This would be a three-stage process: checking that the preliminary decision whether to disclose or not 'is not itself perverse', ensuring that the decision 'is in line with the overall purpose of the Act' and making sure it was consistent with other legislation such as the Data Protection Act, and the Official Secrets Act, whose 'effectiveness' the government expressed concern to 'preserve' (3, 19). This was a 'contents'-based, not 'nature'-based approach (3, 12). Such an approach was unusual, being seen only in New Zealand (see Chapter 9 below). Most other regimes excluded certain classes of documents entirely, such as Cabinet papers.

In place of specific 'class'-based exclusion, seven broad areas were offered protection by a legal harm test. Six of these areas were given the 'specific and demanding' level won by the radicals, that of 'substantial harm', namely 'will the disclosure cause substantial harm?' (Cabinet Office 1997b, 3, 8). These areas were national security, defence and intelligence, law enforcement, personal privacy, commercial confidentiality and matters relating to the safety of the individual, public and environment (3, 11). Irvine emphasised the importance of the test: 'this is very liberal. It is not a mere harm test. It is a substantial harm test' (PASC 1998a, 1).

The exception to the 'substantial harm' test lay in the final 'sensitive' area, one of the compromises in the paper. For information involved with 'high level decision making and policy advice' the paper 'proposed a modified straightforward harm test i.e. would disclosure of this information cause harm?' (Cabinet Office 1997b, 3, 12). Overseas experience found that this area could be 'damaged by random and premature disclosure' and is 'always subject to clear protection and sometimes taking it outside the scope of the legislation all together'. The test of harm would be based on the need to maintain collective responsibility and the impartiality of public officials, as well as the ability to give 'free and frank' advice (3, 12). However, Clark later took pains to point out that policy advice was not wholly excluded: 'let me make it quite clear ... We are not excluding policy advice. It is included within the scope of the Bill. That is very, very important' (PASC 1998a, 1).

Third, the Information Commissioner, appointed to oversee the operation of the Act, was given 'wide ranging powers' (Cabinet Office 1997b, 5, 6). The powers, described as central to the operation of the Act, meant that the commissioner could order disclosure, access any records and report failure to disclose, which equated with contempt of court (5, 12). To further strengthen the commissioner's position, two key decisions were made. First, the role was made independent of Parliament and accountable to the Judiciary (5, 7). Second, rejecting the experience of other countries, the White Paper decided against giving a ministerial veto or 'discretionary' override, believing 'that a government veto would undermine the authority of the Information Commissioner and erode public confidence in the Act' (5, 18). Irvine thought the proposal 'should be applauded for the very strong powers we have given the Information Commissioner' (PASC 1998a, 7).

The paper admitted to various 'grey areas' concerning the issue of cost and time limitations upon processing a request. Furthermore, although the paper was retrospective and thus past documents came within its scope, the Act upheld the thirty-year rule and took pains to support the Official Secrets Act (Cabinet Office 1997b, 3, 19). Taken as a whole, *Your Right to Know* was highly symbolic as a statement of 'radical intent' for the new government, strengthened by a personal preface from the Prime Minister placing it at the centre of its political reform agenda. It was also radical in detail, offering a FOI regime that went further in its level of openness than most comparable laws.

## The reception

Symbolic policies frequently encounter problems when moving from pledge to detail. When the media take an interest, it is frequently to question vague commitments through forensically exposing the lack of detail or presenting the actions as a cynical manoeuvre (Hart 1995). However, *Your Right to Know* was greeted with 'widespread applause ... indeed the scale of the proposed legislation came as a surprise to many' (Vincent 1998, 321). Clark proudly pointed out: 'I don't think there are many White Papers that can actually claim praise from newspapers as far apart as the *Guardian* and the *Daily Mail* but we did that' (CFOI 1998a, 35).

Those lobbyists and specialists who had long pressed for FOI also welcomed it. CFOI felt that the proposals 'should provide a fundamental break with Britain's tradition of government secrecy', particularly the high level of harm test that would provide 'a strong presumption in favour of openness' (PASC 1998c, 1). PASC welcomed 'the proposed Act as a major plank in the government's proposals for constitutional reform and a radical advance in open and accountable government' (PASC 1998a, 1). It also praised Clark's decision to seek a radical option: 'the Government had been subject to a good deal of pressure to legislate on Freedom of Information immediately after the election, on the grounds that if it did not, its will to do so might soon disappear. Dr Clark resisted that pressure in order to create a better thought-out, more liberal measure' (PASC 1998a, 1). As of December 1997, FOI policy represented a notable exception from the general rule of FOI development. It endorsed a radical FOI regime, one that was strongly symbolic and supported across the media. What made *Your Right to Know* possible?

## The victory of the radicals

*Your Right to Know* was a product of extraordinary circumstances. It was passed because a few well-placed supporters used the opportunity to push it when the traditional obstacles to FOI were, at least temporarily, neutralised.

First, crucially, the 'crusaders' in the case of the UK were very powerful ones. Central was the delegated authority of the Prime Minister, which gave Irvine a power that few were able or willing to challenge. Hennessy claims that Irvine persuaded Blair of the merits of radical FOI policy (1998b). Blair's power and support for Irvine were demonstrated on a number of occasions. During the committee debates, Civil Service pressure to exclude policy advice stopped 'as though a tap had been turned' when the Prime Minister expressed his support for Irvine's view (interview with James Cornford 2005). In parallel, Jack Straw failed in his attempts to 'go over' Irvine's head by complaining to Number Ten (private information). Irvine's unique strategy and style of chairmanship also made concerted or united opposition difficult. As well as employing a 'coaxing or bludgeoning style', he was recognised as the most capable chair in government (Seldon 2004, 206). A number of commentators claim that Irvine's skills were strengthened by a 'clever tactic' whereby 'Clark would propose something very radical which would be violently opposed by Straw. Irvine would then propose a compromise which was, in fact, what was proposed all along' (interview with David Hencke 2005). Clark himself speaks of being 'more radical knowing my colleagues would trim me back' (BBC 11/3/2011). Another source claims that Clark's comments and Irvine's compromises were not planned in advance (private information). Whether planned or fortuitous, when they were combined with Irvine's unusual chairmanship style, the interplay between Irvine and Clark succeeded.

Second, the two traditional sources of opposition were neutralised as institutions and actors proved unwilling or unable to counter-mobilise as they had in the past. Across FOI regimes, ministers who take notice or understand FOI are frequently in a minority, and often alone (Snell 2001). In the UK few of the ministers newly arrived in power were interested in FOI (*Guardian* 21/6/1999b). The policy had been 'formally endorsed but not with any great enthusiasm … it became apparent that senior Ministers and the Prime Minister were doubtful [but] the New Labour government was a particularly inexperienced government' and did not grasp fully the implications (interview with Mark Fisher MP 2005). Straw spoke of how the words in the manifesto relating to FOI constituted 'all the serious consideration the party or shadow Cabinet had given' to it (2012, 275). Blair's Chief of Staff Jonathan Powell later claimed that in 2007, seven years after the Act's assent and two years after its operation began, Chancellor Gordon Brown was not aware of its existence (2010, 118).

Disinterest was severely compounded by distraction. New Labour's arrival in power led to 'turf wars across Whitehall, as new Ministers grappled to establish ascendancy' and few had the time or energy to focus on FOI (Rawnsley 2000, 108). Straw speaks of how 'we were all consumed with the new experience of running our own departments, protecting our own business and our budgets' (2012, 279). Many ministers were too busy, and some too anxious about keeping their jobs, to focus on FOI (interview with Jack Straw 2015).

The other traditional source of opposition, the Civil Service, was similarly disinclined to oppose the policy. Until the publication of the White Paper, its resistance was 'spasmodic' and 'disjointed' for a number of reasons (private information). First, not all officials were against FOI, and attitudes had undoubtedly changed since previous attempts at reform (Flinders 2000, 430). Senior officials claimed they were considering some form of information reform, as the then Cabinet Secretary Lord Butler stated:

> When we were coming up to the 1997 election, knowing what the government policy was in this matter, my senior colleagues and I gave some thought to how we could regularly structure submissions to Ministers in a way that would enable us easily to separate the background which was publishable from, as it were, the subjective advice which was confidential … I think that people could very readily adapt to that. (Quoted in Hansard, House of Commons, 4/4/2000, cols 995–996).

In 2002 Richard Wilson reflected on the Major government's Code:

> We are moving into a world where openness is going to be far more important and a far more common feature of the culture we work in than ever before [and] contrary to some of the reporting which we sometimes get, is one that we recognise and welcome because what goes on in Government and what goes on in the Civil Service is insufficiently understood. Openness is a way of promoting trust and I think it is good. (PASC 2002)

The enthusiasm of senior officials can be overstated. It was alleged that some were keen, as in the past, to use FOI reform to more closely guard certain categories of information (private information). Richard Wilson would, according to Straw (2012), be instrumental in persuading Blair to move back on FOI. The willingness of parts of officialdom to get behind FOI was also based on the Civil Service 'misreading' and 'over-emphasising' the strength of support for the proposals among ministers and, in particular, the Prime Minister. Until the publication of the White Paper, the Civil Service 'believed Labour was more committed to FOI than they turned out to be' (interview with James Cornford 2005). On a more pragmatic level, 'no one was willing to go the wall for FOI' (interview with David Clark 2015).

The Civil Service at this point was also disinclined to oppose any policy from the new government, through a mix of eagerness and shock. Powell speaks of how 'many Labour politicians expected the Civil Service to be dyed-in-the-wool Thatcherites [but] the major problem they faced was having to restrain their new found left-wing enthusiasm' (Powell 2010, 23). As well as their eagerness, officials were also in a state of surprise at the very new ways in which Labour governed. The 'New Labour style ... clashed with the formal structured approach of Whitehall' (Riddell 2005, 46). The Millbank model of tight control, the use of 'special advisors' as 'shock troops' and the primacy of communications were all 'imposed wholesale on the ancient system of Whitehall' (Seldon 2004, 424). The governing style was manifested in 'a succession of knee-jerks' (Hennessy 2001, 517). One observer characterised the new atmosphere following the New Labour administration's arrival in power as 'a new government with a whole set of completely different values who worked in a totally different way', so that 'in 1997 people were still all over the place. It all seemed weird and different' (private information). In this atmosphere officials were unsure what to oppose. It was only after the White Paper had been published, when a degree of 'normality' had returned, that 'opposition began to coalesce' (private information).

Finally, the sheer rapidity of the decision facilitated the White Paper. David Clark spoke of it being 'now or never' for FOI and of the need to 'beat down the opposition' and take advantage of the 'goodwill' towards the government (BBC 11/3/2011). Taken together, this meant, as Straw put it, that there was 'little appetite to stop David' (2012, 278). Lord Irvine seized this opportunity to push a radical policy and was thus 'in the right time and place to take up FOI and ram it through'.

## A symbolic victory?

*Your Right to Know* was powerfully symbolic. Crafted quickly, with Prime Ministerial endorsement, it seemed to offer, as Blair later called it, a 'revolutionary' approach and a 'quite extraordinary offer' to open government up (2011, 127). It marked a 'radical departure from the British constitutional tradition', with 'tremendous implications' for UK government and constitutional conventions such as ministerial accountability and civil service anonymity (Flinders 2000, 425). Its scope, said Jack Straw, 'was extraordinary' (Straw 2012, 278). The danger was that it was both unready as a policy and 'simply too radical' (Flinders 2000, 425).

## A workable policy?

The White Paper itself was clear that FOI was 'a policy with "green edges"' and incomplete, marking 'the start of a consultative process on FOI' rather than a 'final policy' (Cabinet Office 1997a, para. 1.9). The White Paper 'needed a lot of work ... there were whole areas that hadn't been covered' (private information) such as the often complex link to the Data Protection and Public Records Acts. According to Mark Fisher MP, who sat on the committee, although it was a 'good' White Paper it was 'less good than it could have been and was far weaker than comparable legislation in Australia and New Zealand. It should have been state of the art [but had] soft areas and weakness due to the awkward path it had taken' (interview with Mark Fisher MP 2005). Campbell made reference to the 'poor work' done by Clark in the summer of 1997 (Campbell 2011, 88). Jack Straw compared the FOI legislation with the Human Rights Act of 1998. He claimed that while the Human Rights Act had been crafted with 'enormous care', the FOI had a 'wholly inadequate conception' and the process itself was 'close to mayhem' (2012, 270, 275).

Patrick Birkinshaw spoke of how the paper was 'refreshingly radical' with no veto, no exclusion of cabinet documents and an Independent Commissioner (1998). He warned, however, that the 'ambition may prove problematic', as there were 'broad exclusions' for important areas such as policing or immigration and concern over the 'highly contested' issue of access to decision-making (1998, 182). Robert Hazell pointed out, for example, that no other country had a 'substantial harm test' which was 'untried' (PASC 1999f). He correctly guessed that the blanket exclusion of Straw's areas was the 'result of special pleading' (Hazell 1998, 4). Hazell described the paper as an 'aspirational White Paper in which the staffing and resource implications are never mentioned ... they have not sufficiently addressed the question of practicalities' (3).

Despite its support, PASC expressed also 'serious doubts' as to whether parts of the White Paper were 'workable' (PASC 1998f, 6). It reported that 'the tight legislative timetable may have meant the proposals were not as fully considered as they might have been', pointing out that key experts had not been consulted and that the FOI unit was too 'overworked' to respond to requests (6). It was concerned about the exclusion of law enforcement, which it thought was 'unacceptable', and about vague provisions relating to 'administrative functions' that could be 'open to abuse'. It was anxious about the lack of clarity in key definitions such as the 'public interest' and as to whether policy advice was subject to 'harm' or 'substantial harm' (29). It also had 'serious doubts' about the interaction between privacy and FOI as well as the proposed £10 application fee and the lack of coverage of important institutions such as Parliament. It warned that 'the Freedom of Information Bill will be an ambitious and highly complex piece of legislation, covering an enormous range of different organisations and requiring consideration of a large number of other Acts' and would need time and attention (1).

*Your Right to Know* claimed to have drawn upon the experience of FOI in 'mature fellow democracies' such as Canada, France and Australia and to contain 'a number of proposals which reflect overseas experience' (Cabinet Office 1997b, 1, 3). The novel 'contents'-based approach to disclosing information was based on the model of New Zealand, where the policy had been developed through a very different process (see Chapter 9 below). Unlike FOI legislation elsewhere, the White Paper did not contain the 'reassurance' of a ministerial veto power of the type seen, for example, in New Zealand, Ireland and Australia (Hazell 1998). It was also based on an untried, legally new harm test set at a higher level than those of comparable regimes that simply need to prove 'prejudice'.

Given that FOI as a policy was 'uniquely threatening' and had 'tremendous implications' for ways of working (Michener 2011), the paper was likely to cause concern among senior figures (Flinders 2000, 422). Straw claimed later that the policy meant that 'almost all information held by government was to be eligible for release' with 'no exception for categories of documents' (Straw 2012, 278). Although the exact workings were rather nuanced, Straw's claim perhaps reflects the interpretation put upon the White Paper by those concerned about it. Straw's view was symptomatic of a belief that the paper thus 'implied' a 'gratuitous disruption to Cabinet government' (Straw 2012, 279).

### An agreed policy?

Aside from the detailed points, 'there were criticisms of a different persuasion' relating to the shortcomings of the process by which it had been formulated (Birkinshaw 2001, 292). Some guessed correctly that it was not yet a fully agreed policy. Clark himself cautioned, 'in all senses the start of the process rather than its outcome … we have slowly got the snowball rolling but it is up to Ministers to keep it rolling' (PASC 1998b, 3–4).

Amid the praise, Clark was keen to point out the support for the policy within government and its status as 'settled':

> Some might think that the White Paper may not really mean what it says [or it is] just a negotiating package put out to test the water … but significant change would

only occur if the consultation process showed this or it proved to be 'unworkable' in practice ... the Sub-Committee have already fully discussed this and are now settled ... it now had the complete and utter endorsement of the government as a whole and is not just the result of an adventurous element going off on a limb. It is the centre of the government's approach to constitutional reform ... this is the considered view of the government. This isn't something that is going to be watered down. (CFOI 1998a, 39)

When questioned by PASC, Irvine appeared a little more circumspect than Clark:

There is a very considerable amount of development on this Bill to be done but it is certainly intended that the basic principles of the White Paper will be reflected in the Bill ... the devil is always in the detail [but] I am not aware of any material changes in principle that will develop. (PASC 1998c, 4).

A number of commentators found that 'the tone of the White Paper was hopelessly optimistic' (Birkinshaw 2001, 292). Professor Hazell summed up the concerns as follows:

The White Paper offers a very generous Freedom of Information regime, probably the most generous yet seen amongst countries that have introduced Freedom of Information. It is almost too good to be true. That is the central concern: that this is an unreal White Paper brought out without the full understanding or wholehearted commitment on behalf of departments or Ministers. (Hazell 1998, 3)

He warned that the White Paper needed 'Collective Ministerial commitment, without which FOI risks being still born' and the 'commitment of other public bodies and agencies, which will not be forthcoming without proper consultation' (3).

Taken together, the combination of lack of detail and questionable support led to a concern that the policy was not going to work as proposed and 'therefore you could deconstruct it'. There was 'a degree of uneasiness that the whole thing went too far'; the White Paper could prove to be the 'high water mark' for a radical FOI policy (private information).

The idea that the paper was 'aspirational' was not lost on the reformers. Irvine described it as 'a general principle' (PASC 1998a, 4). The White Paper could be seen as the radicals 'over-playing' their hand. Clark spoke of how the White Paper was, in one sense, an example of the FOI radicals 'going for broke' and purposely aiming high. He 'knew it was only a white paper' and 'expected that it would be scaled back'. The hope was that even when scaled back, the radical proposals in the paper would still 'make a good piece' of legislation, especially if Parliament, with its strong support for FOI, could exert influence (interview with David Clark 2015).

Time would not be on the side of the radicals. Straw spoke of how the White Paper had been passed by ministers as if in a 'trance' and Blair claimed that it was done 'with care but without foresight' or knowledge of the 'full implications' (Straw 2012, 276; Blair 2011, 127). This 'collective naivety' among ministers was likely to be short-lived (Straw 2012, 278). By December 1997 signs of resistance began to appear. A number of actors close to Blair were already opposed. Campbell records his later opposition in his diary, arguing that an FOI Act would simply be abused by journalists (2011, 603). Oborne quotes Campbell at a forum for senior civil servants in 1997 as saying, 'a FOI Bill is a bad idea. I do not like it and have no intention of allowing it to be introduced' (Oborne and Walters 2004, 154). David Clark later spoke of the 'antagonism of the senior Civil Service' and 'very senior circles' (BBC 4/12005). Dorey (2008) pointed to the wider 'socialisation' of all ministers within the conventions of British central government as they become 'wedded to the orthodoxies of the Westminster model' that emphasise confidentiality (202). The realities of power and the convenience of information control built into UK government would inevitably strengthen what Flinders calls the 'executive mentality', moving ministers towards a more conservative view on FOI (Flinders 2000, 422).

Nor would the wider constitutional reform necessarily continue to provide impetus. The initial 'constitutional hyperactivity', driven by 'popular pressures and long standing pre-election commitments' would, after the first phase, give way to 'fatigue' and concern that reform would both 'take up too much time' and create obstacles (Flinders 2009b, 44). Chris Mullin expressed the view of many observers when he cautioned that the future of FOI was bound up with the future of David Clark. 'If he survives his authority will be enhanced and he'll win on freedom of Information. If he goes, the Bill may go to' (2011, 359).

## Conclusion

*Your Right to Know* constituted a radical signal of intent bound up in the symbolism of a new reformist government. The policy appeared to have bypassed the traditional opposition. A small group of powerful advocates in government had overridden the 'traditional' scepticism of colleagues and resistance and had taken advantage of the fortuitous context to 'short-circuit' the normal process by which FOI was so frequently lost or weakened. Following the publication of *Your Right to Know* in December 1997, it appeared that the UK had avoided the drawn-out, weakening struggle for FOI seen elsewhere. It had scored an important victory, offering an FOI regime that was close to ideal. It was hugely symbolic. The regime offered a break with past secretive practices, as part of a series of wider changes in how politics worked.

Yet the victory was symbolic rather than concrete. The speed and manner of the policy-making had left the policy lacking in detail and support. As time passed, the extraordinary circumstances that helped *Your Right to Know* would fade. Arguably, the policy would have succeeded if it had been arrived at more 'cautiously ... it would certainly have been better to have started in a normal type of collegiate relations' and pushed forward the policy incrementally (private information). However, '1997 wasn't like that...everything was so extreme' (private information).

*Your Right to Know* concluded upon a warning note, recognising the dynamics of FOI reform that could work against it. Overseas experience showed that 'openness must be championed by the government itself if [it] is to become part of the culture rather than some irksome imposition' (Cabinet Office 1997b, 7, 1). It was vital that 'Freedom of Information should not result in a position where all the pressure for open government lies outside of government while a resulting counter-culture of reluctance develops within' (7, 16). The classic difficulty of any symbolic policy now presented itself as the gap between ideal and operation opened up, with the prospect of long, painful battles over details (Hart 1995; Matland 1995).

# 5

# The 1999 draft Bill: the retreat becomes a rout

If the White Paper was the high tide, the strongest possible signal and symbol of radical change, the second phase of the draft Bill in 1999 was the rip tide. The draft Bill, delayed by nearly a year, was the sum of all fears, the concrete representation of an increasingly executive-minded and reluctant government that feared weakening itself and arming opponents.

Whereas the first phase up to and after the White Paper was the mobilising of radical support, the following period of eighteen months was the counter-mobilising push-back. Power within the small group involved subtly shifted, and the longer, slower process of detail gave time for opposition to coalesce around the symbolic fears, doubts and threat posed by FOI. The context also moved towards retrenchment and pull-back as the momentum of constitutional change gave way to caution. This resistance then shaped the policy outcomes (Moe 2015).

As seen elsewhere, time defeated the radical aspirations for FOI. The changes came in two distinct parts. In the first phase, the radical group was broken up and the process was put under the control of Home Secretary Jack Straw in the Home Office. The White Paper slowly became a draft Bill and retreated somewhat from its strong positions. However, despite expectations it remained a reasonably robust policy. The 'retreat' then became a full-scale 'rout' in phase two (Hazell 1999). The CRP (FOI) committee, increasingly dominated by fears of what a too radical FOI could do, combined to dismantle it. The resulting draft Bill was built around an inner core of protections for decision-making and a series of outer or peripheral new repressive or limiting features. Underneath was a changing notion and new 'justifying narrative' of what FOI meant. The law moved from a proposal driven by certain radical features to a broader, less threatening, legalistic vision of a balanced law aimed at services and delivery rather than at central government itself.

Yet time and politics allowed FOI to escape from the committee. The passage, even in its heavily scaled-back form, rested once more on a political calculation. A compromise that the law would be implemented only after a breathing space of five years, ostensibly for records management reasons but premised on the fact that the government would be unlikely to be still in power, gave it time to be accepted.

## FOI: still imminent?

Following the publication of the White Paper the government repeatedly promised a draft Bill. Little progress was made beyond the White Paper between January and July 1998. The opposition increased across Whitehall, and the atmosphere in the consolidation meetings worsened.

The radical phase of FOI came to end in July 1998. According to Straw, by July he succeeded in calling a 'temporary halt' to FOI development during an 'ill-tempered meeting' of the Cabinet committee (2012, 279). Straw had gathered support in advance and 'done some prior organising to ensure the committee came to the correct decision' (279). This halting was followed by the long-rumoured sacking of David Clark in the first Cabinet reshuffle. Clark's position had been tenuous since his appointment. Although Clark may or may not have been central to the development of the policy, his removal would mean that the FOI brief would be vacant. The Cabinet Office FOI unit was broken up and a new group created in the Home Office, under Jack Straw.

Those groups pushing FOI outside the system feared that the policy would be weakened and applied pressure by emphasising the symbolism of an Act. In Parliament a group of 232 MPs signed an Early Day Motion that quoted Blair's 1996 speech:

> That this House welcomes the Prime Minister's statement in 1996 that a Freedom of Information Act 'is not some isolated constitutional reform' but 'a change that is absolutely fundamental to how we see politics developing in this country over the next few years'; congratulates the Government on its Freedom of Information White Paper; expresses concern at the prospect of any delay in bringing the measure forward; and calls on the Government to publish its draft Freedom of Information Bill before the end of the current session and to ensure that the actual Bill is introduced in the coming session. (House of Commons 1998)

Ominously for the government, the sponsoring MPs were made up of Labour, Liberal Democrats and Conservatives. In parallel, Maurice Frankel of CFOI warned in an opinion piece in the *Independent* that 'unfortunately, there are already signs of retreat.' He argued that time was likely to dilute any FOI plans:

> The more used to office ministers become the more plausible the case for caution will seem. New ministers are learning that delivering effective policies with limited

resources is difficult; that they too make mistakes ... that being caught out is unpleasant. Select committees are starting to probe sensitive issues; the press is becoming less admiring and more sceptical; even one or two opposition spokesmen are showing the signs of scoring points. Why arm their enemies just as the pressure is building up? (*Independent* 26/7/1998)

He too raised the symbolism of loss of an FOI Act – 'If the proposals are allowed to falter through lack of enthusiasm, how will Labour answer the cynics?' – and quoted Blair's 1996 speech. Frankel argued that the government would benefit from the signals and symbolism of the White Paper 'as evidence of an overriding commitment to honest, accountable government' (*Independent* 26/7/1998).

### *The retreat: symbolism reversed?*

Behind closed doors key actors and the flow of attitudes were hardening against the White Paper over the next eighteen months. There was a 'rising worry about FOI after the White Paper was published' (interview with Jack Straw 2015). It became apparent that while the radical symbolism may have served to 'reassure' the public of the government's radical intent it also clearly 'threatened' parts of Whitehall. In parallel, the process itself exerted an effect, as the White Paper was hammered into shape as a statute. As time passed, these separate problems became entangled: complexity was a smokescreen for political reversal but also vice versa as legislative shifts were *blamed* on politics.

The counter-mobilisation against the White Paper was based on a series of views of FOI that grew in salience and appeal as ministers and officials questioned the 'feasibility' and 'desirability of FOI', in a steep curve of institutional learning (Hay and Wincott 1998). The first set of concerns were practical, as the complexity of the legislation meant that consideration was needed of details such as time frames or appeal mechanisms. In the UK the policy required time to fill the 'gaps' left by the White Paper and understand how the policy would work and how it would fit or dovetail with other legislation, from privacy to records.

Second, more politically there was a spreading perception that an FOI Act would weaken government. On a political level, FOI requests, by their very nature, bring disruption and spring surprises: they are 'random, citizen-driven, and often hard to predict' (Hazell 1999, 8). Government could foresee the potential obstacles or hindrance that requests could bring, springing surprises on topics or digging and unearthing what Blair called 'skeletons' in the closets of the government (2011).

As well as the politics was a fear that FOI could also damage 'sensitive' parts of the machinery of government. Straw's claim that the White Paper offered to open up 'almost all' was symbolic of the fear that the proposals provoked, and was probably a claim repeated across Whitehall (Straw 2012). As Chapter 7 below discusses, since its passage in Australia in the early 1980s, claims had abounded that FOI had a negative effect on decision-making, creating a 'chilling effect' whereby decisions were not recorded or obscured, while simultaneously threatening the anonymity of civil servants and their ability to give impartial advice (see Hood 2007; Hazell et al. 2010).

Third, the flip-side of FOI weakening government would be to empower the opposition, both formal parties and 'informal' critics in the media. FOI would give them a new tool to exploit and damage or even block government action. In December of 1998 Alastair Campbell 'feared' that FOI would be a 'disaster' as 'an excuse for the media to clog up the whole government machine with ludicrous enquiries the whole time' (Campbell 2011, 603). Blair later reflected that the power that FOI gave to the 'tender mercies of the media' was 'gigantic' (2011, 127) and suggested later that FOI leads to 'battles' between government and media (Justice Committee 2012a).

New Labour were acutely aware of and sensitive to the press and were frequently accused of trying to 'rule by the media' (Rawnsley 2010, 337). Their victory in 1997 had been partly a result of tight control of the media agenda and sophisticated communications strategies (Scammell 2001). New Labour's 'application of profes-sional public relations techniques to the management of image, issues, reputation and internal communication', though not new, represented an increasing intensity and sophistication of information control (McNair 2004, 328). In the late 1990s Labour became synonymous with 'spin', or 'information manipulation' designed to 'enhance the standing of the government or opposition party'. What began as 'aggressive political public relations' as a defensive measure against a biased right wing media gradually 'became increasingly offensive in power' (Moloney 2001, 128). As a result New Labour 'had a culture of secrecy which had been further ingrained by office' (Rawnsley 2000, 376).

By 1998 and 1999 Labour were hit by 'accusations that it is run by spin doctors or disregards Parliament' (*Independent* 26/7/1998). The paradoxical effects of 'spin' were seen as corrosive to much of what FOI sought to achieve: manipulation and control of information, too close relations between government and selected media and, over the longer term, aggression and conflict (McNair 2004). The longer New Labour stuck to such intense media control the less likely it would be to sup-port FOI. As Snell (2002) points out, an FOI regime 'is unpredictable in terms of requestor, type of request, timing and outcome' and 'government information man-agement techniques are apt to be portrayed as excessive secrecy or cover-ups', none of which effects boded well for a media sensitive government (188). FOI was thus in part 'a victim of their approach to control' (interview with Maurice Frankel 2005).

By 1998 the government had experience of scandals and unearthed information. At the end of August 1997 the government lost, as Blair put it, its 'scandal virginity' in a newspaper revelation of his Foreign Secretary's extra-marital affair. This was followed, more damagingly for Blair, by a financial scandal over donations to the Labour Party, a 'far more potent and dangerous' exposé that centred on his integrity (2011, 130–131). The inexperienced Blair government 'came to understand the down side of open government' as one 'embarrassing revelation followed another: large donations by Bernie Ecclestone to the Labour Party, the arrest of Jack Straw's son, the accidental publication of witnesses' names in the Stephen Lawrence inquiry, press publication of Cabinet minutes on the failing dome project' (Brooke 2005, 12).

Just as views shifted on FOI, the contradictions within Labour's constitutional reform programme began to show (Flinders 2009b). David Marquand explained the piecemeal nature of the 'revolution':

> It is very British, this revolution. It is a revolution without a theory. It is the muddled, messy work of practical men and women, unintellectual when not positively anti-intellectual, apparently oblivious of the long tradition of political and constitutional reflection of which they are the heirs, responding piecemeal and ad hoc to conflicting pressures. (Marquand 1999a, 1)

Labour's reforms had been likened to 'a revolution of sleepwalkers who don't know quite where they are going or quite why' (Marquand 1999a, 1). There were signs that parts of the Labour leadership were beginning to wake up. In 1999 Marquand spoke of how the two years of changes pointed 'towards a politics of deliberative and pluralistic democracy, yet its authors seem terrified by the slightest challenge to their authority' (1999a, 1). Labour's first few sessions of 'constitutional hyperactivity', with twenty Bills pushed through the legislature, gave way to 'constitutional fatigue' as the lack of public interest combined with a growing recognition that the changes 'created a range of constitutional obstacles that may later thwart the government' (Flinders 2009b, 44). Between 1999 and 2005 Labour 'initiated a policy of constitutional containment' meaning that 'any reform that threatened the ability of the government at the centre' was 'diluted in its radicalism' (Evans 2008, 80). In other areas the 'clammy hand of centralism' and support for the Westminster model of strong executive control re-asserted itself (Evans 2008). Labour's (albeit vague) manifesto promise of a more proportional voting system met with the reality of Labour's huge majority created by the electoral status quo (King 2009; Evans 2008). Blair created a commission to look into electoral reform, before shelving the proposals as anti-reform factions and views began to dominate within his own party (Dunleavy 2009). The Human Rights Act 1998 also included compromises preserving the sovereignty of Parliament, while the second stage of House of Lords reform, after the symbolic removal of nearly all the hereditary peers, became bogged down, partly over concern as to whether a reformed second chamber would be a stronger check (Bogdanor 2009; Russell 2013). Gradually, some of Labour's 'boldest reforms' were 'in some way limited' (Beetham et al. 2001, 384). As Flinders argues, looking across FOI and the wider programme, New Labour was sliding away from its early open, plural 'Whig' view of government towards a more Peelite ideas 'emphasising strong government' and the 'old' Westminster model (2000, 423). This caused 'deep disillusion across liberal Britain' as the 'coalition' of NGOs supporting change 'fractured', with Charter

88 accusing Labour in 2000 of running an 'executive dictatorship worse than Thatcher' (Rawnsley 2001, 376).

## Key actors

The removal of Clark and other supporters such as Mark Fisher MP broke up the radical grouping. FOI was also deprived of the support of Irvine. The Lord Chancellor had a series of high-profile media problems over, for example, the costs of renovating his apartment and his hubristic declaration that he was as powerful as Henry VIII's Cardinal Wolsey. He repeatedly demonstrated his 'fallibility ... in Blair's eyes', and what should have been a successful defence of the White Paper before a Parliamentary Select Committee was partly taken up with a tense discussion about the costs of redecorating his official residence (Seldon 2004, 208). By the middle of 1998, Irvine looked 'distinctly out of favour', and 'it is Straw who now commands the Prime Minister's confidence' (Egan 1999, 238). The steep decline in Irvine's power and influence was 'never more apparent than [with] the FOI Bill [where] Blair ... failed to support him in his battles with Jack Straw' (238). This left only a small group of pro-FOI junior ministers within the committee (*Guardian* 21/6/1999a). Following this event, 'nobody was the champion of FOI within government' and 'nobody really wanted it. What the government wanted, in effect, was legislation that would change nothing. Nobody, including Tony Blair, wanted to change things' (private information).

The central figure was now Home Secretary Jack Straw. Straw had 'never been happy with the 1997 White Paper' and 'has always been an Executive man' (HL 97 1999a, 63), and he had privately asserted that 'Freedom of Information is for oppositions, not for governments' (Hennessy 2001, 512). The long-term FOI campaigner Tom McNally compared putting Straw in charge of FOI to 'putting Dracula in charge of the blood bank' (Flinders 2000, 426). His views may have been rather more nuanced, as he regarded himself as a supporter of FOI, though of a rather different kind (interview with Jack Straw 2015).

Straw was not alone in his scepticism of the White Paper. From 1998 onwards 'the centre got a grip of the policy' (interview with Jack Straw 2015). Powerful doubters at the top of government included Alastair Campbell, who had publicly declared that 'you'll get FOI over my dead body' (Oborne and Walters 2004, 154). Blair's Chief of Staff Jonathan Powell, later vocal in his criticism of FOI, may well have been against it at the time (Powell 2010). Another of Blair's advisors felt that promising FOI was the 'stupidest fucking thing we have ever done' (private information).

Crucially, Blair had changed his mind. His delegated authority, vital in making the White Paper happen, was now put at the service of the sceptics. 'It was', argued one journalist, 'the Prime Minister himself who ruled that freedom of information should be manacled' (Rawnsley 2000, 376). There are claim and counter-claim of Blair being 'persuaded' against FOI in this period by various leaders. One source has the Irish Taoiseach Bertie Ahern, who was gifted an FOI Act by the departing 'Rainbow Coalition' in Ireland, warning Blair that FOI was the worst thing his government had ever done (private information). Another claims that Blair's doubts were sown following a phone call with the US President Bill Clinton in 1999, when Clinton expressed a fear of writing notes because of the US FOI Act (Hennessy 2003b, 747). Rawnsley also claims, 'The Prime Minister was horrified to learn from Bill Clinton that the President dared not have written advice from his military advisors for fear of public exposure' (2000, 376). What is more probable is that Blair, never an enthusiast for constitutional reform, had simply not 'realised the significance' of the White Paper or 'not paid attention to the issue' (private information). Jack Straw later told how Blair, in handing over the FOI brief in 1998, instructed him, 'I am transferring freedom of information to you and you have to try and pull it back on the original proposals' (Justice Committee 2012c). Straw added that 'I agreed with him entirely. I wanted to pull it back' (Justice Committee 2012c). Straw described Blair as 'getting extremely worried about the eccentric FOI policy to which his government, in a trance, had seemingly signed up to' (Straw 2012, 279). It was becoming clear by this time that Blair's interest in the constitution was limited. Despite its radicalism, he had devoted no major speech to the reforms and later disparaged constitutional matters as uninteresting to the electorate and suited only to debate between academics and intellectuals (Theakston 2005). His rhetoric of change hid a set of more conservative or conventional views (Theakston 2005). Blair wanted a 'modernised and updated Westminster model that preserve[d] the power and dominance of the Executive' (35). This chimed with Labour leaders traditionally taking a 'benign view of Whitehall' as it allowed for the 'accrual of substantial power at the centre ... regarded as essential for pursuing Labour's political agenda' (Richards et al 2008, 488-489).

Straw later took pains to deny that the Civil Service, complicit in engineering the failure of FOI in the past, had been involved: 'this is not game, set and match to Sir Humphrey... Ministers are responsible for this Bill' (PASC 1999d). Even in 1992 Labour's proposals were greeted with the traditional mixture of alarm and scepticism in some quarters (see Chapter 3). Although Straw was correct in claiming that the policy shift came from ministers, some senior officials did appear to be opposed (private information). Straw reports that Blair's doubts were 'encouraged by the Cabinet Secretary', Richard Wilson, who allegedly played a key role in persuading Blair of the dangers and recommended that FOI be shifted to the Home Office in 1998 (Straw 2012; interview with Jack Straw 2015). A number of other permanent secretaries reflected the 'institutional nervousness' of their ministers (private information). Furthermore, Hennessy quotes an anonymous 'very senior Civil Servant' expressing the view that 'we only just got it back in time' (Hennessy 2001, 512). Some of the opposition may have been generational and also based on the departmental 'view' (interview with David Clark 2015).

For all the potential opponents, Clark's removal constituted a 'green light' from

Number Ten to the 'principal opponents [of FOI] to do as little as you think you can get away with' (interview with James Cornford 2005). Increasingly sceptical ministers in the Cabinet committee, from John Reid at the Ministry of Defence and Geoffrey Robinson at Trade and Industry to Frank Field at Welfare, were all against the radical FOI proposals (*Guardian* 21/6/1999a). There was also a larger group of key figures who were disengaged and exercising a veto via indifference. Important figures such as Robin Cook and other potential supporters such as Clare Short continued to stay away: one supporter asked plaintively, 'If only … just one of them had taken some interest, it would have been a different story' (in Dorey 2008, 197).

#### In the Home Office: retreat and revise?

The creation of the draft Bill first took place in the Home Office before going back to CRP (FOI). The transfer to the Home Office was logical given its experience in drafting complex legislation and the close relationship of FOI to data protection (private information). However, it was 'never a ministry to experiment with radical innovation in government', and its historic closed reputation and previous treatment of FOI caused doubts (Birkinshaw and Parry 1999, 540).

According to Straw 'the draft Bill was an attempt to start afresh' on FOI (interview with Jack Straw 2015). The Home Office team attempted to remain as close to the White Paper as possible. Much of the initial difference between the White Paper and the Bill lay in the practical problem of converting a set of principles and aspirational aims into legislation. Straw asserted that the 'devil was in the detail', and the Home Office department, already 'over-stretched', found there to be a 'great deal more work to do' (PASC 1999d). The process was hampered by the difficulty of legislating within the English legal system, whereby rights require close description and matching with pre-existing provisions in other laws. Here, the lack of detail and 'grey areas' within the White Paper proved problematic. The White Paper 'needed a lot of work', as there existed 'whole areas' that the White Paper had not dealt with, such as FOI's relationship to both data protection and the Public Records Act (private information).

The process of legislating began amid media accusations of delay, drawing on the symbolism of FOI and the damage of any of betrayal. The *Independent* spoke of the Labour Party's 'shame' in delaying FOI, with a leader saying that 'secrecy should have no part in a modern democracy' (*Independent* 7/8/1998). The following month it ran stories on 'The Vice of Secrecy at No 10' and, again giving FOI a 'moral' angle, claimed that Labour was preparing to 'Renege on Open Government' (*Independent* 13/9/1998; *Independent* 28/9/1998). The Liberal-Democrat Leader Paddy Ashdown publicly warned Blair 'not to betray voters' on FOI and endanger the Labour Party's relationship with the Liberal-Democrats (*Independent* 24/9/1998). However, in the Home Office the fears of many campaigners were not realised. In fact, the draft legislation 'in many ways stuck quite closely to the White Paper', and the changes were 'just drafting' (private information). Frankel confirms this, having seen various of the Home Office's pre-Committee drafts, which he claims 'were a lot better [in terms of openness] than the draft Bill [with] harm tests and public interests all over the place' (interview with Maurice Frankel 2005). It was in the committee that FOI began to change.

### In the Cabinet committee: the retreat becomes a rout

It was less Straw and the Home Office than collective action of ministers that turned the retreat on FOI into a rout. Mark Fisher explained that 'there was different leadership within government for the White Paper and draft Bill' (PASC 1999c):

> You can start with a presumption of openness and then say ... there are some exemptions ... or you can say [as the Straw group did], here we have a body of government information which is the intellectual property of the government [and ask] how do you set about it and what are the problems? They lead you inexorably to two very different not just approaches to legislation but different terms, feels and often individually different judgements. (PASC 1999c)

Straw's stewardship may have changed the tone and vision, arguably giving sceptics room for manoeuvre in altering policy. He led a 'belated campaign' for its 'full re-appraisal' and saw his 'happy task' as being to 'abandon the extravagance and find a solution that was both plausible and more modest' (Straw 2012, 279–280). While Clark sought a radical White Paper with a 'right to know' above all else, Straw sought an altogether more cautious route, arguing that 'fundamentally, our constitutional reforms must be workable, workable for citizens, workable for interested pressure groups and yes, workable for government as well' (Straw 1999b).

Though Straw described himself as the 'villain' of FOI, the reaction came from CRP (FOI) as a whole (Straw 2012). Straw 'had little difficulty in gaining colleagues agreement to pull back', explaining that 'we had learned a lot in 15 months' (280). Following the demise of the radical group, it was 'open house' within the sub-committee. He claimed that Hazell's comment that the paper was 'unreal' was one of the 'more polite descriptions once cabinet colleagues understood its full implications' (279). The committee's acronym was labelled 'CRAP-FOI', and Birkinshaw and Parry (1999) claimed that it was the only such committee to have more members than the Cabinet as 'everybody wanted to attend to protect their patch' (549). Mark Fisher, who had sat on the committee, described the new atmosphere as being one of 'anxiety and nervousness and worst case scenario' created by 'Ministers and Civil Servants asking "how about a worst case scenario? How do we deal with that?"', each motivated by differing worries (PASC 1999c). Social Security feared being deluged, while Defence was worried about national security (Dorey 2008). According to Hennessy, the 'whole pitch and tone' of the meetings changed as ministers each attempted to protect their 'own patch' (i.e. departmental interests), with a 'great deal of unpleasantness' directed towards the remnants of the radical group and Cabinet Office unit (HL 97 1999a, 63). The atmosphere surrounding the Bill meant a 'lowest common denominator ruling [aimed at] getting something through nobody objected to ... but if somebody objected to something there was no one there to argue against that' (private information). The process became 'very slow and cumbersome' and the atmosphere made it 'very difficult for a sensible discussion to take place' as even minor or non-controversial problems would 'hold things up' and 'make the situation even worse' (private information).

The reversal was made easier by the inconsistencies and flaws within the White Paper. The White Paper 'had the seeds of destruction within it' (private information). There began a series of reversals as the White Paper's most radical components were systematically altered. Irvine's White Paper was dismantled: the inconsistent harm tests were used as a 'handle', and the 'biggest rows' concerned the use of the word 'substantial', inserted by Irvine following the line of the Matrix Churchill ruling but contested as being meaningless or inherently contestable in English legal terms (private information). The term 'substantial' was 'struck out' altogether. Increased protections were lobbied for as 'sceptical Ministers had an interest in making sure they had the exemptions they needed' (interview with Maurice Frankel 2005). Downing Street also attempted to impose a 'blanket ban' on the release of any of its documents, but Straw persuaded them that this might be a step too far (2012, 280). Only the public interest tests, which, the few remaining radicals hoped, would serve a similar purpose to the 'substantial' harm test, survived (private information). Crucially, encapsulating the concerns, a ministerial veto for disclosure, the lack of which was loudly trumpeted by the radicals, was re-introduced to allow government to override the decisions of the commissioner. Straw later claimed that the veto was a deal breaker for the survival of FOI (2012). Supporters aimed to get through what they could and hoped that the Parliamentary process would improve the policy (interview with David Clark 2015; private information).

The opposition within government leaked out to the media. The *Economist* reported that

> some Ministers and senior Civil Servants ... led by Jack Straw ... are staging a concerted effort to water down the provisions outlined in the White Paper [and] have already won some important victories ... the Information Commissioner who is supposed to have the final say has had his wings clipped [and] there will now be an appeals tribunal [rejected in the White Paper]. (*Economist* 30/7/1998)

Elsewhere FOI had effectively disappeared from view into complex committees or been trapped within Parliaments (Snell 2001; Michener 2011). Repeated legislation was lost in India before the 2005 Right to Know Act, and Argentina saw fifteen abortive FOI Bills between 2005 and 2011 disappear between executive and legislature, while Brazilian politicians simply 'sat' on proposals (Michener 2011).

The politics that had weakened FOI policy then served to push it through. One of the crucial issues concerned the time when the policy would take effect. In

Australia, opponents had reportedly pleaded for a long run in as a stalling measure (see Chapter 8). In the UK there was support for a five-year implementation period, similar to the two-year period given in the Human Rights and Data Protection Acts (Evans 2003). It was claimed that this was for records management purposes, in order to give bodies unused to requests time to prepare (Birkinshaw and Parry 1999). This was partially true: for Whitehall 'anything less than five years and you would have had revolt from the key departments' due to the condition of records (private information).

Yet it was also a political manoeuvre. The offer of five years suggested that the law would be in place far into the future: in 1999 the deadline was at least one full government term away, a time when few expected to still be in power. This long implementation timetable gave 'Ministers and Permanent Secretaries the confidence to sign it off ... it sounds very cynical but with a five year implementation period it becomes somebody else's problem' (private information). It may have crossed some ministers' minds that, as seen elsewhere, FOI was an insurance, providing a legally guaranteed means for a Labour Party in opposition to access information (Berliner 2014).

While the fighting took place behind closed doors, the government was keen to preserve the line that FOI was unchanged. According to the Liberal Democrat leader Paddy Ashdown, although Blair admitted to there being a timetable difficulty with FOI, he responded to Ashdown's fears that the White Paper would be 'diluted' by answering, 'I really don't know what you are talking about. As far as I know, the Bill is going to go ahead exactly as originally planned' (Ashdown 2002, 236). Blair's Chief of Staff Jonathan Powell, while informing Ashdown that Clark had left the policy 'in a mess', took pains to reassure him that 'there are no substantive changes [to the Bill] but just some technical work ... our friends will assume that because Jack Straw is now in charge he will water it down. But I can promise you that isn't the case' (Ashdown 2002, 254). Blair was also keen to persuade his own backbenchers that no change was happening, laughing off Chris Mullin's worried question over whether Derry Irvine was the last remaining supporter of FOI in government (Mullin 2011, 384).

### The draft Bill: sum of all fears

Following repeated delay, the draft FOI Bill was published in May 1999. There were signs of expectation management by the government, as one newspaper reported 'sources' as claiming that the Bill will be 'more liberal than expected' and that despite fears it had been 'watered down in behind-the-scenes battles campaigners will be happier than they thought' (*Independent* 30/4/1999). Following the controversial Macpherson report recommending that FOI cover the police, there were attempts by Parliament to lobby for its inclusion (*Independent* 24/5/ 1999). It was then also trailed that police would now be included (*Independent* 13/5/1999). The day before the launch one article pointed out that 'Historically, Labour has a long, and not particularly noble, record of being in favour of more open government when in opposition but not all in favour of it once in government'. While the government was not 'exactly electrified by freedom of information ... T ony Blair does believe in implementing his manifesto' (*Independent* 24/5/ 1999). The Bill was also one of the first by the government to be published in draft as part of an initiative to enhance Parliamentary scrutiny. Bills were to be published in their 'formative' stage with a view to being examined, where possible, by the relevant Select Committee (Norton 2013). Birkinshaw and Parry (1999) identified how this 'pre-legislative scrutiny offered enormous opportunities for feed-in at an open and pretty accessible level' (552).

If the White Paper symbolised radical intent and change, the draft Bill symbolised nervousness, concern and 'constitutional containment' (Evans 2008, 80). The lengthy explanatory document began by outlining that 'FOI is an essential component of the government's programme to modernise politics [which will] radically transform the relationship between government and citizen' (Home Office 1999, 1). It was a 'radical measure [in which] the scales are weighed decisively in favour of openness' (4). The Bill was an 'essential step' but had to take place within a 'change of culture' (1). The government had begun 'delivering' such a change with, among a plethora of government information available, the publication of economic data, defence information and real-time web-based information services (1). Straw argued in a newspaper article that 'We are modernising our constitution to meet the needs of modern Britain – just as we promised in our manifesto. Freedom of Information is a key part of this Government's drive to create a modern and fairer country' (*Independent* 25/5/1999c).

There was a shift in tone, as the document argued that the Bill 'strikes a balance between extending access to information and preserving confidentiality where disclosure would be against the public interest ' (Home Office 1999, 4). The Bill also argued that the 'proposals in the Bill follow the general principle set out in the White Paper'. In went on to explain that there were, however, differences:

> the provisions of the Bill depart in some respect: in some areas providing a more open environment than envisaged in *Your Right to Know*, in others going slightly less far, where, after careful consideration, the original proposals were felt to be detrimental to effective government or would have adversely affected the public interest. (Home Office 1999, 5)

The Bill retained the scope of the White Paper in creating a wide-ranging right of access to government information.The coverage of the Bill was 'slightly wider', bringing both Parliament and the police and, potentially, private organisations engaged upon government contracts, albeit 'subject to consultation' (Home Office 1999, 9). In terms of practical operation, the Bill managed to unite FOI with data protection while also introducing a second level of appeal to an independent tribunal, and also championed the use of publication schemes, the mandatory proactive publication of detailed lists of information (Birkinshaw and Parry 1999). There was also no fee for an application, though a standard £10 charge was considered as mooted in the White Paper (Straw 2012).

However, the Bill contained numerous key differences from the White Paper, bearing the marks of the atmosphere and process that had created it. A number of the 'barometer[s] of the ... nature of the Bill' had shifted, with the White Paper's proposals removed or weakened (Birkinshaw 2001, 295). Overall, the policy moved towards a 'neutral ... evenly balanced regime [with] openness, public interest and the protection of decision making given equal weight' (interview with Maurice Frankel 2005).

First, the 'public interest override' of the Information Commissioner was eliminated, allowing only the power to recommend release (Birkinshaw 2001, 295; Home Office 1999, 8). Although the addition of the tribunal procedure was 'probably a good thing' it threatened to 'lengthen proceedings' (interview with Patrick Birkinshaw 2005). The commissioner could not order disclosure of exempt information on public interest grounds (Flinders 2000, 427).

Second, the Bill eliminated the symbolic word 'substantial' in the harm test, so much fought over earlier. The criterion of 'substantial harm' became the lower threshold of 'would, or would be likely to prejudice matters'. This was presented as a logical tightening: 'after further careful consideration, our view is that a single omnibus substantial harm test cannot work properly for the range of exemptions involved. What is substantial for law enforcement ... may not be in relation to international relations' (Home Office 1999, 8; Birkinshaw 2001, 296). Perhaps most symbolically, a ministerial veto power was re-inserted (Birkinshaw 2001, 296).

Third, the Bill created a number of 'class' and absolute exemptions, a total of twenty-one, some of which were broadly drafted, including those covering commercial interests and investigations and safety issues (Birkinshaw and Parry 1999, 541; Flinders 2000, 427). The exemptions also included policy advice, meaning that there would be no release of 'facts or background' as championed in the White Paper. The accompanying memorandum argued that there had never been an 'expectation that FOI would lead to the disclosure of Cabinet papers and minutes, inter-Ministerial correspondence on developing policy or information about the operation of a private office. The Bill puts this beyond doubt' (Home Office 1999, 8).

However, the Bill went further than reshaping certain parts of the White Paper and was 'characterised by numerous secrecy maintaining devices' (Birkinshaw and Parry 1999, 539); 'novel features' (Birkinshaw 2001, 297) included provisions 'not appropriate to FOI' drawn from the Data Protection Act (interview with Patrick Birkinshaw 2005). Clause 25 gave a wide-ranging power to protect any information that could constitute 'evidence of wrongdoing or serious default' (Birkinshaw and Parry 1999, 542). Another clause, clause 37(1)(a), included an exemption for information through a so-called 'jigsaw' clause, allowing the withholding of information that could be 'pieced together' to expose an excluded subject. Another controversial clause allowed ministers to create new exemptions should they prove necessary (Birkinshaw 2001, 297). One area of particular concern was the discretionary disclosure of exempt information under section14. This allowed a public authority to 'open up' exempt information. However, it did so outside the remit of the regulator, who could only recommend reconsidering. More significantly, it gave authorities the power to ask the applicant the reason for wanting the information and control what the applicant subsequently did with it (Birkinshaw 2001, 297). The Bill also gave a forty-day period to reply, a generous measure of time compared with regimes elsewhere.

As well as what was present, there were also notable gaps. Missing from the Bill was a duty for authorities to assist requesters or a compulsion to give reasons for decisions. Also absent was a so-called purpose clause, seen in many other FOI regimes, which stated the aims of the Act and acted as a legal 'signalling device' that was frequently used to pressure for openness and to inform future appeal decisions (Hazell 1999).

## The response

Jack Straw spoke of how one of the biggest obstacles was the 'expectations raised by the White Paper' (interview with Jack Straw 2015). The draft Bill was greeted with 'near universal hostility' (Flinders 2000, 426). There was 'deep disappointment' and 'outrage' at the contents and the spirit behind it, which provoked 'a vehement sense of betrayal' (Birkinshaw and Parry 1999, 539, 552).

The media had trailed the possible contents months in advance. In February the *Independent* reported on rumours that 'access to secrets will be diluted' (5/2/1999). In the weeks running up to publication the *Guardian* urged Parliament to 'assert itself' against 'Whitehall's traditional steel shutters' and reported that Straw had 'weakened the secrecy Bill' by declaring the harm test 'unworkable' (24/4/1999) and 'trounced' the idea of 'opening up policy advice' (22/5/1999). The *Times* also reported that 'Jack Straw has won his Cabinet battle to water down the long-awaited Freedom of Information Bill' (14/5/1999).

On the day following publication the *Guardian* spoke of how the Bill 'puts key state secrets off limits' and was 'fettered by 21 separate exemptions' and a forty-day time limit (25/5/1999c), while the *Daily Mail* described it as a 'depressing damp squib of a Bill' (25/5/1999) that gave a 'right to know nothing' (27/5/1999). The *Independent* spoke of how 'good government needs scrutiny and challenge' (25/5/1999b) and argued in an opinion piece that 'democracy is poorly served by this disappointing Bill' (25/5/1999d). Another article in the same paper listed Labour's historic failures: 'it was in October 1974, that Labour first made a manifesto pledge to "replace the Official Secrets Act by a measure to put the burden on the public authorities to justify withholding information". Further commitments were made in 1979, 1983, 1987, 1992 and 1996.' It quoted from Blair's 1996 speech and asked 'What was promised? A revolutionary transparency at the heart of Whitehall resulting from the realisation of a 20-year-old Labour Party commitment to freedom of information' and followed up with 'What has been delivered?', discussing the 'major climb-down' on the harm test and listing the twenty-one exemptions (*Independent* 25/5/1999d).

The regional press also criticised the draft Bill. Papers as diverse as the *Birmingham Post* and the Newcastle *Journal* published critical opinion pieces, with the former describing the proposals as 'deeply disappointing' and the latter as 'a pathetic apology for a Freedom of Information Bill' (*Birmingham Post* 25/5/1999; *Journal* 29/5/1999). In another case of constitutional overspill in Scotland, the poor response to the UK was then used to apply pressure to improve on it in the separate Scottish FOI proposals being developed in the Scottish Parliament: 'In Scotland we will have two bites at the freedom of information cherry ... a Scottish Bill will have the opportunity to make redress for some of the notable failures in the UK Bill' (*Glasgow Herald* 25/5/1999).

The media reported the cross-party anger from the Shadow Home Secretary and chair of PASC (*Guardian* 25/5/1999c; *Independent* 25/5/1999a). The importance of FOI to the Labour Party was shown by the fact that it 'was not [just] the left ... Blair loyalists were very upset at the government's disregard', and a number of Labour members openly criticised the Bill alongside Conservative and Liberal Democrat members and peers (interview with Maurice Frankel 2005). It was also claimed that the Conservative opposition was considering taking up FOI as a 'Tory issue' (*Independent* 25/5/1999d).

CFOI called the Bill 'deeply disappointing'. The Bill 'represents an astonishing retreat from the Government's own White Paper published only 17 months ago, with the backing of the whole Cabinet and a preface from the Prime Minister ... In key areas the Bill is weaker than Major's Code' (CFOI 1999, 1). Although the Campaign acknowledged that the Bill was wider in scope and proposed lower fees than the White Paper, it listed the Bill's numerous faults: it 'allows authorities to classify safety information as top secret ... it abandons the White Paper promise of access to internal discussion ... it replaces the White Paper's "substantial harm" test with a lower "prejudice test" ... it contains numerous "catch-all" exemptions allowing information to be refused without any real evidence of harm' (1). The proposal for a forty-day response time 'would make it the slowest and most unresponsive FOI Act in the world', while the discretionary aspects in section14 'violates the basic FOI principle, that access to information is a right which everyone enjoys regardless of their purpose' by asking for the requester's identity and, possibly, their motives (1). CFOI argued that 'the introduction of this Bill would remove existing rights to information and would permit greater secrecy on the part of central government' (1).

Rodney Austin argued that the exemptions and veto meant that the law was no longer a 'Freedom of Information' Bill but an 'open government' law in which information was released with the 'consent of Ministers' (2000, 321). In looking across the positives, Robert Hazell praised the commitment to 'publication schemes' that 'could prove to be a powerful vehicle for greater openness', especially when combined with new technology, and argued that the 'jump' in the number of exclusions between White Paper and Bill was a result of some areas simply being subdivided (Hazell 1999, 11). However, overall the draft 'contains no clear or coherent scheme, and is tortuous and very difficult to understand ... [it] purports to fulfil the White Paper proposals, but so undermines them in the detail that the thread has got lost' (23). Hazell concluded that:

> The distressing feature of the draft Bill is what a mess it has become. It is evident that the difficult process of turning an aspirational White Paper into a more realistic draft Bill degenerated into a downward spiral, in which departments were allowed to plead for additional exemptions and other special provisions with no one seriously holding the ring ... The overall conclusion is inescapable: this is in general a restrictive Bill when judged by international standards. (1999, 23)

Hazell gave a detailed assessment comparing it with legislation in Australia, New Zealand, Canada and Ireland (1999). He identified the 'main restrictive features' as an absence of a purpose clause or a statutory duty to advise and assist requesters and the ability to add to the exemptions by order (7). The government's caution, he argued, might prove counter-productive as it 'erects a Maginot line in the wrong place' and 'the Government risks having the worst of both worlds: the draft Bill will raise expectations, generate a much higher volume of requests than under the Code, but still leave most requesters feeling dissatisfied' (23).

### The symbolism of the draft Bill: radicalism in reverse?

While the details of the Bill unleashed a wave of criticism, it was what the sum of these details signified that became important. The FOI Bill exposed the complexity of creating an FOI policy but also, to many, the contradictions of a radical government in reverse, willing to give away power on the periphery but hoard it for itself at the centre (King 2015; Flinders 2009b). The symbolism was of a government shifting its radical ideas in power, moving towards a preservation of its own centralised power and a protection from potential opponents (Flinders 2009b). However, it was not only a retreat from radicalism but also a denial of power to the people, a refusal to empower the electorate or grant them in full what had been framed as an essential right. While the White Paper was predicated on radical ideas of new politics and empowerment, the draft Bill was based on a belief that cultures would shift, ministers could be relied upon and Parliament (or the executive) 'worked' (Flinders 2000, 429). It was a 'fundamental difference' in tone, view of FOI and 'willingness to alter or change the constitutional equilibrium' (429).

To many observers 'it was felt that the Bill had been the outcome of a pact between forces of darkness in government and an extremely clever, if somewhat context-blind (in terms of openness) draftsman' (Birkinshaw and Parry 1999, 546). Hazell characterised it as a wholesale turning back: 'It would have been defensible for the government to decide on a tighter regime than that set out in the White Paper. But what should then have been an orderly retreat appears to have become a rout' (1999, 23). Mark Fisher described the Bill as 'slightly neurotic' and 'possibly paranoid' (PASC 1999c). The Bill had a tendency to adopt a 'paternalistic model of government, with the government deciding what we need to know' (HL 97 1999a, 64) and was 'soaked in the doctrine of Executive convenience' (Hennessy 2001, 511). The 'essential value' of a statutory right to information would be that it 'removes the discretionary powers of Ministers and officials' (Flinders 2000, 429). Birkinshaw and Parry (1999) argued that the Bill violated the key principles of FOI itself: it 'left absolute control with Ministers in every crucial area', and this 'unique and remarkable' approach 'comes close to making the provisions a discretionary need-to-know regime, not one built on a right to know' (549). The *Times* offered the view that the Bill also took a new direction, as FOI was now

> clearly aimed at patients and pupils rather than litigants and political activists. The institutions which will face the closest examination are schools and hospitals to whom fewer of the exemptions are likely to apply. On the other hand, any government infor-mation which falls into the potentially broad band of policy advice can remain under lock and key, regardless of whether it might affect the workings of government ... a wide safety net for both political and Civil Service acrobatics. (25/5/1999)

Straw himself emphasised the 'local' or 'service' aspect of FOI in an article in the *Independent*:

> In future, parents will be better able to find out how schools apply their admissions policies. Patients will be able to understand how hospitals allocate resources between different treatments, and how they prioritise waiting lists. And citizens will be able to find out more about the actions of their local police force. It's at this local level that constitutional reform matters. (*Independent* 25/5/1999c)

Overall, the Bill sent out a signal of 'reassurance' to sceptics and doubters in govern-ment. Hazell (1999) argued that it went further than that, as 'the signals in the draft Bill for public servants are all consistently negative'. He explained how 'Civil serv-ants are very astute in reading political messages; the messages in the draft Bill will not encourage them to be more open' (22).

Hugo Young in the *Guardian* initially blamed the 'butchers and whisperers' among the Civil Service but later pointed to Tony Blair and senior Labour figures. He claimed that 'two years of power has finally suppressed the clearest ideal Labour formed in opposition'. The draft Bill was a 'triumph for the forces of reaction, a reward for the patience of the mandarin who defeated the proposals by waiting for idealism to fade. The Bill marked 'the definite transition from a party determined to change the world to a government determined its world will not be changed'

(*Guardian* 25/5/1999b). A leader the same day spoke of how the new draft was 'executive minded' and a 'weak minded accession to the norms and prejudices of state power' (*Guardian* 25/5/1999a). The *Independent* characterised it as the end of Labour as a 'party of the people not of the establishment' (25/5/1999c).

Hugo Young then retracted his accusation and instead spoke of how the Bill 'reveals this government, at war with every previous principle, giving the wrong answer to every question'. He argued that

> There are certain measures that tell the world how a government sees itself, what ruling species it belongs to. Is it open or is it closed? Does it trust the people, or suspect them? Is its priority invariably power or, just occasionally, accountability? Is it, at bottom, about control or, ever, about losing control?

The government 'are co-conspirators in a unique piece of legislative wreckage. A party that once said government would be different is exposed as another bunch of hubrists, incapable of imagining that information should enhance anyone's power but their own'. It was, he concluded, 'Blair who sabotaged Freedom of Information', concluding, 'the artilleryman is Jack Straw. But the strategist and general is Tony Blair' (*Guardian* 22/6/1999).

## Conclusion

Complexity and politics had created a different policy, as ministers and officials had weakened the crucial and symbolic parts. In doing so they had also created a new Bill with a new vision. Though in some ways it went beyond the White Paper, the Bill was broadly viewed as the 'sum of all fears' for the most cautious and sceptical sections of the government, with a reduced harm test and a ministerial override, seemingly surrounded with qualifications and restrictions. Its underlying vision had altered as FOI became about services and local matters. Rather than opening up what Jack Straw called 'Kafka's castle' to activists it slammed the gates shut and threw up a smokescreen (Straw 1999a).

The Bill represented only a draft, even if a highly controversial one. Just as the White Paper was a radical 'long shot' or over-reaching aspiration, the Bill was an underwhelming lightning rod or 'trail balloon'. It was, some argued, packed with controversial clauses, legislative 'ballast' to be traded in the legislature (Birkinshaw and Parry 1999). The government had shown itself to be adept at trimming controversy as it went (Cowley 2002). FOI now headed to its final arena before assent or being dropped, Parliament.

# 6

## The Parliamentary passage: asymmetric warfare

As the draft Bill headed towards the legislature, those behind the original White Paper hoped that Parliament could act as a 'backstop' and last line of defence for a more robust law and claw back some of the lost 'radicalism'. By contrast, the government sought a Bill that could be passed through both Houses as quickly and painlessly as possible, with the minimum of disruption or change. As with FOI elsewhere, the contest was also fought within a severe information asymmetry and uncertainty, with the implicit threat of dropping the Bill deployed at strategic moments by the government to divide the radicals.

This chapter examines four key stages of the process that demonstrate the tensions and nuances of FOI's passage. The battle to make the Bill 'stronger' was more successful in its early stages, during the forensic analysis by two Parliamentary committees, than later, when government could more easily deploy threats of dropping, promises of deals and brute procedure. Although it was an unequal struggle, what emerged was a compromise. A number of the 'outer' controversial features were dropped while the 'inner' core protections remained mostly intact.

### The power of Parliament

On the surface, despite the hopes of those seeking a stronger FOI, the chances for a re-strengthening of the draft Bill in Parliament looked unlikely (Straw 2012). The UK Parliament has long been regarded as relatively weak and dominated by the executive (Norton 2013). In the House of Commons, normally secure majorities and a large payroll vote, allied with strong party discipline and loyalty, make defeat rare and concerted opposition problematic. Executive influence is further reinforced by control of the agenda and timetable, bolstered by a relatively new power to cut off debate via a guillotine. By 1999, Labour's huge Parliamentary majority of 179 seats and its strict discipline made any opposition seem futile. The considerable delaying power of the House of Lords was stymied by the chamber's historic lack of electoral legitimacy, leading to a reluctance to oppose policy.

However, underneath the apparent 'supine' nature of Parliament, latent influence is evident. Both Houses carry a strong if difficult-to-quantify influence through anticipated reactions, with government foreseeing problems and adjusting strategy accordingly (Norton 2013; Russell and Cowley 2015). In 1976 Anthony King pointed to the hidden complexity of groupings in the House of Commons: any government faces not only a formal opposition but an 'over the shoulder' threat from its own backbenchers (King 1976). This 'over the shoulder threat' grew between the 1970s and 1990s through a self-reinforcing pattern of rebellion among government MPs (Cowley 2005). By the third Parliamentary session, when FOI was introduced in 1999–2000, there were more rebellions by Labour MPs than in the previous two session put together. The likelihood of another Labour victory at the coming election made it such action 'less risky and far easier' (68). The House of Lords was also becoming a more potent threat: in a classic example of 'overspill' and unintended consequences, Blair's removal of the hereditary peers also gave the second chamber a renewed sense of legitimacy and helped shape its self-appointed role as a guardian of constitutional and civil rights issues (Russell 2013).

## FOI and Parliament

By the time the Bill arrived in Parliament, the battle lines around FOI had been drawn. On the one side stood the executive, with its large and loyal payroll vote, control of the timetable (in the Commons) and the second largest majority in Parliamentary history. Opposed was a loose but wide coalition of cross-party MPs and peers in both Houses seeking a more radical FOI law or 'FOI max', supported by a growing network of NGOs and parts of the media. As a proxy for public interest, this ad hoc and partially tacit alliance provided momentum, expertise and publicity, bringing pressure to bear both inside and outside Parliament, often simultaneously. The alliance sought to frame, or reframe, discussion of the policy back to a more political and radical view of FOI. The radicals pushed the symbolic power of FOI and its positive effects for the government and Britain's democracy, while framing any weakening or failure as a 'betrayal' not only of the government's promise but also of its commitment to democratic renewal and political radicalism.

Yet the power of the radicals was limited. First, the cross-party alliance was wide but fragile. It encompassed Conservative and Liberal Democrat MPs as well as Labour backbenchers, from normally loyal Labour MPs to Conservative openness campaigners and, at times, the leadership of the Conservative opposition (Cowley 2002). While this was testament to the legislature's support for the reform it was an ad hoc grouping in an institution primarily defined by party conflict (Cowley 2002, 67). The highly partisan nature of the Commons meant that such alliances could be brittle. Party loyalties could be, and were, exploited by the government.

It was also fragile in a more fundamental way. As both the government and a number of rebel MPs recognised, FOI was not a heartlands issue. Because it was a voteless policy, any determined opposition lacked the clear groundswell of public opinion behind it (Cowley 2002). This was only partially offset by the 'proxy' support via the media and NGOs. Some feared that campaigns in the *Guardian* to 'open up' were counter-productive, merely emphasising the limited interest and 'elite' nature of the debate over FOI 'as a middle class issue' (68).

Second, the battle in Parliament was fought within the context of severe information asymmetry. The leverage of the 'radical' coalition was limited by one fundamental uncertainty: whether the government would ditch the legislation if it proved too troublesome. As seen in the US and Australia, this concern frequently divided and restrained those seeking stronger laws. The danger was that if the Bill encountered too strong an opposition or was blocked, the government would drop it. For a policy so long in gestation, the possibility was that FOI, if lost 'like electoral reform', could 'be off the agenda for 25 years' (private information).

Exactly how serious the government was about dropping FOI is unclear. Straw claimed in his memoirs that he 'felt like' dropping the Bill or pushing it into the 'long grass' but was overruled by Blair. After that, there was, in fact, no real possibility of FOI disappearing (2012, 281). It was a manifesto commitment, and there was 'no way of abandoning it, especially as it was a principle to recognise the will of Parliament' (interview with Jack Straw 2015). Others agree that there was 'little danger of the Bill being lost' (interview with Maurice Frankel 2005; interview with Lord Goodhart 2005).

However, the very possibility or suggestion of losing FOI was part of a 'process of bluff' in Parliament, an implicit and sometimes explicit threat (interview with Maurice Frankel). Whether the threat really existed is less important than whether some or all of the radicals believed it, or were made to believe it. Whether it was true or not, the threat of dropping the Bill was certainly sent through the whips to rebels at various points. This had the desired effect, creating uncertainty and divisions within those pressuring for a stronger law: should there be an extra push or should Parliament get the Bill, in a lesser or weaker form, onto the statute book?

Third, there was the matter of legislative tactics. The approach of the Blair government, for all its apparent dominance and tight discipline, was to listen to its backbenchers and adapt ideas. Cowley (2002) argues that the usual government tactic at this time for any difficult legislation was to 'publish details of a proposed Bill ... test the reactions and if necessary make concessions' (23). Jack Straw, as Home Secretary, had to shepherd a series of controversial Bills through Parliament. He was expert at 'sounding hard line and consulting like mad', using what Cowley called his 'low political cunning' to get through 'cosmetic changes' and the 'minimum they can get away with' (Cowley 2000, 20; Cowley 2002, 68, 180). His consultative approach with FOI involved attending hostile meetings, publicly and privately offering concessions and, at one point, showing rebel MPs his ministerial red box to demonstrate the difficulties of dividing facts and opinion from policy-making (Cowley 2002).

As well as consultative strategies, concessions could be created from the Bill itself. Draft or early legislation was often prepared with 'ballast' or 'expendable' parts that could be dropped (Cowley 2002). Straw has explicitly denied on numerous occasions that the FOI draft Bill was deliberately created to be amended. Nevertheless, a number of MPs suspected it was, perhaps reflecting their view of the government's attitudes. In his first appearance before the PASC committee Straw was accused of using such ballast: 'what you are doing here is that you are taking that much out only to let this Committee put that much back in again … to be able to say to the newspapers and the *Guardian* in particular, "Look what I have done to the Committee. I have given more than half its recommendations"' (PASC 1999e). Another member alleged that the 'draft Bill has been devised for the sake of robust argument' (PASC 1999e). The 'extreme nature' of some of the points, a number of which Straw later 'conceded' on, 'raised suspicions that they may have been placed in the Bill as part of a premeditated strategy' to gain 'credit' for 'concessions' (Beetham et al. 2001, 384).

Whether by accident or by design, the Bill seemed perfect for just such an approach, as Chapter 5 above shows. The draft contained a core of strong executive protections, a veto override and lower harm tests. Clustered on the periphery was an array of lesser clauses which attracted controversy, such as the 'jigsaw' clause or the power to make new exemptions. These 'peripheral' or 'outer' sections could be easily dropped.

### FOI in Parliament

This chapter examines four key stages of the Parliamentary process that demonstrate the tensions and nuances of the passage of the Bill. The clashes were over not only detail but also 'vision' and the 'fundamental difficulty' that Parliament's 'perspective was different from that of Ministers' (interview with Jack Straw 2015). The government maintained the need for 'balance' and its heavily legal and guarded interpretation. Those seeking a stronger Act pushed for a more radical, political vision and played upon the transformative and symbolic effects of the law and the 'betrayal' of implementing too weak a policy.

Despite the media trailing each stage as a 'defining' event, Parliamentary pressure and scrutiny were effective in inverse order, as the stages became increasingly prey to government tactics. The early scrutiny by two committees led to a number of concessions while the later debates, where whipping and partisan feeling could be exploited, elicited less. What emerged was neither a 're-radicalised' Act nor a 'minimal concessions' law but a compromise between the two.

### The reports of the two committees

Those seeking 'FOI max' were granted greater time and political space than normal. The Labour government in 1997 had championed the idea of pre-legislative scrutiny, whereby Bills were published in draft form so that 'Parliament's influence is maximised' with an additional stage of scrutiny (Norton 2013, 84). It was felt that the process meant that legislation could be discussed in a less partisan setting. Although the government hoped that drafts could then have an easier passage, pre-legislative scrutiny also framed later debates and supplied knowledge to Parliamentarians (Smookler 2006).

FOI was chosen as a test case, and two committees, PASC in the Commons and an ad hoc committee HL 97 in the Lords, were given the chance to examine it at the draft stage. The PASC report began by questioning whether the Bill constituted FOI. Although it did 'create a statutory right to information [it] is so hedged with qualifications and exemptions that it does not cover a large amount of information which the public may want ... in short, [it] perpetuates "the paternalistic model of open government with the government deciding what we need to know"' (PASC 1999f). The committee pointed out that 'in three crucial ways the draft Bill has more in common with non-statutory open government regimes than with statutory Freedom of Information ones':

> First, as long as the disclosure of information could cause prejudice, the authority cannot be forced to release it ... Second, there will be no general statutory obligation to publish reasons for administrative decisions: nor to release the facts and analysis behind policy. Third, matters ... laid down as duties in other Freedom of Information regimes ... are left to be included in a non-statutory code. (PASC 1999f)

For PASC the fundamental problem lay with the removal of the Commissioner's powers of release, and the 'single most important amendment' would be to give the Information Commissioner a public interest override power (PASC 1999f). The report then pushed for a stronger harm test, as 'prejudice ... is not enough to justify exempting information from public access', and it recommended that the test be 'more demanding', closer to the earlier idea of 'likely to substantially prejudice' (PASC 1999f). The 'over-protective and over-elaborate' exemptions regime should be 'much more tightly drawn', the right of access 'should apply as broadly as possible', and, in particular, policy advice should be subject to a 'distinct and separable' division between factual and non-factual information, with the former released and the latter subject to a 'substantial prejudice test' to be reviewed by the Information Commissioner (PASC 1999f). The report advocated the removal of all of the 'novel features' of the Bill and, almost as afterthought, supported coverage of Parliament by FOI.

HL 97 began by criticising the short six-week turnaround time and what it felt was the illogical division of work between two committees (HL 97 1999b). It praised the scope of the Bill, which, it acknowledged, 'goes beyond the White Paper' in giving elements of access to the police and allowing an appeals tribunal (HL 97 1999b). The committee's criticisms echoed those of PASC, taking the view that 'to the extent that the draft Bill represents a move from an enforceable public right of access to discretionary disclosure, it abandons the Freedom of Information principles expressed in the White Paper'. The Bill needed to 'provide a framework for transforming the "culture of secrecy" in British government', and 'the most important single way to restore [FOI] principles is to give the Information Commissioner a public interest override' (HL 97 1999b, 3). The committee further supported a Croham-style distinction concerning policy advice, a harm test of 'likely to substantially prejudice', the removal of the power to create new exemptions under clause 36 and a redrafting of the opening to become a purpose clause.

In its reply, the government robustly defended parts of the Bill. The exemptions were 'small in number, clearly defined and fully justified', and the exemption for policy advice was 'essential' to 'avoid hindering the effective conduct of public affairs' (PASC 1999b). The 'prejudice' test was 'consistent with other legislation' covering access to information, such as the 1998 Data Protection Act and 1972 Local Government Act. The addition of words like 'substantial' or 'significant' to the harm test would 'add an unquantifiable standard which may itself cause confusion' (PASC 1999b).

Underneath its robust defence, the scrutiny wrought a number of concessions. The two reports led to the dropping of the section 36 power to create new exclusions and of the power of authorities to place conditions upon how information is released. The government also offered to insert an amendment meaning that authorities must balance the public interest in considering disclosure, and committed itself to a lesser purpose clause through a rearranging of existing parts to create a 'presumption in favour of disclosure'. There were other smaller, if important, changes over partial release, reducing the response period for requests from forty days to twenty, and covering Parliament under FOI for its administrative work (PASC 1999b). However, PASC professed itself to be 'disappointed that the government had not amended the basic structure and scheme of the draft Bill' and pointed to the lack of change over the presumption in favour of disclosure, the ministerial veto and the 'too weak' harm test (1999a).

According to Lord Goodhart, a member of HL 97, 'the most effective work done' to improve the Bill was in the two committees (interview with Lord Goodhart 2005). The two reports set the ground for later debate and framed the issues and dividing lines, over the veto, policy advice and exemptions that would follow the Bill throughout Parliament (Smookler 2006). The reactions to the Bill in the hearings were significant not only because 'both were in tune with each other' but also because 'they produced very well informed Parliamentarians who then played a leading part in the legislative process' (interview with Maurice Frankel 2005).

In parallel to the scrutiny, support for a stronger FOI began to build outside of Parliament. In June the *Guardian* reported 'mounting pressure' as forty-two Labour and Liberal Democrat MPs expressed support for a stronger law, while CFOI and Charter 88 began campaigns on the theme of greater openness (*Guardian* 21/6/1999b). Three days later the *Guardian* claimed a 'tidal wave' of support with the poet laureate, the National Union of Journalists, peers and lawyers all signing up (24/6/1999).

PASC ended its report with what could be seen as a challenge to all sides. FOI was 'of historic significance', or 'that, at least, is the potential', but 'the draft Bill needs to be strengthened. This can be readily done. It requires only a combination of political will and the draftsmen's pen', and 'a failure to make the draft Bill better … would represent a missed opportunity of historic proportions' (PASC 1999f).

### Interregnum: what is FOI for?

As the government digested the reports and prepared the Bill, a debate broke out within the Labour Party over the symbolism and meaning of FOI. The discussion revealed the very different visions of FOI that now confronted each other.

In June of 1999 Jack Straw spoke at an awards ceremony for CFOI, where he was heckled. Straw defended the government's record on constitutional reform, arguing that 'we have been accused of not going far enough' but that the Bill must be 'workable for citizens, workable for interested pressure groups, and yes, workable for good government as well' (Straw 1999b). He again repeated the argument that what mattered was the passage of the law itself, which would then, by its presence on the statute book, trigger further change: 'my critics underestimate the degree to which the culture will change simply by putting on the statute book a clear legal right of information' (Straw 1999b). He also again drew a picture of FOI as a 'localised', individualised tool:

> We want schools to explain much better how they apply their admission criteria; health authorities to provide better details of how they allocate their resources between different treatments; the Prison Service to provide information on the performance of different regimes; hospitals and general practitioners to explain better how they prioritise their waiting lists; National Health Service trusts and health authorities to provide information on their administrative procedures governing Private Finance Initiatives. Those, of all the many other examples, will be guaranteed by the Bill. (Straw 1999b)

He offered a somewhat convoluted reassurance that the Bill would not be dropped: 'it would be, to say the least, eccentric, if we had decided not to deliver on this. Because we have not decided not to deliver on it' (Straw 1999b).

The new justifying narrative was then taken up by Phillip Gould, one of the major architects of the New Labour project, who argued publicly that those pressing the government for a stronger FOI Bill misunderstood New Labour's radicalism (*Guardian* 24/8/1999). Critics were 'wrong' in claiming that FOI was 'not far reaching enough'. The party was leading a 'new modernised progressive agenda' that was able 'to deliver results rather than ideology', and FOI was part of a delivery of 'populist' instruments allowing 'new forms of contact with the electorate'. New Labour was not 'betraying its progressive past' but 'making a progressive future possible'. Gould pointed to FOI as a 'practical' instrument to engage, and saw arguments over 'principles' (and presumably details) as a distraction that undermined Labour's attempt to create reforms that delivered 'results'.

Tony Wright MP, a Labour chair of PASC, responded with a counter-vision. FOI was political and, as a 'badge' of identity, said much about what Labour wanted to be. Labour must use FOI to demonstrate its new approach to politics. The party's 'command of the political landscape' gives it a chance to show that politics can be done differently', and the FOI Bill would be a 'good place to start'. He went on to warn that 'the party will insist' on a 'radical re-strengthening' of the policy (*Guardian* 29/9/1999). Other parts of the media kept up the pressure on the government, again framing FOI as a 'test' of the government's trust and commitment. The *Independent* focused on Blair himself, asking 'We've Seen the Caution, Mr Blair, Now Where Is the Radicalism?' and claiming that FOI was being 'smothered' and electoral reform stalled (27/9/1999). In parallel, 112 MPs, including four Select Committee chairs, tabled another motion calling for tougher powers for the Commissioner, including the power to compel authorities to release information (House of Commons 1999).

Further 'friction' and institutional pressure came from unexpected directions. In an unintended overspill from the devolution programme, the new Scottish government issued its own separate FOI proposals which contrasted sharply with the UK draft, which had emerged out of coalition negotiations between Scottish Labour and Liberal Democrats who shared power (John 2009). The Scottish proposals retained the higher harm test of 'substantial prejudice', stronger public interest tests and a commitment to publish policy background information (House of Commons Library 1999). They was followed in March 2000 by further criticism of Labour's local government reforms, which were designed to create executive-controlled local councils as oppose to the old committee-based decision-making structures. This would, the media claimed, lead to more 'closed door decisions', backing up its point with a list of examples of secretive local authorities (*Independent* 15/3/2000). A final drop of overspill came in the wake of the debate, when the London mayoral candidate Ken Livingstone, an ex-Labour member then running against the Labour Party, promised to publish online the meeting minutes of his new mayoral office (*Independent* 17/4/2000).

Amid this pressure, a confidential Cabinet memorandum by Jack Straw was leaked to the *Guardian* in which the government appeared to be considering numerous concessions. Straw proposed that 'the Commissioner should have an express power to recommend a discretionary disclosure', that there be 'a slightly clearer balancing provision' and that 'a public authority will expressly consider whether the need to maintain the exemption outweighs the public interest in the disclosing'. In addition, he suggested a removal of the 'jigsaw' clause and reportedly 'asked his Civil Servants to draft changes to allow the release of information used in Whitehall to come to policy decisions', though he was 'adamantly against releasing policy advice'. These amendments would allow the government to 'get the Bill through' and 'have a policy that is defensible in Parliament' (*Guardian* 11/10/1999).

### A victory and a repulse: the Commons report stage (April 2000)

The report stage revealed the depth of feeling as the FOI radicals sought a series of concessions. However, it also revealed the strength of the government's position and its power to control, undermine and divide the MPs seeking change.

The significance of the debate on the Commons report stage was anticipated by parts of the media, which framed it as a symbolic clash. Hugo Young described the coming vote as a 'defining confrontation' after 'two decades of argument about citizens' rights to be informed about the way they are governed'. It stood as a struggle 'between the virtue and vice of power [which] poses the pretensions of New Labour as a party of reform against the instincts of a no-longer-new-Labour as a party of government' (*Guardian* 4/4/2000). The media highlighted reports of a rebellion 'of up to 60 Labour MPs' (*Evening Standard* 5/4/2000). The government was keen to win Commons votes with a minimum of 100 (*Sun* 14/4/2000) and 'feared winning by less' as a 'pyrrhic' victory would be construed as a defeat (interview with Maurice Frankel 2005). Two leading Labour FOI radicals, Tony Wright and Mark Fisher, predicted that the Bill 'would face a rough ride in the Commons especially over the Ministerial veto [and that] Ministers were "on the ropes"' (*Guardian* 3/4/2000). During the preceding month Straw had met potential Labour rebels on a number of occasions (Cowley 2002).

In the debate itself the two ministers leading the debate played rather different roles: Mike O'Brien offered a robust defence, and Straw, who followed, then made more conciliatory noises. The debate over the two days focused upon what Mark Fisher called 'the twin pillars on which the Bill is constructed', the veto power and the exclusion of policy advice, though it covered many other areas (Hansard, House of Commons, 5/4/2000, col. 1004). It opened with a clear rebuff from the government of one of the FOI opposition's key demands, the insertion of a purpose clause. This proposal was firmly and quickly rejected by Mike O'Brien, who argued that FOI policy 'requires not a purpose clause, but a Bill' (Hansard, House of Commons, 4/4/2000, col. 843). O'Brien went on to defend the second area of contention, the government veto power, arguing that 'democracy must mean something … only a qualified person can have a full understanding of the issues involved in the decision making process of a public authority' and that to give the Commissioner an override power would be 'illegitimate', creating a 'democratic deficit'.

By contrast, Straw was more conciliatory when he took over, offering an unexpected concession. To the surprise of the FOI radicals, Straw restricted the veto power over disclosure to Cabinet ministers and the Attorney General rather than all ministers and local councillors as originally proposed: 'I accept the burden of the argument that has been put to me. Therefore, I propose-it will have to be done in the other place, but it will be done – that those parts of the amendments that speak of Ministers of the Crown will be replaced by a definition of a Cabinet Minister' (Hansard, House of Commons, 4/4/2000, cols 921–922). After limiting the veto power, Straw then gave a further concession, that 'other colleagues should be consulted, other than on quasi-judicial decisions' (col. 922). Later on in the House of Lords, the possibility of judicial review was discussed in the committee stage, and the minister in charge, Lord Falconer, reminded peers that the veto 'decision is subject to judicial review' and that the Commissioner 'will have a locus to seek such a review' (Hansard, House of Lords, 20/4/2000, col. 828). Straw also moved somewhat over the Information Commissioner's power of disclosure, offering to insert an override power and make the public interest test mandatory:

> As a result of the representations, we have in many ways fundamentally changed the structure of [clause 2] ... We have strengthened the tests – that is a matter for another debate in respect of factual information – but we have made it a duty, not a discretion, on the public authority to consider whether the public interest in disclosure outweighs the public interest in the matter not being disclosed. (Hansard, House of Commons, 4/4/ 2000, cols 918–919)

Mark Fisher later saluted his 'courage' and 'good sense' (Hansard, House of Commons, 5/4/2000, col. 1006). It appears that Straw had taken a political risk in making these concessions without consulting Cabinet, announcing that 'it was necessary to get the Bill through' and allegedly assuming responsibility for it even before a phone call to the Cabinet secretariat (private information).

The following night the radicals hoped for further concessions. Little was forthcoming despite one MP reminding the government that FOI was based on a 'manifesto commitment' and 'a White Paper promise' (Hansard, House of Commons, 5/4/2000, cols 998–999). The centre of the debate turned on access to policy advice and whether there could be a distinction between 'facts' that could be disclosed and 'advice' that could not. At points it became a rather abstract seminar over whether it was possible to define a fact or opinion: Straw argued that 'the difficulty ... is essentially a linguistic one, about what is meant by factual information. The word fact encompasses a huge sphere of human activity. "Words and Phrases Legally Defined" states: "Everything in the cosmos is a fact or a phenomenon"' (col. 1027). Robert MacLennan rejected this reasoning, and argued that the issue was 'fundamental to the nature of democracy ... as if power is distributed to the people, the people will have the power. We are engaged in a fundamental constitutional argument about the role of the House and the Executive. It is not a little problem of definition or of finding the right words' (col. 1012). Tony Wright then pointed to other countries with FOI legislation, asking if the Home Secretary was 'suggesting that they know what a fact is in Ireland and in New Zealand, and that they have discovered what a fact is in Scotland, but that we in the United Kingdom have not quite managed to work out what a fact is at all?', and Richard Shepherd quoted an official claiming that 'The only thing that has to be protected from exposure is rows between Ministers-that is the really sensitive area' (cols 1015, 1028).

The debate then ranged from data protection to the power of the Commissioner to the openness of the security services. Two former members of CRP (FOI) also intervened: Mark Fisher argued that if the government maintained its 'amazing defensive edifice' and 'enormous rampart' then 'the Bill will cease to be an FOI Bill' (Hansard, House of Commons, 5/4/2000, col. 1005), and David Clark spoke of how he was 'mystified by the government's continuing retreat' (col 1013). Despite his refusal to back down, Straw ended the discussion on a somewhat more concilia-tory note: 'we want the greatest possible openness in the operation of government … the search for a better form of words will be difficult, but it will continue and we shall not close the door on it' (col. 1029). Wright explained how 'The Home Secretary illuminated … a fundamental choice in approach between open govern-ment and freedom of information. Open government happens when a Government decide to behave in a more open way. It is a gift, or a grant, from a Government. Freedom of information is achieved when rights are claimed by citizens, and bestowed on them' (col. 1031).

During the debate the long-time openness campaigner Richard Shepherd claimed to have identified Straw's tactics, praising his 'extraordinary performance' and 'the devices that lay behind it – softly, softly here, concede there, do this, say that, talk about drafting difficulties' (Hansard, House of Commons, 5/4/2000, col. 1015). Straw also invoked party divisions, contrasting Labour's openness with the previous Conservative administration: 'I am interested to hear a member of the pre-vious Government professing expertise on freedom of information, when the cam-paign guide on which he fought the election said "The only group in Britain who are seriously interested in a Freedom of Information Act are inquisitive left-wing busy bodies"' (col. 1029). He would, he said, 'take with a pinch of salt the Conservatives' late conversion on the issue' (col. 1029). The Conservatives, Straw felt, were merely using the issue to cause the government difficulties (Straw 2012).

The debate had demonstrated the cross-party support for a stronger FOI. Wright spoke for himself and Tony Benn, saying that they 'could not remember an occa-sion when Parliament had been so roused collectively by an issue across party lines' (Hansard, House of Commons, 5/4/2000, col. 1031). He made a cross-party appeal:

> I confess to being a serial loyalist. The problem is that there comes a moment when we have to decide whether we can accept the formula that the Government are offer-ing on issues that affect the workings of our democracy and the rights of our citizens.

There are not too many such moments during a Parliament, but this is one on any test. (col. 1030)

A total of forty-one Labour MPs rebelled at various points over six different areas, including rebellions of twenty-four over the veto power (Cowley 2002, 68–69). The opposition had succeeded in getting a concession on the veto, an important potential amendment of one of the 'core' parts of the Bill. Perhaps more importantly for the future, but less noticed, the government strengthened the Commissioner's power over disclosure and made a public interest test for partial exemptions mandatory (Hansard, House of Commons, 4/4/2000, cols 918–919). However, MPs were not agreed on what they had achieved. In an interview with the *Guardian*, David Clark believed 'Jack Straw's concession is a massive step forward' (*Guardian* 7/4/2000). The Liberal Democrat Simon Hughes described the government as giving 'small but welcome concessions' (Hansard, House of Commons, 5/4/2000, col. 1002). Another MP, rather less convinced, quoted a newspaper editorial: 'Alastair Campbell, the Prime Minister's press secretary, has frequently said that we will get a Freedom of Information Act over his dead body. He need have no fear; the Home Secretary is giving us neither freedom, nor information, nor any Act worth the name' (col. 1018).

A further question is whether the government fully understood the changes. Straw's legal training gave him a clear insight but there was later surprise over judicial review of the veto in 2015, indicating that succeeding governments may have believed that the wording of the veto gave them an 'ultimate' defence. Similarly, later examination by the Justice Committee revealed that the government viewed sections 35 and 36 as effectively absolute exemptions, despite the giving of a mandatory public interest test for this and a number of others exemptions (Justice Committee 2012d).

However, the limits of the FOI radicals had been revealed. The very fact that the Labour majority remained over 100 demonstrated the unequal nature of the battle. Potential rebellions had been halved by Straw's actions and, perhaps, the conflicting doubts of rebellion and FOI. Straw was described as conducting a 'seminar with his MPs' and taking a 'consultative approach' culminating in his rewriting of policy (Cowley 2002, 69). The government's concessions over the veto and public interest tests had been matched by robustness, for example, over policy advice or the insertion of a purpose clause.

Moreover, the fragility of the FOI radicals had been exposed. At times, the debate had descended into argument over Conservative hypocrisy for denying FOI when in government and had confirmed the view of 'party strategists … that the openness issue is a preoccupation of worthies and pointy heads, neither gaining nor losing heartland votes' (*Guardian* 7/4/2000). Cowley (2002) quoted the concerns of Labour rebels that it was 'an issue for intellectuals not the majority of my constituents' and that 'no one cares about it outside of the [London] M25 beltway'

(68). Labour whips had reflected this view during the vote, declaring, 'government this way ... other way for Tories, Liberal Democrats and left-wing intellectuals' (Paxman 2003, 169).

Media reaction was divided, though all focused on the government's growing caution. The *Independent* addressed Straw with a headline stating that 'FOI is Ours by Right, Mr Straw, not at Your Discretion'. The policy was a product of the 'deep seated conservatism' of the Blair government, while those seeking improvements spoke for the 'radical liberal tradition'; the paper cautioned that while 'FOI is never going to be a central issue in a general election ... this does not mean Mr Blair and Mr Straw can ignore it' as voters 'recognise and reward integrity' (7/4/2000). The *Times* took a less optimistic note, calling the Bill a 'mournful ghost' that had for the government 'clearly been one devolution of power too far'. While Straw had already 'thrown a few bones the rebel's way', it 'is left to the Lords to breathe some living freedom into this mournful ghost' (5/4/2000). As the Bill joined the queue for the Lords, concerns again were raised over its future. The government was forced to postpone the Queen's speech as a series of Bills created a 'logjam'. FOI and the similarly controversial 'right to roam Bill' on access to land were caught in the middle. The government publicised a somewhat double-loaded reassurance in the article that FOI 'is still strongly backed. It has not been dropped' (*Guardian* 29/9/2000).

## The House of Lords outflanked

FOI, said the long-time supporter Lord McNally, would be 'an important test of the new House of Lords' (Hansard, House of Lords, 20/4/ 2000 col. 837). The chamber retains considerable powers of delay and a membership of experts, many with legal expertise. Following Labour's reforms of 1999, removing the hereditary element, the House had also become increasingly assertive, particularly over what it viewed as constitutional or civil rights issues (Russell and Sciara 2008). The post-1999 makeup of the Lords also meant that no party had a majority and Conservative and Liberal Democrat peers could use their numbers to defeat the government (Russell and Sciara 2008). Lord Peter Archer, chairman of HL 97, predicted that 'if there are no concessions ... I'm pretty sure there will be a pitched battle in the Lords', and it was the belief of another peer that the FOI Bill 'would "ping-pong" around Parliament, forcing concessions' (*Guardian* 7 April 2000). The government had already faced a slew of hard-fought issues in the Lords over the European Parliamentary Act 1999 (rejected five times by the Lords in 1999) and the lowering of the age of consent (Ganz 1999).

Like the Commons debate, the final debate in the Lords was heavily trailed as another defining moment where a 'Tory–Lib Dem alliance' could extract concessions (*Independent* 11/11/2000). Conservative peers, showing 'surprising resilience', were buoyed by a pro-FOI speech by their leader William Hague (*Guardian*

14/11/2000). Hugo Young predicted that the government must compromise, as 'if it fails, its humiliation before its own constituency will be corrosively damaging' (*Guardian* 14/11/2000). The Lords had pushed a series of changes including a Parliamentary oversight committee for FOI and a harm test for the veto (House of Commons Library 2014).

Yet the defining confrontation and gridlock did not come to pass. The government effectively 'outflanked' opposition through a deal with Liberal Democrat peers. Before the session, Liberal Democrat peers had tabled four amendments asking for a rebalancing in a 'dead heat' over the public interest test, a requirement that authorities have 'particular regard' for the public interest, a statutory duty for authorities to assist applicants and a requirement that authorities inform applicants of an estimated time in any delay (CFOI 2000a). Following 'very strong negotiations', the government accepted the four amendments and the Liberal Democrat peers agreed to pass the legislation (private information).

The Liberal Democrats were roundly criticised for their action by campaigners. Young described them as 'compliant, abject, half-baked' and demonstrating a 'shocking ... willingness ... to assist in the butchery' (*Guardian* 14/11/2000). CFOI professed to be 'deeply disappointed' as 'it seemed likely that significant changes would be secured in the Lords due to the apparent "all party agreement" on the need for changes' (CFOI 2000a). Although the amendments 'represent progress ... the question is whether they represent such substantial progress, in terms of outstanding issues, as to justify ending any real pressure for further improvements. In our view, they do not' (CFOI 2000a). The leader of the Conservatives in the House of Lords, Lord Strathclyde, wrote a letter to the *Guardian* claiming, 'the record shows clearly we would have defeated the government if the Liberal Democrats stayed with us' (*Guardian* 17/11/2000). According to CFOI, the agreement left 'outstanding issues' over policy advice, the ministerial veto, exclusion of information related to accidents and the lack of a purpose clause (CFOI 2000b, 4–8). Young claimed that the 'worst flaws' of the Bill, namely the 'protective catch-all' ministerial veto and exclusion of policy advice, would now remain (*Guardian* 14/11/2000).

So why did the Liberal Democrats concede? Across FOI regimes the same dilemma appears: do supporters risk losing a Bill by pushing too hard or accept a lesser law on the statute book? One possibility is that they fell victim to the government's hints that the Bill would be dropped. Liberal Democrat peers felt 'they had a very weak hand because the government was going to walk away from it' and did what they could (private information). Another more political explanation is that the Liberal Democrats made a tactical mistake, accepting the amendments because they did not trust their erstwhile Conservative allies and it was 'better to accept the amendments rather than risk the Tories letting it through' (private information). The Lords stage, perhaps most of all, showed the fragility of the FOI alliance and its difficulty in leveraging change and the power of the government. Mistrust, party politics and information asymmetry again stymied the concessions. The Bill then passed through the Lords to the final Commons stage.

### Guillotining in the Commons (27 November 2000)

The government circumvented the Lords through tactics. It then ended the FOI Bill's passage through brute procedure when it was guillotined in the Commons and given a four-hour final debate to discuss more than 100 amendments. To further complicate things, another controversial Bill, the Countryside Rights of Way Bill, was considered at the same time.

Straw justified the double debate and guillotine as necessary for FOI's survival, pleading the pressure of the legislative log-jam: 'the Freedom of Information Bill and the Countryside and Rights of Way Bill would have no chance of being enacted without the guillotine motion' (Hansard, House of Commons, 27/11/2000, col. 666). He then explained that 'the Freedom of Information Bill has been the subject of very extensive pre-legislative and legislative scrutiny, including two days of fine debate at the beginning of April [with] 40 hours in Committee in this House and two full days on the Floor of the House at the beginning of April this year, as well as 28 hours in the other place'. He pointed to the concessions already granted on the veto, public interest tests and reduction of the discretionary element (col. 670).

Contrary to the hopes of FOI radicals there was no final 'push'. Instead, the debate became rather confused. Members had tabled 118 last-minute amendments in a final 'heave' to further 'improve' the Bill (*Guardian* 28/11/2000). Arguments over FOI overlapped with arguments over the Countryside Rights of Way Bill, about which the Conservatives felt strongly and which had itself gathered 283 amendments. Tony Wright pointed out that many members used the remaining time to criticise the guillotine rather than debate the Bills, asking, 'why on earth are we spending all this time talking about our inability to discuss matters?' (Hansard, House of Commons, 27/11/2000, col. 706). After 10 o'clock, with the Countryside Bill passed, the FOI debate ranged over the actions of the Liberal Democrat peers and focused, rather tangentially, on the coverage of the National Assembly of Wales. Wright warned parts of the radical group that 'they should realise that, in the end, they have produced more a mouse than the Freedom of Information Bill that many hon. Members on both sides of the House loudly called for' (col. 743).

The dilemma that had underlain the opposition was brought to the fore. In the weeks preceding the Bill the whips sent the 'message', though 'initially disbelieved', that the government was 'threatening to drop the Bill' (interview with Maurice Frankel 2005). The radicals were split over whether to continue fighting and jeopardise the Bill or to simply allow it, whatever its defects, onto the statute book. Tony Wright, supported by the *Guardian*, took the view that more pressure would bring further concessions (interview with Maurice Frankel 2005). However, some 'Labour backbench opponents who felt the Bill was still too weak made it clear they would be supporting the government', with David Clark 'defending the need to get the Bill on the statute book' (*Guardian* 28/11/2000).

The Bill was passed and received assent on 30 November. After twenty-six years as a manifesto commitment and four years of uncertainty, FOI was on the statute book. The five-year implementation process could now begin.

### Coda

Following assent, the FOI Act continued to gather controversy during its five-year hiatus between assent and implementation. Using John Major's Code of Access, two *Guardian* journalists claimed that plans to gradually roll out FOI after eighteen months, as against the original five-year timetable, had been shelved. According to the report, originally 'Central Whitehall departments were to open up by June [2002], with police forces following in 2003 and all other state bodies by the end of 2004', though other sources claimed that this had always been the plan (*Guardian* 26/10/2001; see Chapter 5 above). Although responses indicated that 'openness is nonetheless spreading through a few parts of Whitehall … some departments resorted to traditional evasiveness, others eventually handed over detailed internal documents disclosing the PM's behaviour'. It was reported that 'Mr Blair – said to be no enthusiast for opening up government – wants legal rights for Whitehall information-seekers to be delayed, on the grounds other bodies like councils, schools and hospitals need time to prepare voluntary plans to publish information all together in a "big bang".' Responsibility for implementing the Act, in a stroke of managerial irony, was passed back to Lord Chancellor Irvine but 'the government appeared to have "stalled" and slowed implementation of FOI once more' with a new deadline of 2005 (*Guardian* 26/10/2001).

### The FOI Act 2000

The Parliamentary process was never likely to produce a dramatic turnaround in FOI, but more a sustained but messy compromise. The radicals had been effective in reverse order to the process. The pre-legislative scrutiny and early debates appeared to exert a stronger, if less obvious, effect than the supposedly more dramatic later stages, gaining concessions and shaping later discussion. As the process went on government was more able to deploy its formal powers and structural advantages, not least its majority, while also exploiting the continuous uncertainty over whether the Bill would be dropped. The later 'defining confrontations' or 'last ditch' battles in the Lords and finally in the Commons were severely limited by, in turn, politics and procedure.

The Act that emerged from the lengthy Parliamentary process carried neither the radicalism of the White Paper nor executive mindedness of the draft Bill. The proposals had undoubtedly been changed and Parliament made a difference during the marathon debates (interview with Jack Straw 2015). A later review in

2016 concluded that 'the Act was substantially amended during its parliamentary passage' (Independent Commission on Freedom of Information 2016b, 3). Many of the peripheral clauses had been dropped, including the 'jigsaw' clause and the power to make new exemptions. The wide discretionary aspects that seemed undermine the spirit of FOI had also been cut back. A series of small but important changes had introduced a statutory duty to advise and assist and had cut the forty-day time limit on responses in half. The opposition had also made some inroads into the 'core' protections. The Information Commissioner's power appeared strengthened and the veto power reduced, albeit from a comparatively wide scope, to a ministerial exercise that matched that in most other Commonwealth countries. The public interest tests would also prove symbolically and practically important.

However, the central tenets of the executive protections, the inner ring of defences for government, remained in place. The lower harm test remained, as did the ultimate override of the executive veto. The exemptions, particularly on policy, stood as well. In some senses, the compromises left the law 'insufficiently clear' and led to legal 'uncertainties' (Independent Commission on Freedom of Information 2016b, 3). One legal critic concluded that the new law represented a 'denial of democracy' (Austin 2004, 415). So why did the government not drop it and how would it work in practice?

# 7

# FOI in the UK: survival and afterlife

The development of FOI is a classic case of 'back room in-fight and front stage dissembling' (Kennedy 1978, 115). It is a tale of mobilisation and counter-mobilisation within institutional settings and of a small group of decision-makers, insulated from electoral pressure, changing their attitudes (Hacker and Pierson 2014).

The first 'radical' stage created a proposal designed to fulfil Blair's 1996 promise, in what amounted to a lightning strike against tradition. The rapid production of the paper was the key to its success, as the radical group overrode and took potential resistance by surprise. It produced a political vision of FOI as a giving-away of power, in a policy loaded with symbolism – with no government veto, no broad Cabinet exclusion and a strong harm test. The White Paper encapsulated the radical, anti-establishment ideas of constitutional reform, imbued with ideas of empowerment, democracy and change.

The second stage took a very different form. The loss of the radical group's power and new leadership meant 'normalcy' returning. The draft Bill proposals were a much altered legalistic balancing of interests, built around a 'core' of protections for government and a 'periphery' of controversial provisions. The new vision was of the law as a whole acting as an 'agent of change' and shifting cultures. Shorn of its radical elements, the redesigned FOI became to an individual instrument of information seeking (Terrill 2000).

Parliament saw a clash between these two perspectives. The subsequent battle was unequal, as the radical alliance used the symbolism and fear of betrayal to exact concessions, while the government used its resources, and an implicit threat to drop FOI, to push its chosen policy through. The Parliamentary opponents did reduce the 'peripheral' controversial parts but made fewer inroads into the 'core' of protections.

FOI in the UK can be seen as a tale of two tactics. A White Paper was launched and pushed amid optimism, general confusion and inattention. The Bill, by contrast, was created in an increasingly executive-minded environment, by a government appreciating its own power and recognising the strength of its opponents; it was caught in a trajectory of what it would claim to be a 'realistic' logic of power.

### Why was FOI not dropped?

In the UK the New Labour government had the best chance of passing FOI, perhaps the only chance, in a generation. As Chapter 6 has explained, the possibility that FOI would be lost was made explicit on several occasions before crucial votes, though it is unclear how real this threat was. Straw claims that the 'slow progress' towards the Lords stages 'became the break point', as 'I'd had enough of FOI' (2012, 281). He explained that 'I had half thought that the best thing might be to bin the whole Bill or kick it into the long grass with a royal commission' (2012, 281).

Superficially, Labour could have easily dropped FOI. Throughout the period during which FOI became law Labour possessed a landslide majority and seemingly unending popularity in polls, accompanied by a largely supportive press and divided Conservative opposition. The political costs of 'losing' a minor policy such as FOI appeared low. Widely perceived as an intellectual issue, FOI was not a vote winner and, the *Guardian* and *Independent* aside, large parts of the media were uninterested. By 1999 Labour had been able to park or freeze progress in other areas of constitutional reform when they proved too difficult, inconvenient or divisive. Voting reform was put on hold, as was later the more complex and politically limiting 'stage two' of House of Lords reform (Flinders 2009b). So why was FOI not dropped?

### *The commitment*
The first reason why FOI was not dropped was a prosaic and rather honourable one, commitment to the manifesto. As McDonald and Hazell point out, Labour

> came to power determined to implement its programme. This, it might be observed, is true of any new administration. But there was a particular edge to New Labour's commitment. This was a party which had been out of power for eighteen years, which had wearied of the charges of betrayal which critics had levelled at the Wilson and Callaghan governments and whose leader had spoken often of the need for sustained achievement over two successive terms. (2007, 6)

Peter Mandelson spoke of Labour's concern that 'to retain the country's trust, we had to show we were keeping our bargain with the voters', and stated that it was 'haunted by the history of one term labour administrations' that had failed to do so (2010, 226). Straw referred to the manifesto as a 'holy text' over which 'immense care' had been taken (2012, 281). FOI was 'in the manifesto and it would have been lame' not to have completed it. There was also a respect for the political and Parliamentary process, and, as time went by, it was felt that time and energy had been expended and the policy should be finished (interview with Jack Straw 2015).

Moreover, despite its incoherence the constitutional reform programme itself was created to be interlocking:

> The programme ... was one which was intended to be delivered in its entirety. Some had criticised the manifesto's economic and social policies for lacking ambition and radicalism. Neither charge could fairly attach to the constitutional pledges [and] they ... were to be delivered come what may. (McDonald and Hazell 2007, 6)

The reforms were designed to be 'interconnected' (Matthews 2015, 329). The overspill and different linkages that were spread between them meant that change fed change and triggered unintended and unexpected consequences (King 2009; Flinders 2009b; Evans 2003). FOI benefited from the co-evolution and overspill and the, albeit brief, atmosphere of radical change (John 1999).

It was connected to the central aims of the programme as a whole. If, as Straw explained, the constitutional programme was based on themes of decentralising power, creating a more open society and promoting democratic innovation then FOI clearly helped fulfil all of these objectives (2010, 360). Referendums in Scotland, Wales and Northern Ireland, local elected mayors and citizens' juries all sought to re-invigorate democracy and create what Blair had called a 'laboratory' of new democratic 'experiments' (King 2009). The sum was a political system that was less representative and more participative – with FOI a missing piece of the openness needed to make it work (Bogdanor 2009).

FOI also fed into the wider championing of citizens' rights in the reforms (Klug 2010). The new Human Rights Act was seen as a 'floor' onto which could be built greater rights, including FOI. Articles 8 and 10 of the Act have been used since to advance the idea of access to information as a human right (Birkinshaw 2006; McDonagh 2013). In a speech outlining the programme in 1999, Straw explicitly linked FOI and the Human Rights Act:

> Taken together, the Human Rights Act and the proposed FOI Bill, will move us from the notion of 'the ruler and the ruled'. It marks the end of the 'citizen as subject' idea [and] puts in place a modern dynamic relationship between the individual citizen and the state. (1999a)

What Straw outlined as the underlying premise of the entire reforms strongly mirrored the claims of FOI itself: to help 'break up traditional centres of power' and 'make those in power accountable' (2010, 360).

### The benefits of inattention

FOI also survived, secondly, through inattention. Edelman speaks of how laws are passed partly due to their 'symbolic effect' and partly through 'rational reflection'

(1985, 41). FOI inclined very much to the symbolic, and partially survived through inattention and disinterest, as another thing to be done by a busy new government distracted and preoccupied by far bigger issues after eighteen years out of power (Straw 2012). Although actors took action against it, their focus on FOI was sporadic and often fleeting. From Tony Blair downwards, key figures were unaware of the change or gave it little thought, from the outset to the formulation. Peter Mandelson complained of Blair's lack of focus on any issue at this time (2010). The CRP (FOI) committee was full but was populated by lesser ministers and sparsely attended by important ones. Even after FOI was passed little detailed thought was given to what might be the result – and some major figures seemed still unaware of its existence years later (Powell 2010). Certain implications were not fully absorbed or believed. FOI's very votelessness or lack of centrality may have saved it from the scrutiny and attention that could have stopped it dead.

### The politics of pressure

The third reason was political. The government, the whips and the opposition all recognised that FOI contained no votes. However, a series of proxy forces applied consistent pressure for change and blocked, at least partially, any line of retreat.

The legislature was a powerful force, with support spread across Liberal Democrats, Conservatives and, most importantly, Labour backbenchers in the House of Commons and up to the House of Lords. Numerous influential individual MPs and peers were advocates. The formal institutions, such as PASC or the ad hoc HL 97, brought expertise to bear while supplying MPs and peers with cadres of well-informed members. Outside Parliament an experienced coalition of lobby groups headed by CFOI supplied expertise, knowledge and influence. CFOI, Charter 88 and Liberty in turn were supported by major newspapers such as the *Guardian*, the *Independent* and, to a lesser extent, the *Telegraph* and *Times* as well as the regional press.

This pool of networked 'opinion formers' could, and did, generate attention and controversy that translated into headlines and sustained campaigns. They had proved themselves an effective force in the 1980s and 1990s, criticising government secrecy and helping achieve concrete change with lobbying and Private Members' Bills. Dropping FOI would be unlikely to make them quietly back away. Loss would be likely to simply reinvigorate them, and their power to generate problems could prove damaging: 'It would make a fuss', with the issue likely to be raised 'and be asked about in Prime Minister's Questions', providing a common cause for 'Lib-Dems and Tories' who 'would vote with Labour rebels' (interview with Jack Straw 2015). Given the commitment to the manifesto and pressure, it was also recognised that in the future, if FOI was dropped, 'It would have had to be put back in the manifesto and life would not get any easier for the government' (interview with Jack Straw 2015).

## Symbolism of FOI

The fourth reason was the symbolism. 'Names', Edelman argued, 'are important symbols' (1985, 206). The problem on one level was purely linguistic: it is difficult for a government to outright oppose a law giving 'freedom of information' or a 'right to information' and expressly deny a right to the people. Such a change would be difficult to back out of or refuse once offered.

FOI carried a powerful moral credibility, symbolising the new government's commitment to a new approach and working 'in the open' and its desire to 'legislate morals' not for the public but for itself and its officials (Gusfield 1968). It was pitched as a decisive break with the past, in contrast to previous governments' refusal to be open. Attached to this were ideas of increasing public trust and partnership, a theme across the constitutional reform programme that also attached to Blair himself as leader (Curtice 2010; Rawnsley 2000).

FOI was also linked to the government's self-image as a radical administration prepared to make decisive changes to the political system. FOI symbolised to itself what New Labour was, a 'badge' of its intent and approach. For Labour, the very radicalism that attracted support for FOI made it difficult to drop. FOI had been trumpeted as an anti-establishment, transformative tool, a weapon of accountability and a new, central right to be given to all in a mature democracy. Dropping FOI would make it the party of conservatism and rather than radicalism – and Labour prided itself, throughout its three terms, on its radical approach. Hugo Young described it as a 'test' of New Labour's own image, as a struggle 'between the ... pretensions of New Labour as a party of reform against the instincts of a no-longer-new-Labour as a party of government' (*Guardian* 4/4/2000).

Finally it was also about a recognition of a new, more direct democracy, as a tool of individual self-empowerment (Bogdanor 2009). While claims were made for 'breaking up' power, many of the constitutional reforms actually transferred power to other elites at regional or local level (Straw 2010; Bogdanor 2010). FOI, along with use of referendums and new human rights, was one of the few changes to grant a genuinely populist instrument of use to the public. It was also one couched in the language of 'rights' to which the public were *entitled* or which they *should* be given as part of a modern democracy.

For Blair, there was also an issue of personal credibility. As CFOI hoped, he had left several very public hostages to fortune, including his 1996 speech and the preface to the 1997 White Paper. Straw recalled, 'I saw Tony [Blair]' who was 'exasperated as I was'. However, Blair had 'made a categorical promise in the John Smith memorial lecture' as well in the manifesto commitment and had let the White Paper (called the 'David Clark extravaganza') go 'public' (Straw 2012, 281). 'How credibly', Blair asked, 'could we explain dropping a Bill with our names on it which was close to completing its passage through Parliament?', and he concluded that 'we'd better let the Bill go through' (281). As Blair feared, his own earlier words were used repeatedly in Early Day Motions, newspaper editorials and campaign literature.

The *Guardian* and *Independent* repeatedly quoted the 1996 speech, with the former printing large extracts of it alongside its analysis of the draft Bill. CFOI turned extracts of it into a small pledge card.

Dropping the policy and not having FOI would signal a number of damaging things. First, loss of FOI would mean that Labour wished to be secretive, like its Conservative predecessors. 'Why', a voter would potentially ask, 'would you drop FOI unless you wanted to keep something secret', or 'what is it they do not want us to know'? Labour would be 'power-hoarding' and not 'power distributing'. As seen below, later governments attempting to reform FOI faced exactly these questions.

Second, it would reverse the 'moral' signal. Hugo Young predicted that 'if it [FOI] fails, its humiliation before its own constituency will be corrosively damaging' (*Guardian* 14/11/2000). Blair had cast the new reform not only as a mode of empowerment but also a means to hold the government to account and show it as more 'clean'. It was a commitment based on 'trusting' the public and the public 'trusting' it. By reining back, Blair would be reneging on being more open or ethical. It would also be denying a right that, as Blair himself had reiterated in the preface to the White Paper, was a central right across most developed democracies – and, it could be pointed out, one that existed for local government and the Scottish Parliament. The government had already seen how the symbolism of FOI could be used to attack the government by those pushing for a stronger law. As early as 1997 Campbell's diaries record the concern at the top of government when the media criticised delays to the White Paper (Campbell 2011). FOI came to be treated, particularly by the media and opponents, as a 'test' of credibility, using the language of betrayal or failure of either Labour's values, promises to the people or commitment to reforming politics.

Any politician could see that, while FOI was voteless, dropping the Bill would mean that such attacks would continue. Blair saw how damaging the 'secrecy' epithet was to Major and how, while few voted on the basis of it, it influenced perceptions of the government as vaguely dishonest (Blair 2011). He could also see how such a view built over time and how 'drips' could erode reputation. Just as 'sleaze' became the word that haunted Major, so dropping 'Freedom of Information' could become a recurrent trope for him. Every secrecy scandal or cover-up would lead to a repeat mention of FOI and consequent hammering-home of hypocrisy and betrayal by opponents. The House of Commons and Lords could continuously send Private Members' Bills, and Select Committees could continue to highlight it in their reports as they did in the 1980s and 1990s, supported by highly organised alliance of NGOs. The press, about which Labour was uniquely sensitive, would endlessly remind the public about the 'loss' of FOI until it became a trope. While few among the electorate would ever recognise the detail, the words 'Freedom of Information' themselves could be resonant enough to be damaging. The odour of secrecy could linger and begin to stick.

These factors worked together, driving momentum even against politicians' better judgement or wishes. While FOI was not electorally potent there was enough symbolic capital in it to make dropping it damaging, sending out the wrong signals and messages, possibly leaving a disreputable atmosphere and handing a weapon to opponents. As a matter of practical politics and symbolic resonance, it appeared better to have a weak FOI on the statute books than to attempt it again later, at a worse time, or have a forever 'lost' Bill as a permanent reminder of Labour's perfidy and stain on its honesty.

### FOI in operation, 2005–15

The Coalition government expressly warned that 'the formative years of open government will be difficult, tricky and uncomfortable' (Cabinet Office 2012, 6). By 2015 the UK Act had existed across governments of three complexions: Labour, Liberal Democrat-Conservative coalition and Conservative. Has the Act survived or thrived? More importantly, how have the competing visions of FOI been borne out in practice? Is the Act an individualised, localised and legal tool? Or is it simply, as one critic argued 'a sheep in wolf's clothing?' (Austin 2007, 387).

Evaluating the impact of FOI requires multiple methods, sometimes combining quantitative and qualitative approaches (Meijer et al. 2015). It involves mapping use through requests made, alongside more intangible changes to culture or behaviour. It is about not only what is happening but what actors believe to be happening (Meijer 2013; Darch 2013). Studies have sought to measure laws in numerous ways, from statistical analysis to design experiments (see Hazell and Worthy 2010; Meijer et al. 2012; Michener 2015d). Like other changes, FOI comes to symbolise more than the sum of its parts, positively for those outside government and sometimes negatively for those within (Kreiss 2015b).

As user-driven legislation FOI Acts are inherently disruptive and dynamic. They are disruptive in their sheer unpredictability, over what and who can be asked and what can be opened up: as one former Cabinet Secretary put it, 'the great cost from FOI is uncertainty' (Justice Committee 2012b). They are also dynamic, altering over time through a potent combination of use, legal rulings and reform, with technology adding a further fluidity: 'decisions and interpretation' can mean that a law departs 'from the original intentions behind the legislation' (Independent Commission on Freedom of Information 2016b, 3). FOI adds to the chaos and uncertainty in a rapidly changing political information ecosystem (Stubbs and Snell 2014; Chadwick 2013).

The divisive symbolism of FOI also carries over into its operation. In the UK, as elsewhere, an FOI laws stands to supporters outside as a powerful signifier of democratic freedom, accountability and as a counter-availing tool against the corruption and malign intent of those who govern. Inside government it frequently comes to be viewed as a symbol of counter-productive and perverted change which impinges on decision-making and encourages abuse and 'shallow' exposure (Heclo 1999).

### The Act in retrospect

FOI laws often operate differently in practice. In the UK some of the most feted or criticised parts of the Act had a lesser impact than expected. One example was the publication schemes, which were to be the 'catalyst' for culture change, pushing the vital proactive side of the disclosure of information (Home Office 1999, 9). The schemes were rapidly overtaken by the advent of the internet search engine and are now largely unused and neglected (Hazell et al. 2010). The veto power under section 53, the make-or-break point of the law, has also been deployed sparingly, though it has caused controversy and, unintentionally, constitutional crisis. Fears that the 'catch-all' sections 35 and 36 would be used to continually block release appear to have been unfounded. According to the first Scottish Information Commissioner, even the lower harm test, perhaps the issue at the centre of the battle fought in the committee room, has proved to make little difference when compared with the higher test in Scotland, especially as the Information Commissioner's Office (ICO) in the UK can order disclosure (Dunion 2011).

By contrast, other parts of the FOI regime have been the source of unexpected outcomes. The appeal system has proved to be a robust forum for important decision-making. Although the ICO and Information Tribunal rule on few cases in relation to the overall numbers, around 1% and 0.25% respectively, a series of decisions on MPs' expenses, the Iraq war and coverage of private emails have made successive Commissioners advocates for FOI (Hazell et al. 2010; Burgess 2015). The Tribunal, now renamed the First Tier Tribunal, which some feared would slow the process, has emerged as a 'strongly pro-disclosure force' (Austin 2007, 404). The public interest tests in sections 35 and 36 that survived the push-back from the White Paper to the Bill have now become a symbol of the strength of the UK FOI (Burgess 2015). Even the scope of the Act provided unexpected effects: the seemingly absent-minded addition of Parliament's administrative activities led to FOI's most high-profile exposure.

### Patterns and use

In the UK, the Act applies across more than 100,000 public bodies, from 10 Downing Street to the village parish council and across the NHS, schools and libraries. As well as the UK Act, the Freedom of Information (Scotland) Act covers devolved matters in Scotland, which are overseen by a separate appeal system. The practical operation of FOI is an 'iceberg effect', with a minority of high-profile requests attracting attention and headlines while a hidden stream of more everyday 'micro-political' actions are processed within (White 2007; Richter and Wilson 2013).

The UK FOI Act has been relatively well used, with request numbers rising steadily across central government by around 5% a year from 30,000 in 2005 but seemingly plateauing and then slightly dropping to 46,000 by 2015 (Institute for Government 2015c; Institute for Government 2015a). Use is heavily orientated towards local government, with 70–80% of requests, or nearly four in every five, made to local councils, totalling in excess of 200,000 per year (Worthy 2013; Worthy and Hazell 2016). Here the vision of the draft Bill is borne out in part: FOI is primarily a local and individualised tool. Many of the local requests appear to be micro-political and concerned with focused matters of personal interest, though often overlapping with politics (Worthy 2013; Richter and Wilson 2013). In 2007 the Constitutional Affairs Select Committee concluded that the 'real value' that FOI provided was to 'people's lives, public service and the environment' (in Austin 2007, 400). Under the separate Scottish FOI regime the former Scottish Information Commissioner similarly spoke of how 'the real worth of freedom of information [is] to be found in the pages of the local rather than the national newspaper' (Dunion 2011, 458).

Yet there are high-profile requests and 'disruption' at the iceberg's tip. As the radicals hoped and the sceptics feared, at central and local government requests have centred on departments or areas dealing with controversial reforms, such as the Department for Work and Pensions or the MOJ (Institute for Government 2015c). These requests appear to come in 'waves' around particular media issues, while coverage is 'self-generating' and attracts further interest (Justice Committee 2012d).

## Who is using FOI?

Despite its powerful justifying narrative, research points to there being no 'average user' of FOI (Meijer et al. 2012). Any claim by politicians that the UK FOI Act is for the person on the street is belied by the complexity of user groups. Rather than being the mass public instrument talked of by politicians, FOI is driven by a 'vanguard' with an ad hoc collection of users following in their wake (Dunion 2011). This diversity appears to hold from local government to health bodies and higher education bodies (Richter and Wilson 2013; Ministry of Justice 2011). Their variety lends FOI an unpredictable quality and, like other mechanisms of participation, it produces sudden 'bursts' of exposure in 'leptokurtic' patterns that puncture the 'information equilibrium' of political institutions (Yasseri et al. 2013) (see Table 7.1).

The 'public' here is actually composed of a small group of activists, already involved in politics, and a looser, less politicized network of the curious or locally engaged. NGOs are also keen users, stretching from national or even international campaign groups to ad hoc grass-roots activists, though they are sometimes

**Table 7.1** Estimated top four FOI requesters in the UK by category, 2010

| Category of requester | Local government (%) | Central government (%) |
| --- | --- | --- |
| Public | 37 | 39 |
| Journalists | 33 | 8 |
| Business | 22 | 8 |
| Academics and researchers | 1–2 | 13 |

reluctant to interfere with pre-existing relationships (Spence 2010). In contrast to the US, business appears to have little use for FOI at central government level but uses it a great deal locally (Worthy 2013). A very small group of MPs and a few members of the House of Lords also regularly deploy FOI as part of their 'armoury' of weapons to hold government to account (Worthy 2014b). Although they constitute a small group, journalists have a large influence (see Cain et al. 2003; Hayes 2009). The media act as innovators, generate stories and frequently pick up others' requests. Despite the fears of Alastair Campbell, only a few have the time and patience to use FOI, which proves somewhat slow in relation to journalistic deadlines (Hay and Wincott 1998; Burgess 2015).

However, the negative symbolism of FOI is potent within government, where it seen as a counter-productive hindrance. Straw describes FOI as being 'cursed by ministers and officials alike' (2012, 269). Politicians appear to suffer from a mixture of disappointment at FOI failing to meet their expectations, and concern that it is either opening up sensitive areas of decision-making or being abused (Dunion 2011). The view within government is shaped in part by the media. In an insight into how those at the top see FOI, Tony Blair alleged that the Act was misused mainly by the media:

> The truth is that the FOI Act isn't used, for the most part, by 'the people'. It's used by journalists. For political leaders, it's like saying to someone who is hitting you over the head with a stick, 'Hey, try this instead', and handing them a mallet. (Blair 2011, 516–517)

His Chief of Staff Jonathan Powell repeated this erroneous claim, saying, 'unfortunately the number of requests lodged by the public was dwarfed by those from journalists, and their aim was not illumination but harassment' (2010, 197). In 2015, the Leader of the House of Commons Chris Grayling spoke of its abuse by journalists: 'It is, on occasion, misused by those who use it as, effectively, a research tool to generate stories for the media, and that is not acceptable' (*Guardian* 29/10/2015). David Cameron also spoke colourfully of how FOI is one of a series of participative and 'checking' instruments making government more difficult, part of

> What I call the buggeration factor, of consulting and consultations and health and safety and judicial review and FOI [the Freedom of Information Act] … Just generally, if you want to do something, build a road, start a new college, launch a programme to encourage people to build more houses – it takes a bloody long time. (*Times* 28/3/2015)

### The hopes of FOI: democratic effect?

The hopes of those pushing FOI were that it would strengthen democracy in the UK, particularly in terms of transparency and accountability. In its post-legislative scrutiny in 2012, the House of Commons Justice Committee concluded succinctly that it had done so:

The Freedom of Information Act has enhanced the UK's democratic system and made our public bodies more open, accountable and transparent. It has been a success and we do not wish to diminish its intended scope, or its effectiveness. (Justice Committee 2012d)

In March 2016 a government-appointed Independent Commission on Freedom of Information offered a similar view:

The Act is generally working well, and it has been one of a number of measures that have helped to change the culture of the public sector. It has enhanced openness and transparency. The Commission considers that there is no evidence that the Act needs to be radically altered, or that the right of access to information needs to be restricted. (Independent Commission on Freedom of Information 2016b, 3)

Has the Act succeeding in pushing the FOI radical's aims of increasing transparency or accountability or improving trust?

### Transparency?

The FOI Act has made UK public bodies more transparent. It has also opened up the workings and actions of a swathe of other public bodies, with Parliament perhaps the most spectacular example (Hazell et al. 2010). In this sense it has reversed deeply engrained secrecy habits and cultures. In a measure of its unpredictability, it has also played a role in opening up a whole range of other institutions, from universities to the monarchy.

FOI exists on a paradox: as an instrument rooted in distrust, it requires the public to trust that the targets will co-operate and is reliant on how those who are requested behave (Prat 2005; Terrill 2000). Has it then 'legislated morals' for public bodies? The Justice Committee concluded that 'The Act has contributed to a culture of greater openness across public authorities ... We welcome the efforts made by many public officials not only to implement the Act but to work with the spirit of FOI' (2012d, 4). The new transparency has led to a greater willingness to publish proactively and encouraged better relations with stakeholders (Hazell et al. 2010; Justice Committee 2012d). Fears of mass resistance have proved unfounded. There is little evidence of systematic avoidance, though 'game playing' has undoubtedly occurred, from outright refusals to attempted circumvention of the law through, for example, use of private email accounts (Burgess 2015). To further complicate matters, the rise of transparency has been paralleled by the growth of 'spin' and 'blame avoidance' (Hood 2007). It may be that certain requests lead to greater subterfuge, whether through simply hiding information or more sophisticated 'spinning' of release (Roberts 2005; Hood 2007; Heald 2012).

Further pressures for transparency have come from unexpected quarters: in an example of constitutional 'spillover' the UK Supreme Court, established in 2005, made a series of pro-openness rulings over Parliamentary expenses, rights of access and the government veto. Straw recognised that the FOI Act had 'ignored the internet' in its drafting but technology has proved a powerful driver, not only shifting expectations but fostering innovations such as mySociety's online requesting portal *WhatDoTheyKnow* and more broadly keeping the issue high on the agenda through Open Data innovations (Straw 2012; Worthy 2015a; Bailur and Longley 2014).

The effect of transparency is not uniform. There is unevenness, with some departments and bodies more open than others, interspersed with a few notorious resisters. Local government is generally more transparent than central government because of its decades of experience with other access legislation (Worthy 2013). Exactly how open a body is can depend on individual cultures, enthusiasm or ability, and, while political ideology appears to have little bearing, leadership is key (Worthy 2010; Worthy 2013). At the lowest level of parishes, awareness and resources may be a significant obstacle (John et al. 2015).

### Accountability?

A second of the radical hopes for FOI was that it would make government more accountable. The first decade of its operation is replete with examples of accountability initiated by FOI. The law has created a constant, if irregular, answering of questions on important national issues, from extraordinary rendition to reform of the NHS, and locally through a stream of questions over planning and car-parking (Worthy 2013). It may also be indirect, building pressure or attracting enough attention to lead to disclosure by other means, as was the case with the legal advice on Iraq, which was subject to forty failed FOI requests before being leaked to the media (Hazell et al. 2010). In its ultimate form, FOI is linked to a string of resignations from the Scottish Parliament, the Northern Irish Assembly and local government. In 2012 Walberswick parish council resigned en masse over a stream of 100 FOI requests that the council could not afford to process, following claims that local people were excluded from meetings on a new housing development (BBC 3/10/2012; BBC 6/2/2013).

By far the most-high profile accountability came with the MPs' expenses scandal of May 2009. Parliament was not intended to be covered by FOI, having been left out of the White Paper, and was then considered for partial inclusion in the draft Bill following a PASC suggestion. It was then added, seemingly as an afterthought without any debate (Hazell et al. 2012). After five years of dogged pursuit by three journalists and an ICO, Tribunal and high court ruling, details of all MPs' expenses sought by FOI were leaked to a national newspaper (see Worthy 2014a). In the ensuing coverage five MPs were imprisoned and nearly a quarter of all MPs stepped down. The scandal also generated a wave of similar expenses requests to the police, the health service and universities.

Underneath the rare headline-grabbing exposés, FOI accountability is sporadic and unexpected and requires the right context and tools in order to work (Worthy 2010). On a day-to-day level, it is most useful as part of wider, long-term information-gathering campaigns by NGOs or activists. It also works best alongside other tools, supporting, for example, the patient digging of MPs and activists over the UK's involvement in extraordinary rendition, who used FOI in the UK and US as well as Parliamentary questions to expose government evasions (Worthy 2014b).

### Trust?

If secrecy provokes distrust and suspicion, it is the hope of reformers that transparency triggers the opposite (Bok 1986; de Fine Licht 2014b). Alongside transparency and accountability, FOI, like much of Labour's reform agenda, was intended to improve trust and legitimacy (Bromley et al. 2002; Bromley et al. 2001). New Labour's 1997 manifesto explained how 'our mission in politics is to rebuild this bond of trust between government and the people' (Curtice 2010, S66). Advocates hope that FOI at least deters distrust and leads to more informed citizens, while sceptics argue that media 'abuse' means it has further undermined trust in government: Blair claimed the 'irony was that far from improving our reputation, we sullied it' (2011, 127).

FOI can have serious counter-productive consequences through its tendency to exposure and release of limited, often de-contextualised, information in a contentious political environment (O'Neill 2006; Flinders 2015a). The Coalition government concluded that improving trust through FOI may not have been an entirely 'realistic' objective (Justice Committee 2012d, 6). Trust is also known to differ in its long term and short-term effects, and any shift takes time (Whiteley et al. 2015; Van de Walle et al. 2008). Measuring trust itself is highly problematic, as judgements are frequently complicated by perceptions of democracy and policy performance, heuristics and causality (Whiteley et al. 2015). Experimental studies of the link between openness and public trust have found it is also heavily context-dependent and can vary according to policy area (de Fine Licht 2014a; Grimmelikhuijsen 2012 and 2009).

The FOI Act came amid decades of declining political trust, evidenced by continued falls in perceptions of government competence and politicians' truth telling since the late 1980s and early 1990s (Whiteley et al. 2015; Ipsos MORI 2015). Labour overall had 'relatively little success in restoring levels of trust' with a further decline between 2000 and 2013 (Curtice 2010, S71; Whiteley et al. 2015). Recorded trust fluctuated around a low base between 2005 and 2015, with the percentage of voters trusting politicians to put the national interest first dropping from 26% to 17%, and those trusting politicians to tell the truth ranging from 8% to 10%, with a drop down to 6% during the MPs' expenses scandal (National Centre for Social Research 2015).

Deeper investigations have found little change specifically due to FOI. The Justice Committee concluded that FOI had 'no generalisable impact' on trust (2012d, 17–18). Other studies found it had neither increased nor decreased trust in central government (Worthy 2010). At local government level, traditionally more trusted than central government, trust is more heavily influenced by performance and 'community visibility' than openness (Worthy 2013). Aside from these relatively small studies, mapping any larger shifts in public attitudes due to FOI is complex. A survey in 2002 found that FOI had no positive effect on trust; indeed among those broadly trusting government, support for a public right to know fell from 19% in 1996 to 13% in 2000, though this was before FOI was implemented (Bromley et al. 2002, 4–5). A series of tracker surveys between 2005 and 2010 by the Ministry of Justice found that 'respondents tend to disagree that public authorities are open and trustworthy' since the introduction of FOI (2010). Such blunt findings need to be approached with some care. Even the seemingly clear case of a decline in trust triggered by the MPs' expenses scandal shows nuance, as the disclosure of Parliamentary corruption was to many a confirmation of their representatives' poor behaviour rather than a revelation, and afterwards levels of trust in MPs began to shift upwards (Hansard Society 2010; Fox 2012). In a low-trust environment like the UK FOI is likely to be lost among the distrustful noise (Flinders 2015a). An alternative way of viewing FOI is perhaps as an instrument of 'democratic distrust' or a safety net for scepticism, going back to Bentham's system of distrust (Schudson 2015, 237).

The idea that information equals increased trust over-simplifies how the public approaches politics and the numerous biases, dissonances and expectations through which information is processed (de Fine Licht 2014a and 2014b; Grimmelikhuijsen and Meijer 2014; Grimmelikhaujsen 2012). The assumption underlying transparency, that we are rationally influenced by what is released, is not always borne out in reality (Bauhr and Grimes 2014). Voters' perceptions are 'weighed down' with 'deeply engrained' views associating government with 'inefficiency and inflexibility', and any change due to new information appears 'short lived' and subject-specific (Marvel 2016, 143, 145). Experiments point to voters having systematic negativity biases and an inclination to focus on poor performance while ignoring positive achievements (Boyne et al. 2009). James and Moseley (2014) found that information on poor performance had a far more negative effect than any positive impact from publishing better results, and was accentuated greatly by media coverage (506–507). Research has also pointed to a crucial distinction between uninformed and misinformed voters: while the uninformed can be persuaded, the misinformed 'hold wrong information [and] do so confidently' and 'tend to resist facts' (Kulinksi et al. 2000, 792). Attempts to 'enlighten' them may create a 'backfire effect' as correction increases and reinforces misinformed views, especially in controversial areas (Nyhan and Reifler 2010; Nyhan and Reifler 2015).

### Democratic overspill and public awareness

Whether FOI has helped create or added to a 'new politics' is even more difficult to measure. On one set of metrics neither FOI nor the wider reforms have reversed the historic trend towards political disengagement. From public attitudes to voting to party membership, voters are increasingly 'disgruntled, disillusioned and disengaged' (Fox 2012; see also Flinders 2015a). Any democratic overspill or unforeseen effects are not systematic or evenly spread. The MPs' expenses scandal, triggered a year before an election, did not lead to any substantial change in voting patterns, in part because the electorate did not act on the information and because the first-past-the-post system is not conducive to such forensic use (Pattie and Johnston 2012; Vivyan, Wagner and Tarlov 2012 and 2014).

There have been some democratic effects, most notably the creation of a new independent body controlling MPs' salaries and allowances, the Independent Parliamentary Standards Authority (IPSA). In 2015 a Recall Act allowing constituents to trigger elections for errant MPs was introduced explicitly as a result of what happened in 2009 (Wright 2015). The scandal triggered a Labour manifesto commitment to introduce Proportional Representation, a Conservative commitment to reduce the size of the House of Commons and strongly informed the debate around the 2011 Alternative Vote referendum. Another FOI to the House of Lords led to changes to tax status of members of the House of Lords (Worthy 2014b).

More broadly, whether as a local, personal instrument or as part of an ecosystem of accountability, FOI is one of a series of tools that has opened up the 'political information cycle' to new actors (Keane 2009; Chadwick 2013). FOI may be an ideal instrument for a new individualised, post-representative way of doing politics, within a new ecology of openness and informational engagement (Richards and Smith 2015). Here FOI may fit with an increasingly 'anti-establishment' attitude that challenges the essentially elitist, power-hoarding and majoritarian model of British politics (Flinders 2015a, 244). Over time, FOI may prove to be part of the 'bridging' reforms between the 'old' and 'elite centred' representative democracy and the 'information challenges' and 'bottom-up insurgencies' of a new, more complex, British politics (Richards and Smith 2015, 48).

The question is also whether the Act's decade of existence has ended its isolation among the public. Public awareness and approval would buttress support and protect the Act from attempts to weaken it. Although use is high relatively speaking, FOI is not a 'mass use' instrument as fewer than one in 1,000 people ever make an FOI request (Hazell and Worthy 2010). In terms of wider public awareness, an opinion poll in Scotland found that 78% of respondents have heard of the Freedom of Information (Scotland) Act, similar to a survey in 2011 where 80% had heard of the Act (Ipsos MORI 2013). Five years into FOI 81% of UK respondents were aware of a legal right to know, though nearly 40% could not name the legislation in question (Ministry of Justice 2010). Knowledge of the Act has moved upwards constantly, peaking at 89% in 2009 (around the time of the MPs' expenses scandal) and dipping back to 82% by 2014. Of those asked, 17% could name the Act unprompted, compared with 5% for the Data Protection Act and 1% for the Official Secrets Act (ICO 2014, 9, 25–26).

Little is known about any deeper views the public may have. As seen elsewhere, the popular reaction to FOI appeared lukewarm as Table 7.2 shows, though this was before the introduction of FOI and, possibly more importantly, the MPs' expenses

**Table 7.2** Perceived impact on the public of selected reforms in the way Britain as a whole is governed (%)

| Reform | Improved it a little/a lot | Made no difference | Made it a little/a lot worse |
|---|---|---|---|
| Reforming the House of Lords | 11 | 69 | 8 |
| Introducing FOI | 25 | 59 | 3 |
| Creating the Scottish Parliament | 19 | 53 | 13 |
| Creating the Welsh Assembly | 15 | 56 | 12 |

*Source*: Bromley et al. 2002, 3.

scandal (Bromley et al. 2002). What views the public have appear to be in favour of greater openness. In 2014 75% felt the Act should cover private bodies working on behalf of public authorities (ICO 2014). 76% of Scots who were asked felt that private prisons should be covered, with 79% believing that housing associations should be as well (Scottish Information Commissioner 2015).

There is some awareness, albeit vague, of FOI laws and transparency. The best that can be said is that FOI is a somewhat fuzzy presence on the political landscape.

### FOI fears: closing down government?

While FOI has clearly achieved some goals and fulfilled some hopes, what of the concerns as the Act was created? How well have the protections, such as the veto or exemptions, worked and has it led to a chilling effect?

#### The veto power

The veto was the lynchpin of the FOI revisions and a 'central feature of the Act' (Elliott 2015, 6). Straw and Blair both saw it as a 'deal breaker' for the survival of the policy, as a final line of defence for the government (Justice Committee 2012d). Removed from the White Paper and re-inserted into the draft Bill, the final FOI Act gave government a veto to prevent the release of information, even if the appeal system ruled in favour, in situations where the public interest had been weighed and 'exceptional circumstances' existed (interview with Jack Straw 2015; House of Commons 2014).

Austin argued that the presence of the veto 'undermines the claim that the Act creates a legally enforceable right of access' (2007, 398). Straw argued back that any use would be naturally limited by a 'political reluctance'. So it has proved (Justice Committee 2012d). It is true that each use is seen as signalling lack of faith in the system (Justice Committee 2012d, 17–20). Nevertheless, the veto carries a 'backlash potential' as it naturally draws attention to the particular topic, generates headlines and makes the government appear secretive. In the UK, for all the concern and struggle, the veto has been used only seven times to prevent the release of information. As Table 7.3 shows, UK use has been very much restrained by international standards, and this may be indicative of support for the system (Hazell et al. 2010). The overall lack of use challenges claims that the decision-making process is severely undermined by FOI. The seven times it has been used illustrate the sensitivity of the areas:

- The legal advice on military action in Iraq;
- Background decisions relating to Scottish devolution (twice);
- NHS Risk Registers;
- Prince Charles and the government;
- Cabinet minutes where the war in Iraq was discussed (House of Commons Library 2014).

The first use was by Jack Straw himself, a visible demonstration of the short-sightedness of the five-year 'breathing space'. Moreover, Straw was vetoing a decision in which he had been closely involved as Foreign Secretary, over the invasion of Iraq in 2003, following controversial decisions by the appeal system to (partially) open up the Iraq war Cabinet meetings (Burgess 2015).

In 2015 a Supreme Court ruling re-ignited the old concerns. A request by a *Guardian* journalist to see pre-2010 correspondence between the Prince of Wales and government departments was vetoed following a case at the Upper Tribunal. The requester's appeal was eventually upheld by the Supreme Court after a six-year court battle (*R (Evans) v Attorney General* 2015). The complex case hinged upon the 'constitutional dubiousness of the override power', whether a court could 'strike down a government decision under power granted by Parliament' and whether a government could 'overturn an independent judicial tribunal' rather than the ICO (Elliott 2015, 2). In a 'radical' majority verdict, the Supreme Court ruled that the use of the veto 'cut across two constitutional principles' and 'fundamental components of the rule of law, namely that a decision of a court is binding between the parties and cannot be set aside, and that decisions and actions of the executive are reviewable by the courts, and not vice versa' (Elliott 2015, 2). The executive could have such a power only with clear legislation, and 'section 53 is a very long way from being clear' (2). The decision appeared to greatly limit what constituted 'exceptional

**Table 7.3** Comparative veto or override use in the first four years of FOI legislation

| Jurisdiction | Number of veto uses |
| --- | --- |
| Australia | 48 |
| New Zealand | 14 |
| Ireland | 2 |
| UK | 0 |

*Source*: Hazell et al. 2010, 271.

circumstances'. As well as kick-starting a detailed and controversial review of the law (see below), the ruling became one of the 'landmark public-law cases of the early twenty-first century', raising 'fundamental' questions around the rule of law, sovereignty of Parliament and the separation of powers and illuminating the 'complex constitutional environment FOI inhabits' (Elliott 2015, 1; 6).

In March 2016, although the Independent Commission recommended a narrower, redrawn veto power, the government decided to leave the veto power legally unchanged: 'In line with the Commission's thinking, the government will in future only deploy the veto after an Information Commissioner decision. On the basis that this approach proves effective, we will not bring forward legislation at this stage' (Cabinet Office 2016).

### Exemptions and decision-making

In 2001 Democratic Audit argued that the new FOI Act was so hedged with exemptions as to be potentially worse than Major's Code of Access (Beetham et al. 2001). The 'unduly wide' exemptions undermined the entirety of the FOI principle (Austin 2007, 397). However, little of the concern over exemptions has come to pass. Exemption use has remained reasonably static, with personal information and environmental information used five times more than any other (Ministry of Justice 2011; Institute for Government 2015). The frequently criticised protections under the Act for policy-making, sections 35 and 36, designed to create a safe space for discussion, have proved to be less of a problem than envisioned. Though they were the second most frequently used in the early years, their use fell sharply from 2005 to 2007 and jumped recently only in connection with controversial policy (Hazell et al. 2010; Ministry of Justice 2011; Institute for Government 2015). The Information Commissioner argued that 'the safe space is respected, both by the Commissioner and by the Tribunal' and the Independent Tribunal concurred (ICO 2015; Independent Commission on Freedom of Information 2016b).

Concerns over the exemptions now lie with government. Straw argued in his memoirs that 'eccentric' decisions by the UK ICO had 'whittled away' the safe space, while the former Cabinet Secretary Gus O'Donnell called for greater clarity around decision-making material, in particular Cabinet documents and advice to ministers (Straw 2012; Justice Committee 2012b). However, Straw was part of the commission that concluded no change was needed (Independent Commission on Freedom of Information 2016b). Jonathan Powell also felt that the Commissioner had continued 'pushing the boundaries' around decision-making and believes that 'owing to a mistake in the legislation' the ICO is both judge and advocate (2010, 197). Powell even suggested that a future Prime Minister should reverse 'counter-productive elements' of the Act (197).

By contrast, the Justice Committee concluded that the protections for policy were sufficient:

given the clear intention of Parliament in passing the legislation that it should allow a "safe space" for policy formation and Cabinet discussion, we remind everyone ... that the Act was intended to protect high-level policy discussions ... the realities of Government mean that the ministerial veto will have to be used from time to time to protect that space. (Justice Committee 2012d, 75)

CFOI argued back that the safe spaces had been protected by the ICO and Tribunal but that it had taken each case in terms of its context, its timing and the particular frankness of the detail (CFOI 2015). The Independent FOI Commission examined the protections for policy-making and 'sensitive areas' but concluded later that 'It is the view of the Commission that – generally – section 36 affords an appropriate balance of protection for sensitive information held by public authorities' areas' (Independent Commission on Freedom of Information 2016b). It remains a point of contention, bound up in the further problem of the so-called chilling effect.

### The chilling effect

The negative effect of FOI on policy discussions has proved a tenacious story, linking back to the 1980s in Australia when it was feared that FOI would lead to 'hidden filing' or 'post-it-note' cultures (Hazell 1989). Straw referred to the threat numerous times during committee hearings. The area is replete with anecdote from numerous senior figures. In the UK, Tony Blair claimed that FOI had led to more caution over recording decisions, concluding that FOI was:

> not practical for government ... if you are trying to take a difficult decision and you're weighing up the pros and cons, you have frank conversations ... if those conversations then are put out in a published form ... you are going to be very cautious. (*Guardian* 1/9/2010)

Jonathan Powell stated that FOI had led to a 'reduction in the amount of confidential work done on paper' (2010, 198). David Cameron also hinted that it was disrupting decision-making and was, as he put it, 'furring up the arteries of government' (BBC 7/3/2012). Officials appear to agree. The former Cabinet Secretary Gus O'Donnell claimed that it has 'hamstrung' government, though when pressed he could only offer three isolated examples: two hypothetical and one based on the coalition negotiations 2010 (Justice Committee 2012d). O'Donnell's successor as Cabinet Secretary, Jeremy Heywood, while praising the Act, agreed that FOI was 'sand in the machine' and that 'there are some extra costs that come with the freedom of information act, there are some chilling effects, there's no doubt about it whatsoever' (Institute for Government 2015b). The claim is also regularly made at local government level. In 2016 Suffolk County Council was accused of 'dodging' the keeping of a paper trail in meetings (*Thetford, Brandon and Watton Times*, 13/1/2016)

Research points towards a minimal effect. The Justice Committee (2012d, 32) 'was not able to conclude, with any certainty that a chilling effect has resulted from the FOI Act'. In central government there was concern, with isolated instances but no general trend (Hazell et al. 2010; Waller et al. 2009). At local government level similarly there appear to be a few exceptional cases but no systematic effect (Worthy 2013; Shepherd et al. 2011). In both Scotland and England there was some concern at informal recording but also some evidence of a positive professionalising effect on records (Taylor and Burt 2010; Richter and Wilson 2013). FOI appears to have had no impact on the anonymity or quality of advice of officials. A 2010 study found that the Phillips Review of 2000 into BSE revealed identities at a lower level than any FOI request.

One key concern was the protection of Cabinet documents, which was a worry in 1997 and again in 2005 and 2010 when suggestions were made to exclude all Cabinet documents as a class. However, few requests are made for such high-level documents and, while there was change to the 'principle' of Cabinet confidentiality, one detailed study concluded that FOI had no effect on the practical decision-making process (Waller et al. 2009). Gus O'Donnell explained that the unintended openness of Cabinet was triggered by

> first, the amount of leaking that goes on from different Cabinet members; and, secondly, the propensity of a number of the Cabinet members to write their memoires rather quickly and include things they probably should not ... People know when they make a very clear profound disagreement in Cabinet that quite often you find within a few days it has emerged one way or the other. (Justice Committee 2012b)

Leaks, one study concluded, remained a far more potent threat to Cabinet than any FOI request (Hazell et al. 2010). Cabinet confidentiality exists in a constitutional grey area and remains a malleable and fluid concept, summed up in Callaghan's famous distinction: 'You know the difference between leaking and briefing. Leaking is what you do and briefing is what I do' (House of Commons 2004).

Looking at the evidence for any chilling more generally, the 2016 Commission cross-examined Gus O'Donnell but the chairman concluded that he 'struggled to find is actually cases, clear cut cases, where a lot of information has been released and discussions of the kind ... have been damaging' and argued that the ICO's case-by-case approach and possibility of veto use for truly sensitive cases had worked well (Independent Commission on Freedom of Information 2016a). The questioning led to a fascinating discussion between two former home secretaries and one Cabinet Secretary, taking rather different views of the evidence for any chilling:

> LORD HOWARD: Do you have any direct experience of ministers avoiding putting things into writing in order to escape the provisions of the legislation?
> LORD O'DONNELL: I mean, in a sense, how could I? Minister A phones Minister B on his mobile phone and I'm not involved in that process at all. That's what I mean. The whole evidence thing you're asking for is virtually impossible ...

LORD HOWARD: Not at all. You might have suggested to a minister that a meeting's necessary to discuss a particular decision and you might have been told, 'No, I don't think we need one' and you might be able to form quite a good judgment that that was the reason why the meeting wasn't taking place. Have you ever come across something like that?

LORD O'DONNELL: Yes, is the short answer, and yes, I've had occasions where – I mean, I think the area of contingency planning. You know, I think there are various reasons why ministers are very reluctant to commission planning for outcomes that they do not want to happen.

JACK STRAW: But is that directly related to FoI?

LORD O'DONNELL: That's a combination of FoI and leaks, let's be honest.

JACK STRAW: Yes, because I can recall in the early part of the 1997/2000 government, well before FoI was a serious prospect in people's minds, that there were some ministers who were very reluctant to go in for contingency planning on any basis because they were just reluctant to. It was nothing to do with FoI. (Independent Commission on Freedom of Information 2016a, 84–86)

### Proving the effect?

There are two problems with examining any chilling. The first is the methodological difficulty of proving or disproving it. Anecdote abounds, but finding hard evidence for such an effect is by its nature very difficult, as it requires proving a negative, detailed process tracing and asking interviewees to admit unprofessional conduct. One study found that many comments were jokes or light-hearted quips and that officials were more concerned with the consequences of not having a record if their superiors or a judge asked for it than with obscuring the record (Hazell et al. 2010).

Second, as the extract above shows, it is also very difficult to prove that any changes are a result of FOI. Isolating FOI as a causal factor among so many others is problematic. Straw spoke of how decision-making had altered radically in the last decade, moving to informality because of a growing use of technology (Justice Committee 2012c). When asked about the chilling effect in 2012, Gus O'Donnell answered that at 'a formal meeting like a committee meeting or a Cabinet meeting … we did not reduce the coverage of those minutes. They were accurate', but added, 'we tended to put it in rather plain prosaic language because there could be *leaks*' (Justice Committee 2012b). There is also the age-old politics of what is recorded, relating to both avoiding controversy and changing styles. Concerns over the non-recording of information go back far into the past. As the Justice Committee pointed out, the 2004 Butler report raised serious concerns over Tony Blair's use of informal meetings and 'sofa government' a year before FOI became operational.

Here the concrete effects of FOI intermingle with what actors believe is happening. It is impossible to say whether there is or is not an effect. It is likely that there is one at the margins but it is not widespread (Hazell et al. 2010). However, the evidence is far outweighed by the disproportionate and self-reinforcing concern created within government. These concerns may have a powerful signalling effect on bureaucracies, and the Information Commissioner warned that 'if mandarins keep talking about a chilling effect, theirs is a self-fulfilling prophecy' (ICO 2015).

### The battle lines of FOI: expansion and dismantling

Given the continuous conflict and uncertainty, most FOI regimes exist in a constant state of change and flux. Taken together, as Table 7.4 shows, these divergent pressures frequently lead to a continuous series of attempts to 'dismantle' or 'expand' information regimes, sometimes working in parallel (see Knill et al. 2012; Knill et al. 2009). Proposed changes to FOI have a 'magnetic' effect and cluster together: when one alteration is proposed others are rapidly added or proposed to take advantage of any window of reform. Winds of change towards openness or closure then blow across all areas and reveal new issues. However, attempts to either extend or curtail FOI frequently run up against the forces of symbolism, complexity and resistance that shaped laws in the first place. Table 7.4 illustrates the varying strategies and degrees of action involved in rescinding or rebooting FOI laws.

In the UK, the history of the first decade of FOI appears to be a constant 'push' and 'pull' of attempted strengthening and weakening. There have been a series of attempts at 'dismantling' parts of the FOI law, with roughly one attempt floated every eighteen months to two years. They began under Blair with a proposed introduction of fees or change to the cost limits (2006), followed by an attempt via a Private Member's Bill to remove Parliament from the law (2007) and, under Brown, the proposed removal of monarch and heir (2010). The Conservative-Liberal Democrat Coalition then mooted a clampdown on 'industrial users' (2012–13), and the Conservative government suggested amending the veto (2015). Only the removal of the monarch and heir, pushed through at the end of the 2010 Labour government with little publicity, was successful. The other attempts were stopped by a powerful barrage of press criticism, cross-party opposition within Parliament and sustained campaigns.

Alongside these overt attempts has been a low hum of complaint about how

**Table 7.4** Expansion and dismantling in FOI regimes

| Type of action | Expansion | Dismantling |
|---|---|---|
| Signals | Public praise or support | Public criticism, veto use, formal messages |
| Resources | Abolition of fees | Cuts in funding or stringent fees |
| Alterations | Expansion of access, link to other openness | Restrictions on access to classes of documents, reform of appeals system |
| Rescinding or rebooting | Ceating new success or law | Eating away at law – possible complete repeal? |

much FOI 'costs'. Costs are often discussed within the context of whether the Act is being 'abused' by the media or troublemakers (*Daily Telegraph* 9/12/2015). There appears to be some support from officials themselves for some form of charging (*Civil Service World* 2/11/2015). Methodologically, however, it is almost impossible to obtain a precise figure. Estimated costs per request range from £160 (Ministry of Justice 2011) to £255, with internal studies by public bodies putting costs as low as £36 and £19 (Colquhoun 2010).

Yet in parallel, there has been expansion and strengthening. Following Brown's arrival as Prime Minister in 2007, there was a limited extension of FOI to a number of new bodies in 2009–10, including examination boards, alongside a reform of the thirty-year rule under the Public Records Act. The FOI Act was amended again to cover datasets and protect research in 2012, with further extension to cover Network Rail in 2015 (triggered by a legal change in designation). As with the dismantling, the promises appeared less than the reality, with extension limited to a few bodies and pursuit of a lesser option of using FOI 'clauses' in relation to private contractors.

Outside Westminster, the Scottish devolved government has twice pushed limited expansion of its own Freedom of Information (Scotland) Act, with some small extension to leisure trusts in 2012 and housing associations, independent schools and private prisons in 2015–16. At the time of writing the Scottish FOI has not exempted the royal family. In parallel, private utility companies appear to be covered by FOI's sister legislation the Environmental Information Regulations (EIR) in the UK and Scotland (Act Now 2015).

The inquiry of the Independent Commission of 2015–16 illustrated the depth of division between supporters of expansion and dismantling. The Independent Commission was created by the Cameron government with a remit that was widely viewed as skewed towards some form of dismantling, looking into veto reform, stronger protections in the area of decision-making, the chilling effect and the potential 'burden'. The Commission appeared to be composed of those predisposed to strengthening protections, including Jack Straw, who had spoken publicly of the need for better protections and a possible charge for requests, as well as another ex-Home Secretary, Michael Howard, and a selection of senior officials. In an illustration of the 'clustering' effect of change, press rumours circulated of an interest in introducing up-front fees and the possibility of universities being excluded from the law. The Commission's call for evidence received 30,000 submissions and, prompted by CFOI and the media, generated criticism from civil society and the church and across the media, with a 38 Degrees petition gathering 192,236 signatures.

From within government, the Commission's investigation was framed around unintended consequences, abuse and burdens of FOI. The Justice Secretary, Michael Gove, spoke of the need to review the operation of the original Freedom of Information Act. Some of the judgments that have been made have actually run contrary to the spirit of the original Act … It is vital that we get back to the founding principles of freedom of information. Citizens should have access to data and they should know what is done in their name and about the money that is spent in their name, but it is also vital that the conversations between Ministers and civil servants are protected in the interests of good government. (Hansard, House of Commons, 23/6/2015, col. 752)

Some health authorities and local authorities used the inquiry to argue that FOI was burdensome and was taking resources away from 'vital services'. The Local Government Association, in its own submission to the Commission, claimed that 'requests from journalists and researchers for a specific research or media purpose, [were] often provided as a round robin request to fish for news stories' while others were 'effectively using the FOI route as a short cut to undertaking proper research' (House of Commons Library 2016).

Outside government, as with the passage of the law itself, campaigners emphasised the power of the right to access and beneficial consequences of the Act, while questioning the integrity and ethics of those seeking change. As a measure of the extent to which FOI has become a powerful symbol in its decade of existence, the Commission generated unified criticism across the media, with more than 300 articles mentioning the Commission explicitly in 147 different national, regional and local papers (House of Commons Library 2016). The media opposition went far beyond the 'traditional' FOI-supporting *Guardian*, involving right-wing Conservative papers such as the *Daily Telegraph* and, most effectively, the *Daily Mail*, alongside a range of regional and local newspapers.

The media drew on the symbolism of FOI to assert that it was a public right, and that any government wishing to change the law was secretive. It also highlighted what FOI had done and questioned both the cost of and motives for any change. The *Daily Mail* focused upon Cabinet Secretary Sir Jeremy Heywood, labelled 'Sir Cover-up' (25/9/2015) and Leader of the House of Commons Christopher Grayling, 'Minister for Hypocrisy', as he had championed and used the law in opposition but criticised it in power (30/10/2015). The Press Association ran a 'Hands Off FOI' campaign, attracting 430,000 signatures for a petition via Change.org. A personal submission to the Commission from the head of Associated Press argued that 'curtailing FoI will inevitably contribute to even greater voter cynicism about an elitist political class protecting its own interests, rather than the public's' and was 'entirely antipathetic to the mood of the times, in which voters expect more, not less transparency in the way they are governed' (*Daily Mail* 10/12/2015). Headlines in the national and regional press gave a flavour of how the media defended FOI and attacked those seeking to push back:

- 'We must Fight Watering Down of Freedom of Information Act' (*Belfast Telegraph* 10/7/2015)

- 'A Tax on Journalism: New Campaign to Keep Vital Freedom of Information Act Free for All' (*Birmingham Post* 29/10/2015)
- 'Greater Secrecy "will put Britain back in Dark Ages"' (*Times* 8/12/2015)
- 'It's Our Right to Know' (*Daily Telegraph* 9/12/2015)
- 'Freedom of Information Act MUST be Protected, Says Daily Mail Editor' (*Daily Mail* 10/12/2015)
- 'The Great Public Backlash over Bid to Curb Freedom of Information Law' (*Daily Mail* 11/12/2015)
- 'It's Our Right to Know What Government is Up To' (*Daily Telegraph* 17/12/2015)
- 'FOI Class Act' *Sun* (21/1/2016)
- 'Britain has Sinister Cover-Up Fetish ... We Must Fight It' (*Sun* 14/2/2016)

Opposition MPs in Parliament reacted by forming of a cross-party counter-commission in December 2015 championing the expansion of FOI, and there was vocal opposition from the Labour Party, the Scottish National Party and within the Conservative Party itself, including a group of backbench MPs labelled the 'Runnymeade Tories' and grassroots associations (Worthy and Hazell 2016; House of Commons Library 2016). Political leaders in Wales and Scotland also spoke against the change, as did a former head of the Civil Service and the UK Information Commissioner (*Daily Telegraph* 17/12/2015).

Instead of proposing dismantling, the Commission's final report in March 20116 opted for minor tweaking. It came down firmly against introducing up-front fees. It then recommended tighter deadlines for public authorities to respond to complex requests and conduct internal reviews; some minor rationalisation of the exemptions for policy formulation; and legislation to clarify the executive veto. In some areas it was expansionary, recommending that all contracts worth £5 million or more per annum with private contractors be regarded as part of the Act, rejecting the case for universities' exclusion and urging the publication of more data on senior pay and perks across the public sector (Independent Commission on Freedom of Information 2016b).

The government's response was to agree. It had found itself facing powerful opposition from across the media and Parliament, as well as from its own backbenches and grassroots, and it was increasingly unwilling to push any dismantling. Even before the Commission reported there were signs that the government was reluctant to make any changes as the press campaign gathered pace. Its fear of reputational damage was reinforced by its precarious position in the legislature, where it had a working Parliamentary majority of only sixteen, and the fact that it had so publicly pushed openness in the past. In an elegant backing down, the government described FOI as 'one of the pillars on which open government operates'; it acknowledged the 'keen public interest', opted for no legislative change and agreed to publish statistics, update guidance and push greater publication of 'pay and perks' (Cabinet Office 2016).

## Conclusion

FOI has simultaneously fulfilled and disappointed both sides. FOI is both a legalistic mechanism and a highly political instrument. Its focus is primarily local, individualised and personal. At its 'tip', FOI is a highly politicised and unpredictable force, with ripples and consequences that may have differing behavioural effects on those in government. It has triggered, irregularly and unpredictably, democratic change, from new laws to new institutions, and has undoubtedly made public bodies more transparent and accountable. It has not, however, increased trust or fully rooted itself within the population. Government appears reasonably 'safe', despite its fear of damage to sensitive areas, though politicians continue to claim otherwise.

The legislation was never likely, on its own, to drive wholesale radical reform or shifts of the kind envisioned. Yet legal rulings, political change and technological innovation make for a highly unstable, dynamic and unpredictable system. It may be that these 'moving parts', combined with the repercussions of events that FOI causes, from local council to MPs' expenses, have a far stronger effect than instruments in the original design.

# 8

## The US, Australia and India: two firsts and the greatest?

This chapter examines the passage of three of the most influential pieces of FOI legislation: the world's first modern law passed in the US in 1966, one of the first pieces of FOI legislation in a Westminster-style system in Australia in 1982 and the landmark Right to Information (RTI) Act 2005 in India. Symbolically, the three laws involved passing a powerful 'right' to the 'people' and a deepening of democracy, bound up in 'transformative' narratives. Each was a case of small groups inside and outside government manoeuvring between shifting groups of officials, politicians and advocates. As in the UK, the symbolism of the proposed laws threw openness onto the agenda and cut off retreat lines.

The nuances of the cases bear comparison. All the laws that emerged were born from compromise and internal struggles and were a product of very particular circumstances, powered by elections, coalitions and events. Parties and party control were crucial, and legislatures and bureaucracies provided a continuous force. At certain times, the symbolism made FOI appear inevitable, a matter of when, not if, as politicians appeared trapped by their own rhetoric and promise unwilling or unable to stop.

### The US

The enacting of the world's first modern FOI Act in 1966 has become the 'quintessential' struggle for openness (Fenster 2012b). The narrative is that of one valiant crusader, supported by parts of the media, doggedly fighting for more than a decade against entrenched interests across three administrations (Snell 2001). The 'justifying narrative' combined a claim to free speech and press freedom with a 'people's right' to access information.

Underneath this is a more nuanced story of partisanship, political compromise and deft manoeuvre as the symbolic force met institutional resistance (Kennedy 1978; Schudson 2013a). The 1966 FOI Act (FOIA) was 'conceived in partisan planning, went through its gestation period immersed in public relations and saw the light of day ... because of a political deal' (Archibald 1993, 726). The Bill was pushed in the challenging context of Cold War secrecy and was also shaped by the process (Schudson 2013a): 'it was the result of the legislative process and as such was a compromise' (Archibald 1993, 726). The central mystery is not that the Bill was ever passed but why President Johnson chose, on several occasions, not to kill it.

The roots of openness in the US go far back. Claim and counter-claim from legal scholars hold access to information to be (or not to be) a constitutional right flowing from either the 'logic' of the First Amendment, a combination of the First, Fifth and Ninth or, alternatively, the constitutional silence on the issue (see Emerson 1976; Peled and Rabin 2010; Moon 1984). Advocates found support for FOI in statements from founders such as Alexander Hamilton, Thomas Jefferson and, most famously, James Madison, though their actual views may have been more nuanced and limited than openness activists claimed (Wald 1984; Schudson 2015).

Open meetings were a resonant local model and part of the founding myth of American democratic practice (Hood 2006). Access to meetings legislation had long been a feature of many state decision-making processes, with some laws going back centuries (Schudson 2015). Arguably, the first step towards national FOI was the creation of the Federal Register of 1935, which mandated the keeping of updated lists and codification of the growing number of US regulations (Feinberg 2001). In a carefully choreographed mixture of 'values, politics, law, administration and theatre', a concurrent series of Supreme Court cases, a ready-made model Bill and judicious persuasion overrode President Roosevelt's concerns (Feinberg 2001, 359). The push was made by a small group of academics and legal scholars, supported by a number of FDR's advisors and led by the archetypal transparency advocate Justice Brandeis.

This was then followed by the Administrative Procedure Act of 1946, a law that required public notice of new rules and offered the chance for those interested to comment, with an appeal that constituted a 'rough guarantee of access to information' (Roberts 2006, 13). Section 3 of the Act allowed information not otherwise barred from disclosure by statute to be made available by published rule 'to persons properly and directly concerned except information held confidential for good cause found' (quoted in Fenster 2012b, 463). Roosevelt had vetoed an earlier version, fearing it to be a tool for 'powerful and organised interests' against the individual (Roberts 2006, 14). The law was more symbolic than functional, but represented a first step towards FOI.

## The beginnings and the long struggle, 1946–66

Although FOI is widely seen a phenomenon of the 1960s, its roots are older (Schudson 2015). The idea of FOI had been circulating since the 1940s and the term was used by both FDR and Truman in different contexts (Fenster 2012b). In the 1950s the idea began to take on a powerful democratic significance.

FOI began with a small group of media advocates (Kennedy 1978). According to Fenster (2012b) self-interest overlapped strongly with altruism, as the US press sought to fill the space for press exclusives following the inter-war demise of a number of international press cartels. American journalists championed openness through the Associated Society for American Newspapers (ASNE) at the world's first FOI conference, offering a heavily media-influenced definition of any law that carried a 'very tangible self-interest' (Fenster 2012b, 459): 'Freedom of information implies the right to gather, transmit and publish news anywhere and everywhere without fetters' (Kennedy 1978, 32).

The pressure flowed into domestic politics. In 1953 ASNE appointed Harold Cross to look into FOI, and he began his famous book with the words:

> Public business is the public's business. The people have the right to know. Freedom of information is their just heritage. Without that the citizens of a democracy have but changed their kings. (Fenster 2012b, 460)

The pressure for change then found an outlet within the US legislature. 'FOIA', argues Schudson, came out of a battle between the branches of government and emerged from a 'long but incomplete and inadequate effort by Congress to control the Federal bureaucracy' (2015, 57). From the mid-1950s onwards politics 'slowed and shaped' the law (Kennedy 1978, 114). In 1955, Congressman John Moss, a Democrat who had been on the receiving end of government secrecy as a 'political weapon', persuaded his superiors to form a sub-committee on government information. Moss is now seen as the archetypal crusader, a resilient champion who spent eleven years pushing the idea (Lemov 2011). Though 'not a colourful figure, not much of a self-promoter and no legislative craftsman', he was a 'bulldog' (Schudson 2013a, 2). He was also progressive who was also able to work cross-party and had a powerful friend in Speaker Sam Rayburn (Lemov 2011). Most importantly, Moss was a Democrat in a now Democrat-majority House against a Republican President: his campaign would have been far less acceptable had the President been a Democrat (Archibald 1993). However, initially this also proved a barrier because 'as long as Eisenhower was president, Moss could hardly find a Republican co-sponsor for his proposed reforms' (Blanton 2006).

In 1950s America there was little public or political interest in FOI, and over the next eleven years Moss battled to place FOI on the agenda. To give it the attention it lacked, Moss sought to prove that secrecy was a 'pervasive problem' that needed to be 'solved' by equally eye-catching, absurd or 'silly stories' such as denials over the existence, and then numbers, of mice in the nose cones of test missiles (Lemov 2011, 54; Schudson 2015). Moss and his media allies turned the government's rhetoric against it, using 'cold war rhetoric to pry information from the government' (Schudson 2015, 45). Echoing Goebbels's 'Iron Curtain' phrase, later popularised by Churchill, Moss repeatedly spoke of an 'information' or 'paper curtain' across US government, and even found examples of information available in the USSR but not in the US (Schudson 2013a). Despite the powerful narrative, FOI failed to catch the imagination of the electorate, and there was 'no sign that the issue ever attracted powerful support or opposition from the public' (Schudson 2013a, 7). It did, however, reach into national and local newspapers and editorials, while a growing number of state-level 'sunshine laws' began to open up local and state government (Pupillo 1993).

By the early 1960s Moss's committee had amassed a powerful evidential case against government secrecy. However, the arrival of a Democrat President led to accusations that Moss was toning down his critique, amid claims that Kennedy was apparently sympathetic to greater openness, with his promise to not 'withhold' information from 'Congress or People', but was opposed by his bureaucracy (Schudson 2015; Archibald 1993). Politics then intervened from the other direction as Republicans took a greater interest in the issue. A young Congressman named Donald Rumsfeld became the right's champion of FOI, co-sponsoring the Bill, and the minority leader Gerald Ford expressed support (Kennedy 1978; Lemov 2011).

A series of Bills that followed were lost in the early 1960s, having been directed into committees that simply let them disappear (Archibald 1993). With Lyndon Johnson now in the White House, a two-pronged FOI push from a House and Senate Bill took a different turn, and 1965 and 1966 saw an intra-party struggle (Kennedy 1978, 115). Either as a result of luck or, more likely, a deal between Moss and his chair, the Senate FOI Bill, actually technically an amendment to the Administrative Procedure Act came to his committee rather than meeting the usual dead end (Archibald 1993).

Moss faced the classic dilemma between the 'best possible FOI Act and no law at all' (Kennedy 1978, 119). He made no amendments, in order to give the Bill speed, and then undertook an intricate series of negotiations, further weakening an already 'weak and complicated' proposal. In detailed discussions with the Department of Justice that Moss described as 'very rough' he gave, for example, concessions over wider interpretation of exemptions in the accompanying House report (Kennedy 1978, 115; Lemov 2011). The Assistant Attorney General publicly argued that government information was 'just too complicated, too ever changing' to be covered in one law (Kennedy 1978, 130). Johnson then reportedly asked for some form of Presidential veto power (Kennedy 1978). He appeared poised to kill the Bill, claiming at one point that it was 'unconstitutional' in its restrictions on both executive and legislature, with the AAG telling Moss that the President 'will not sign it' (Lemov 2011, 66). As well as the 'asymmetry' of not knowing if the Bill would be lost, Moss was weakened by political reality, as both he and Johnson knew there were not the votes to overturn a Presidential veto (Kennedy 1978).

Behind the scenes, the attitude of government bodies again proved crucial. Not all were content, and it was reported to Moss that the Department of Justice had told Johnson, in LBJ's own words, that the Bill would 'screw the Johnson administration' (Kennedy 1978, 118). However, several Federal agencies told the Department of Justice that the new language that Moss agreed 'clarifies the Bill and substantially relieves our earlier concerns'. A memo to the President outlined how 'the departments and agencies have been concerned about this Bill for many years, but have come around to the view that they can live with it, and the attached agency reports do not recommend disapproval' (Blanton 2006).

The considerably weakened Bill then landed on the President's desk or, more accurately, was sent to his ranch. Owing to Congressional adjournment, Johnson needed only to not sign it for it to be subject to a pocket veto. Yet on 4 July 1966 he did so, famously not allowing cameras, writing 'no ceremony' on the agenda and not even listing it in his daily diary. He offered a somewhat ambiguous message of support that 'undercut the thrust of the law' (Blanton 2006).

### Why did Johnson sign?

As a politician Lyndon Johnson was not one to appreciate of the virtues of openness, and his career was marked by an 'obsession with secrecy' (Kennedy 1978, 144). His mode of operation was built upon restricting knowledge and strict information control interspersed with preferential openness (see Caro 2002). His greatest success as Majority leader in the Senate, passing the apparently ineffective Civil Rights legislation 1957 that broke the power of the Southern senators, was based in part on secret, backroom deals (see Caro 2012). Nor was he a supporter of the press, the key advocates of the FOI Bill. On the very morning of his predecessor's assassination a committee had begun to investigate his dubious financial affairs following diligent press investigation (Caro 2012). His Press Secretary Bill Moyers famously characterised his attitude to FOI:

> LBJ ... hated the very idea of the Freedom of Information Act; hated the thought of journalists rummaging in government closets and opening government files; hated them challenging the official view of reality. (Quoted in Blanton 2006)

Johnson had earlier threatened to kill the Bill and, it was alleged, asked Moss why he was 'trying to screw' him (Lemov 2011, 53). A Senator close to LBJ inserted an extra protection for private oil company exploration apparently at the President's behest (Lemov 2011; Kennedy 1978). The question is why Johnson, who could have had the Bill stopped in the House or simply not signed it, chose not to do so (Lemov 2011; Kennedy 1978). As perhaps the ultimate 'veto player', why did he decide not to kill FOI? (Berliner 2010).

The media had a powerful influence, pressuring the President directly at his ranch with a series of op-eds, telegrams and 'last minute calls' (Lemov 2011, 68). Although the ferocious press criticism over Vietnam had yet to appear, the idea of a 'credibility gap' between Johnson's claims and reality had already begun and Johnson could well imagine how counter-productive vetoing FOI legislation, widely supported by the press, would be (Patterson 1996; Dallek 2005).

A number of Johnson's key advisors were hidden champions for FOI, including the White House counsel Milton Semer and Press Secretary Bill Moyers. While Moyers contacted the press and advised pressurising the President, Semer gave Moss suggestions, such as 'exploit the fact that the President is under pressure from the bureaucracy to veto' as a way of arguing that the Bill would actually help the President bring the 'permanent bureaucratic interest' more under control (Blanton 2006).

Politics also exerted an effect on Johnson. As the mid-term elections and a severe defeat loomed, Johnson feared that vetoing the FOIA could influence the elections in some way (Dallek 2005; Lemov 2011). He saw that the Republicans supported the Bill and the potential for partisan attacks to be made from it (Archibald 1993). Resignation may also have played a part: Johnson had also recognised the realities of the Presidency in pushing for a raft of change early in his term and facing declining influence thereafter (Patterson 1996).

Finally, the symbolism played into the broader agenda of the Johnson administration. Although FOI sat uneasily with Johnson, it exactly fitted the new 'rights consciousness' he had begun (Patterson 1996, 562). Johnson had initiated a 'rights revolution' in 1964–65. With civil rights the centrepiece, new citizens' powers had been created in education and health in 1965, with a slew of follow-up regulation on the environment and consumer rights in 1966 (Dallek 2005). It was also part of moves towards targeted transparency over labelling and standards, and new consumer rights with laws over truth in packaging (Schudson 2015). The statement that accompanied the signing drafted by Moyers, reflected on the importance of information to democracy and was signed, in a final act of symbolism, on 4 July 1966. Ever the politician, Johnson saw the possibility of reflected positivity and, as Moyers described: 'he signed the f_cking thing, as he called it, and then set out to claim credit' (Lemov 2011, 68).

### Ford and the FOIA, 1974

As a result of comprises in its creation, the 1966 Act was 'difficult to interpret and badly drafted' (Davis 1967, 761), failing, for example, to deal with executive secrecy, containing wide exemptions for law enforcement and being primarily used in its early years by 'private interests' for 'private gain' (Archibald 1993, 316). It was widely viewed as a 'paper tiger' (Wald 1984, 658) and a 'shadow' of later legislation (Roberts 2006, 55). A later head of the Justice Department's Legal Counsel described it as a 'relatively toothless beast' (Roberts 2006, 55), and the operation was worsened by administrative responses marked by 'foot-dragging, lack of enthusiasm and outright evasions' (Kennedy 1978, 140, 144). An investigation by Moss's former committee found that users, and particularly the media who pressed so hard for it, were deterred by serious delays, excessive fees and the use of a battery of administrative and legal instruments to deny release, including mixing confidential and open documents to exempt whole files (Lopez et al. 2002). In 1973 a Supreme Court ruling in *Mink* appeared to offer government a wide discretion in classifying information, locking in place a government power to keep secret whatever it wished (Kennedy 1978).

The symbolic catalyst for a new law was Watergate. By the time of Nixon's resignation a number of Bills to amend the Act were in process. Edward Kennedy had taken the chairmanship of the Senate sub-committee on information, and his Bill expanded the definition of 'agency' and, challenging the *Mink* ruling, proposed giving judges the power to sanction officials and examine classified documents in camera. The proposed amendments were now supported by a far wider group of NGOs and media organisations, led by the campaigner Ralph Nader and covering civil rights and consumer groups, the Bar Association and organised labour (Archibald 1993; Kennedy 1978).

Despite his attempts to create a fresh and 'open' new start, the new President Ford was influenced by the secretive and anti-press attitudes of Nixon's advisors whom he kept on (Hamilton 2011). Although Nixon appeared willing in his final days to sign amendments, Ford was undecided. His Chief of Staff, the former FOI champion Donald Rumsfeld, and Deputy, Dick Cheney, argued in favour of a Presidential veto, as did the CIA and a number of government departments: it was alleged that the FBI ended negotiating to make it 'as bad as possible' and so easier to block (Roberts 2006; Lopez et al. 2002). In October 1974 Ford did what LBJ had not dared do and vetoed an FOI law. Ford's veto message mixed politics and costs: it expressed concerns over exposure of military secrets, the power of judges deciding upon classified matters and the short administrative turnaround of ten days. He used words that would become familiar in FOI struggles, speaking not only of the changes as 'unconstitutional' but also of the Act as a 'burden' and 'unworkable' (Lopez et al. 2002).

The exact political results of Ford's veto were unclear. Ford had begun his Presidency committed to openness and set a tone in his inaugural address, proclaiming that 'our long national nightmare is over' and making a public pledge for 'truth':

> I believe that truth is the glue that holds government together, not only our Government but civilization itself. That bond, though strained, is unbroken at home and abroad. In all my public and private acts as your President, I expect to follow my instincts of openness and candour with full confidence that honesty is always the best policy in the end. (Ford 1973)

The White House aide Ken Cole wrote to Ford of the symbolic costs of opposing FOI on 25 September 1974:

There is little question that the legislation is bad on the merits, the real question is whether opposing it is important enough to face the political consequences. Obviously, there is a significant political disadvantage to vetoing a Freedom of Information Bill, especially just before an election, when your Administration's theme is one of openness and candour. (Lopez et al. 2002)

However, one unnamed administration source felt that the issue of FOI had little political consequence and asked, 'who gives a damn except the Washington Post and the New York Times?' (Kennedy 1978, 186).

The immediate consequence for Ford was political embarrassment as the veto was overturned by 371 votes to 31 in the House and, more narrowly, by 65 to 27 in the Senate (Lopez et al. 2002). Senator Kennedy spoke of how Ford's promises of open government had failed and stated that his veto would 'perpetuate the insidious secrecy' of the Watergate years' and the 'anti-media, anti-public, anti-congress secrecy of the Nixon years' (*Congressional Record* 21/11/1974). Congressman Moorehead, chair of Moss's old committee, spoke of the legislature offering Ford a 'golden opportunity … to dramatically fulfil his 2 month old pledge of open government' that could 'strike a ringing blow for credibility of government' and help 'reverse the publics cynical distrust' (*Congressional Record* 20/11/1974). Whether it had any electoral effect is unclear, but media criticism made much of Ford's claims of to 'run an open White House' and urged voters in the mid-term elections to think on this (see Lopez et al. 2002). ASNE urged editors to 'demonstrate who gives a damn', and editorials were run across the regional and local press (Kennedy 1978, 186).

Ford's veto was a pyrrhic and ultimately damaging 'victory'. As he was one of the few politicians to oppose FOI outright, the immediate damage appeared limited. The veto did, however, undoubtedly help erode Ford's 'moral capital'. Although there is little polling evidence for any shift in attitudes, his veto probably contributed to a continuing disastrous decline in popular support, one of the steepest of modern times, which had begun with his earlier pardon of Richard Nixon (Gallup 2006; Hamilton 2011).

### Australia: Westminster FOI

The campaign for FOI in Australia was launched by symbolic and powerful rhetoric from successive prime ministers, being justified first as a radical anti-establishment marker and then as a democratic instrument. It was championed by a radically reformist and modernising government and then carried on by its successor. As in the US, FOI pressure built slowly over a decade (Snell 2000). The 'Australian experience began largely in response to an external reformist movement battling an entrenched and, with a few notable exceptions, non-receptive bureaucracy' (Snell 2000, 579). The political consensus that FOI was a 'good' thing meant that successive prime ministers championed it, partially for its symbolism and partly in the belief that it might be electorally effective. The heavy symbolism did not translate easily into concrete policy, as the energy of a few internal and external crusaders was diverted into detailed discussions in committee back channels and lengthy processes: 'politicians lost control of the debate. The agenda was being steered by the bureaucracy' (Terrill 2000, 99). The opposition and process 'shaped the possible', moving from a policy based on the US FOI law to a more home-grown legislation, constrained by the 'overarching argument … that FOI represented a threat to the Westminster system' (Stubbs 2008, 671). Politicians lacked the 'vigour and vision' to push it, and officials were divided, rather than uniformly opposed (671).

### Whitlam's openness, 1972–75

The arrival of FOI in the US attracted some minor interest in Australia, provoking scholarly debate and a series of books in the late 1960s (SSCCLA 1978). The first clear commitment came as a result of small group of activists and their 'casual' lobbying of senior members of the Australian Labor Party in the early 1970s (Snell 2000; Terrill 2000). The Labour leader Gough Whitlam's interest was aroused by the shadow minister Clyde Cameron and his private secretary Jim Speigelman, later an author of a landmark anti-secrecy book in 1973. However, rather as in the case of New Labour in the 1990s, FOI was a cause that attracted lawyers, and its support was the preserve of a 'few individuals' (Snell 2000), with other ministers and senior figures 'barely even aware of the subject' (Terrill 2000, 21, 19).

Whitlam committed himself to FOI in his famous 'It's Time' speech of 1972:

> We want the Australian people to know the facts, to know the needs, to know the choices before them … Australia has suffered heavily from the demeaning idea that the government always knows best … this corrupting notion of a government monopoly of knowledge and wisdom has led to bad decisions and bad government. The Australian Labor Party will build into the administration of the affairs of this nation machinery that will prevent any government, Labor or Liberal, from ever again cloaking your affairs under excessive and needless secrecy. Labor will trust the people. (Whitlam 1972)

Whitlam's promise was bound up in whole series of wide-ranging social and political reforms after twenty-three years in opposition (Whitlam 1972; Stubbs 2008). Terrill argues that FOI was 'central to the image that the ALP [Australian Labor Party] wished to project of itself as an alternative government' that was 'anti-Vietnam', reformist and intent on 'recapturing popular politics' (2000, 19, 21). It also paralleled the rise of other citizen-based accountability mechanisms under Labor's 'New Administrative Law' reforms, including the strengthening of judicial review and the creation of an Ombudsman (Stubbs 2008, 669). The publication of Jim Speigelman's book on secrecy then coincided with the visit by the US FOI advocate Ralph Nader (Snell 2000; Terrill 2000). Whitlam later undertook to 'introduce a Freedom of Information Act along the lines of the United States legislation' (SSCCLA 1978, 6).

Carrying the Prime Minister's clear support, the FOI policy initially moved quickly, with a new committee given the relatively 'straightforward' task of creating a law on the US model (Terrill 2000, 100). In a parallel symbolic move, ministers had been asked to follow Whitlam's instructions to release departmental reports as quickly as possible (Terrill 2000).

Both policies then rapidly hit obstacles. The Interdepartmental Committee (IDC) on FOI proved a 'fiasco'. Although a final draft of a Bill appeared to be ready, the FOI proposals were criticised by the heads of the Treasury and Defence, who described FOI as policy that would 'enable partisan interests', 'foster an adversary situation' and cause governments to fall. Blocked by 'fussy' points, 'pedantry' and 'polarised viewpoints', the policy was unable to move further (Terrill 2000, 103–105). The report on FOI that emerged was a brief eighteen-page document that failed to press fully for FOI, describing it as a 'complex' and 'far reaching' policy with consequences for a Westminster system. It proposed to protect Westminster government, giving individual veto powers for ministers and excluding draft documents. Whitlam himself described the paper as 'insipid and negative' (Terrill 2000, 106), and the *Canberra Times* called it 'unimaginative, bereft of practical detail and short on supporting argument' (quoted in SSCCLA 1978, 7). The accompanying commitment to publish departmental reports also began to dry up.

Whitlam later claimed that 'the government devoted many hours of discussion to FOI legislation but not sufficient to overcome the resistance of the most senior and respected public service administrators' (Terrill 2000, 99). While ministers were 'drawn into the minutiae' in a way that 'empowered the bureaucracy', parts of the bureaucracy were by no means opposed to openness: some had suggested inserting court powers over documents or publishing FOI-related papers as decisions were made (Terrill 2000, 99). However, it was the government itself that slowed FOI, amid Whitlam's ambivalence and a lost champion when Attorney General Lionel Murphy moved to the High Court (Terrill 2000, 99; Fraser and Simons 2010, 404). In a final push that would prove helpful for FOI later, the government set up a Royal Commission into Australian Government Administration. Despite the promises and action, the Whitlam government left FOI amid 'marginal change' and 'general failure' (McMillan 1977, 381).

### The Fraser government

Reflecting on the Act in the 1980s, its advocate Senator Alan Missen spoke of how emerging cross-party support for FOI made a crucial difference as 'there is value when from both political sides there are promises, even though governments tend to backslide. But if they have made those promises, they find it very hard to avoid' (Missen 1984).

In 1975 the new National-Liberal government committed itself afresh to FOI legislation. The new Prime Minister Malcom Fraser described FOI as a 'new ortho-doxy' (Terrill 2000, 109). Bayne (1993) concludes that Australian politicians may have seen FOI as a 'vote getter' for a 'marginal' or 'swing voter', and those on the right linked greater openness to the influence of Public Choice ideas in controlling bureaucracy (211). Gone was the anti-establishment symbolism of Whitlam but, instead, Fraser made the democratic case for FOI:

> If the Australian electorate is to be able to make valid judgements on government policy it should have the greatest access to information possible. How can any com-munity progress without continuing and informed and intelligent debate? How can there be debate without information? (Quoted in SSCCLA 1978)

Like Whitlam, Fraser pushed for FOI as part of a broader tranche of legal reforms and the creation of new powers of checks and redress (*Canberra Times* 21/3/2015).

In his memoirs Fraser portrayed his Cabinet as pushing for FOI against the resistance of officials, in particular Geoffrey Yeend, the head of the Department of the Prime Minister (Fraser and Simons 2010). Fraser set up a second IDC and pushed urgently for action just as the Whitlam-created Royal Commission reported with a complete draft FOI Bill and a minority report in favour of FOI (SSCCLA 1978). The draft Bill went further than any previous proposals, limiting ministers' powers to block requests, empowering the Administrative Appeals Tribunal and cutting the response time for a request down to ten days.

According to Fraser the policy then ran 'straight into public service resistance' (Fraser and Simons 2010, 404). In a note to Fraser, Yeend warned of FOI bring-ing 'administrative chaos' and 'dual filing systems' and, in a note marked 'not to be filed', wrote: 'were I not under threat of my advice being made public I would be questioning the wisdom of the whole legislation. It is a can of worms.' There followed 'more delays and more reconsideration', and Fraser admitted to there being 'misgivings' in Cabinet (Fraser and Simons 2010, 405). The eighteen-month wait between the IDC and the Bill was a result of 'complex issues' and 'behind the scenes debates' as ministers that feared the Attorney General would 'go too far' and was 'pressing for a more liberal Bill' (Curtis 1983, 13). In a measure of their worry, the entire Bill had to go before the Cabinet and not just the legislative committee (13).

Outside government, a campaigning group for FOI, Freedom of Information Law (FOIL), was created involving academics, lawyers and unions (ALRC/ARC 1995). There was also concerted action by members of the legislature, particularly in the Senate, to question government secrecy, and upward pressure as various state governments, including those of New South Wales and South Australia, began to consider openness laws (SSCCLA 1978; Snell 2001). None of this served to 'gal-vanise the public or attract press support' (Terrill 2000, 112). The campaign was limited, in the view of one campaigner, by Australia's lack of a large 'tenacious press' and its 'political inertia' (McMillan 1977, 391).

The new government Bill that emerged from the government committee was presented as 'a major initiative by the Government in its program of administrative law reform. It is, in many respects, a unique initiative. Although a number of countries have FOI legislation, this is the first occasion on which a Westminster-style government has brought forward such a measure' (ALRC/ARC 1995). McMillan described it as a 'pyrrhic victory' for FOI reform, a change 'bought at too great a cost' and intended to cause the 'least disruption', with wide ministerial powers to prevent release, a non-retrospective scope and wide exemptions (1977, 432–433).

Though the Bill passed in the House, it found the Senate more of an obstacle. The SSCCLA (1978) conducted an extraordinarily thorough and wide-ranging review of FOI, covering both its philosophical and its practical consequences. Its report challenged a number of the concerns over FOI. It rejected the claim that any FOI Act within a Westminster system would weaken it or, as one witness put it 'cut fundamentally' at it (SSCCLA 1978, 25). FOI would, instead, strengthen ministerial accountability and make government 'more adaptable': it is 'not that FOI would change our system of government: it is rather our changing system of government is creating pressures for FOI' (26–27). The committee saw no evidence that administratively government could not 'cope' with FOI and recommended lesser exclusion powers and a stronger role for the appeal system (SSCCLA 1978). However, the Bill continued to face resistance from officials: in 1980 Yeend told the Prime Minister that the proposed law went 'further than any other country' and was an 'experiment', and that 'whatever the politics of the decision it is certainly a gamble in the administrative sense' (Fraser and Simons 2010, 405). According to Fraser he pleaded for a delay until 1983, when the government would be out of power.

In the Senate, FOI advocates had some 'good luck' as 'the Government was losing its majority and majority would then be in the hands of the Australian Democrats and the Labor Party' (Missen 1984). Facing eight amendments and after suffering a series of defeats in various votes, the government began negotiating and agreed to thirty-five of them.

> There were about eight or nine Liberal Senators supporting the amendments to the Bill. Because the Government wanted to get its Bill through and an Act in operation ... I suppose we really 'blackmailed' the Government into accepting some amendments. (Missen 1984)

In an echo of what later happened in the UK, Senators were 'abused by the Labor and Democratic Senators for accepting a compromise. However, it was a deliberate choice to take a Bill that was not strong enough ... and hope that, in the new parliament, we could improve it' (Missen 1984). Again as in the UK, the negotiations were done against a backdrop of uncertainty and fear of losing the Bill: 'If we had insisted on all the amendments being passed, the Bill would have gone back to the House of

Representatives where it would never have passed. The Fraser Government would have rejected amendments and it would have gone backwards and forwards for some years' (Missen 1984). Fraser saw the Act as his distinct legacy:

> Soon after his fall, Fraser was asked about his greatest achievements, and nominated, somewhat to my surprise, the passage of the FOI Act. Planned by Whitlam, its cause had languished through most of the Fraser years until it came into effect on the eve of his departure. (*Canberra Times* 21/3/2015)

The changes that the Senators hoped for came sooner than expected. In 1983, the new Hawke government initiated a series of reforms to the Act, reflecting the earlier draft Bill and Senate Committee. The long-time advocate Attorney General Gareth Evans oversaw reforms that gave the law greater retrospective reach, strengthened the appeal system to override ministerial exclusions and cut the time limit for replying from sixty to ten days (ALRC/ARC 1995; Terrill 2000).

## The radical right to know in India

The India RTI Act 2005 created its own radical symbolic narrative as one of the world's best-known and most emulated pieces of transparency legislation. The story of the RTI Act as an equaliser and weapon of anti-corruption forced on a government by grassroots activists has proved 'compelling', and the Indian legislation has been described variously as 'revolutionary', a 'watershed moment' (Calland and Bentley 2013, S80) and the beginnings of a 'socio-economic revolution' (Roberts 2010, 926). The truth is more complex and deep-rooted (Sharma 2015). India's RTI had been on the agenda since the 1970s, shaped by elections and wider political movements, supportive officials within government and hidden champions (Sharma 2015). Competing symbolic appeals acted upon different groups: to grassroots activists RTI was a weapon of anti-corruption and anti-poverty while within the government reformist elements saw it as a way of deepening democracy and 'joining' other advanced democracies.

Before the 1960s interest in greater openness was 'sporadic', emerging only in response to controversy (Sharma 2015). Nehru asked, 'why should we hide ... things? Are we to live behind purdah and wear a veil'? (in Singh 2007, 21). The case for RTI emerged slowly from electoral pressure as Congress Party dominance ended, combined with the shock of the war with China in 1962, the rise of civil rights and a general sense that Indian institutions of representative democracy were not democratic enough (Singh 2007; Singh 2011).

The RTI movement began in the 1960s, focused on the Supreme Court in the 1970s and 1980s and ended with an academic- and intellectual-led campaign in the 1990s (Sharma 2015). The first symbolic move towards an RTI law came not from below but above, with a Supreme Court decision of 1975 in *State of UP v Raj Narain* ruling that 'The people of this country have a right to know every public act, everything that is done in a public way by their public functionaries. They are entitled to know the particulars of every public transaction in all its bearings' (Singh 2011, 23). This was followed by further rulings in 1982 that the RTI flowed directly from article 19 of the constitution and then in the mid-1980s that environmental information should be opened up following the Bhopal gas leak (Singh 2011).

In 1989, drawing on ideas circulating from the 1970s, the first non-Congress government in India's history committed to an RTI law, perhaps as a symbolic means of renewal. However, no law appeared and Prime Minister Singh reached for the standard excuse: he had 'sought a suitable draft' but 'bureaucracy had frustrated him at every step' (in Singh 2007, 43). This appears rather far from the truth. A workshop on developing legislation had been held for officials, with some tentative exploration of existing FOI legislation around the world. Indian officials were keenly aware that no developing low-income country had, as yet, passed such a law. It appears that the short life of government, rather than any overt hostility, cut progress off. The tentative moves ignited change in parts of the bureaucracy, which began moving gradually towards greater openness (Sharma 2015).

In 1990 the RTI movement changed form again. A series of campaigns in Rajasthan against local corruption began to attract attention and rapidly coalesced into a powerful, and powerfully symbolic, grassroots force using the transparency of public meetings to generate change. The campaign has entered transparency folklore as a classic agitprop jamboree of bottom-up political action (see Singh 2005). By the 1990s the movement 'cut across' numerous areas of 'concern' uniting, albeit sometimes uneasily, civil rights and anti-poverty activists as RTI became inextricably connected to 'right to life' and resource issues (Jenkins and Goetz 1999; Singh 2007, 19). The pressure led to a series of state-level laws concerning access to information, beginning with Tamil Nadu in 1997 (Singh 2011).

Despite local movement, the lack of national government action coincided with a unique period of single-party rule by Congress in the early to mid-1990s (Sharma 2015). Nevertheless, by the middle of the 1990s 'articulated political support was de rigeur' in manifestos and post-election deals (Sharma 2015, 111). In 1996 the National Campaign for the Right to Information (NCRI) was established and a draft Bill was created as a second Unity government arrived in power. The 'dominant mood' in government was hostile but, recognising that 'it was never politically expedient to openly oppose transparency', the government set up a committee under a retired judge (Singh 2011, 11). Sharma argues that the committee was not simply, or even mainly, created as a result of external pressure. Reform elements within government wanted to have the 'first' developing world law, as a symbolic means of 'keeping up' with other advanced democracies (Sharma 2015). There was a growing sense within government that openness was necessary, amid recognition of government 'failure' where the state was increasingly seen as a 'problem'. The mid-1990s also saw an increasing pressure on India internationally from the World Bank and transparency groups.

At this point, India began an 'inexorable', if bumpy, journey to an access to information law (Sharma 2015). In May 1997, the committee, drawing on laws from around the world and following detailed discussion, recommended an FOI Act. It presented a draft law, preferring the 'wider' connotations of 'Freedom' rather than a 'Right' to information, which it feared had litigious consequences. In 1999 the then Minister for Urban Development unilaterally declared an open document policy in his department. The opening was classic 'gap' in policy that could be levered for change (Thelen 1999). Although this unilateral action was rapidly reversed by the Prime Minister, the reversal was then used by NCRI as the basis for a court appeal to 'drive a wedge' in government policy (Singh 2011, 13). The Supreme Court ruled in favour of the campaigners and ordered a transparency law.

Institutional resistance exerted an effect. Writing in 2002 Mathur warned that 'the longer the delay ... the more anaemic its effect' and identified a recurring pattern whereby 'each successive draft Bill' was a 'watered down version of an earlier Bill' and a 'bundle of compromises' (2002, 54). What became the FOI Act of 2002 differed from the earlier proposals of the National Campaign for People's Right to Information (NCPRI) in the nature of the appeal system, the removal of individual sanctions for non-compliance and added exemptions. The inclusion of private sector bodies was also dropped (Sharma 2015). In a final twist, the law was passed but not commenced and so sat, inactive, on the statute book.

In 2004 a new United Progressive Alliance, a coalition government of Congress and left-wing parties, assumed power, and its Common Minimum Programme committed itself to ensuring that 'The Right to Information Act will be made more progressive, participatory and meaningful' (Singh 2005). The new process was as significant as the new name. It was overseen by a National Advisory Council (NAC), a non-constitutional body sitting outside government that short-circuited political and bureaucratic decision-making. The NAC was headed by Sonia Gandhi, both a transparency advocate and a powerful figure with huge political and moral authority (Singh 2011, 21).

In a complex choreography of manoeuvre and counter-manoeuvre, Gandhi led calls for amendments to the FOI Act of 2002 with a letter to ministers. However, opponents sought to commence the earlier, weaker version. The decision was then made to offer a new RTI Bill. There was symbolic import in the new shift back to a 'right', as one activist outlined:

> The key to the change in approach is reflected in the title. 'Freedom of Information' suggested an act of dispensation by authority; 'Right to Information' an inalienable 'right' of every citizen – a truly revolutionary change from the era of secrecy. (Bhattacharjea 2005)

The Bill went to the government and was again watered down, most significantly in its coverage, being restricted to central government rather than state, regional and local levels where the vital information that energised the grassroots campaign was held (Sharma 2015). The draft was then sent to a Parliamentary Standing Committee, which sought to strengthen the proposals (Pakanati 2011). The committee recommended a new purpose clause, binding RTI within the Constitution of India as a democratic ideal. It also clarified the contested claim that central government could legislate to cover regions and sought to ensure that the Bill would not fall victim to the legal loophole that the earlier FOI Act did (Pakanati 2011).

Again the set of proposals that left the committee were amended to create a more limited law. Protests from activists were accompanied, in a final crucial intervention, by a visit to ministers from Sonia Gandhi that succeeded in re-extending the scope (Sharma 2015). After this the law easily passed its legislative stages. It received a Presidential signature, though not before the President had sought reassurance that his own correspondence would be protected (Singh 2011).

## Conclusion

Access to information legislation is powered by a complex interaction of politics and symbolism. The symbolism serves to attract the attention of important constituencies, frequently the media and activists or even courts, though almost never the electorate. The venues for FOI then shift across court rooms, newspapers, government offices and legislatures, which supply pressure and interpretations. Nor is the symbolism a constant, as different groups interpret what it means for different ends (Stubbs and Snell 2014; Fenster 2012b).

While the symbolism drives the issue onto the agenda, it is rarely powerful enough to drive it onto the statute book. The natural laws of the legislative process and entropy converge to steal momentum as politics, internal battles and negotiation make for a slow stop-start pattern. Factions within government either support, oppose or resign themselves to change, and the various sides fight, compromise and position themselves for leverage. At this point events such as elections or hidden champions appear to throw the agenda forward and out-manoeuvre opposition.

The cases show how symbolism does, however, start a process that governments find hard to stop. Though they may temporise, even for the duration of a government, it appears difficult to remove openness from the agenda. More importantly, the symbolism of openness and the consequences of opposing something so clearly 'positive' mean that politicians are reluctant to openly oppose it or 'kill it' in any overt way. Gerald Ford's futile and counter-productive veto appeared no end of a lesson, and Lyndon Johnson was reluctant to stop the US FOI, even when simple negligence would have sunk it. In this sense, the symbolism sets off a chain reaction that cuts off a government's line of retreat of, as it mobilises constituencies in favour of it who make retreat potentially costly.

# 9

## Ireland and New Zealand: a legacy and an assault from within

This chapter examines two very different cases. FOI in Ireland emerged from a secretive culture propelled by scandal and very specific coalition politics of the early 1990s. Bequeathed to a new government, it was severely cut back and then rebooted. New Zealand's Official Information Act (OIA) represents perhaps the most unusual story, of a committee of the great and the good, composed of the normally 'vested interests', pushing a radical and decisively different sort of openness law.

### Ireland: corruption, coalition and cutting back, 1990–2014

The emergence of FOI in Ireland is an apparently simple story of a scandal opening up a secretive society. The details are more political. The arrival of Ireland's 1997 FOI law was driven, above all, by corruption and exposure (McDonagh 2015). Although open government campaigns had been up and running since the early 1990s, it was an investigation into corruption in the beef industry that triggered political support for FOI from successive governments. The law was also powered by the unique political makeup of the Ireland's 'Rainbow Coalition' and co-evolved with a wave of wider political and administrative reforms (McDonagh 2015). In contrast to the developments in many other countries, it was 'handed' as a 'legacy' issue to the government that followed, which very rapidly fell out of love with it. Having been gifted legislation, it then made one of the clearest attempts to restrain, if not 'dismantle', an FOI law.

Among the different cases in this book, the Irish government appears one of the most resolutely secretive. The emergence of FOI in the 1990s, alongside a range of other oversight mechanisms, represents one of the 'most powerful and radical changes in Irish political history' (Foley 2015, 186).

For much of the twentieth century, the Irish state was heavily centralised and, as a by-product, resolutely secretive. As in the UK, the Westminster-style system created an 'atmosphere of secrecy' (McDonagh 2015). In a state founded in rebellion, war and tension, the habit of conspiratorial, closely guarded information control was engrained, and the new republic was an 'inheritor' of 'official secrecy' and a 'fragile democracy' (Foley 2015, 188). At the centre of the secretive culture was a 'catch-all' Official Secrets Act modelled on the UK that, while 'rarely used', carried a 'powerful chilling effect' (Foley 2015, 189). Other influences, from the Roman Catholic Church to the long running Northern Irish problem, further reinforced secrecy and the 'closed' nature of government, which had spread across political and social life from film censorship to the use (and abuse) of broad emergency powers. As late as the early 1990s Irish ministers governed with an 'omerta-like adherence to secrecy', and a Supreme Court ruling raised Cabinet confidentiality to an 'absolute constitutional principle' (Adshead 2015, 36). There were few counter-availing powers against the seemingly all-encompassing control. The relatively weak powers of scrutiny held by the Dáil (the Lower House of Parliament) were worsened by a sometimes convoluted accountability philosophy, whereby politicians were seen as scrutineers of the bureaucracy on behalf of the public (MacCarthaigh 2005).

Pressure for greater openness began in the early 1980s not from without but from within: in 1985 the chair of the Association of Higher Civil Servants called for greater openness in government. In parallel, members of the lower and upper Houses tried to initiate legislation to highlight the issue, though a Private Member's Bill by Senator Brendan Ryan 'did not generate widespread publicity' (McDonagh 2015, 46). In parallel, the courts had been used by individuals to press for access to information (Kearney and Stapleton 1998). By the early 1990s a reform group of activists, journalists and academics had formed a campaigning body, 'Let in the Light'. In a high-profile event it attracted Carl Bernstein and Salman Rushdie to speak in favour of legislation. Outside of the direct push for FOI laws, the influence of Europe and New Public Management ideas were gradually pushing wider administrative change, as seen in the creation of an ombudsman in the early 1980s.

Many FOI regimes have been created by scandals (see Darch and Underwood 2010; Blanton 2002). In Ireland it was the Beef Tribunal of 1991 that truly pushed FOI onto political agendas and into manifestos (McDonagh 2015; Foley 2015, 190) and created a temporary 'political consensus on the need for freedom of information legislation' (Doyle 1997, 67).

The Tribunal emerged from a *World in Action* television investigation into corruption in the Irish beef industry that exposed the powerful culture of secrecy in Ireland and, as importantly, the weaknesses of existing accountability mechanisms. After an investigation of three years at the cost of €62 million, the judge famously observed, 'if the questions that were asked in the Dáil were answered in the way they are answered here, there would be no necessity for this inquiry and an awful lot of time and money would have been saved' (McDonagh 2003). The scandal triggered 'three supreme court cases, the loss of a Prime Minister, a Parliamentary committee and the introduction of FOI' (Foley 2015, 190).

As well as from scandal, FOI emerged from the fluid coalition politics of the early 1990s (Kearney and Stapleton 1998). Michener (2015d) argues that coalition politics frequently produce stronger FOI legislation than single-party government does. In Ireland's case a junior partner, the Labour Party, pushed for a law in its first partnership with Fianna Fáil. The Taoiseach Albert Reynolds committed himself to look into FOI and spoke of the need to 'let the light in' (McDonagh 2003). However, partially as a result of the Beef Tribunal, the government fell before any action was taken.

Unusually, a new left-leaning 'Rainbow Coalition' was then formed without an election. Its coalition programme 'A Government of Renewal' gave a clearer promise to pass FOI legislation (Kearney and Stapleton 1998). Transparency and openness became a 'mantra' for the 'Rainbow Coalition' (Felle and Adshead 2009, 10). The Taoiseach John Bruton spoke of how 'the government must go about its work … as transparently as if it were behind a pane of glass' (OIC 2008, 11). As part of this, a new FOI law would be a 'profound change' that would 'turn the culture of the Official Secrets Act on its head' and bring about a 'permanent shift in the balance of power' (Fitzgerald 1996, 8–11). The new 'mantra' sent out a series of political signals: it helped boost the legitimacy of a government that was unelected and, more specifically, acted on the apparent lessons of the ongoing Beef Tribunal. For the Labour Party, a previously 'unhappy' junior partner, championing the Act served to create a more 'co-operative style of governing' that would simultaneously create an 'adequate check' on its partners (MacCarthaigh 2005, 88).

The context was also crucial. FOI was 'part of a broader response to concern about the performance and accountability of public authorities in Ireland' and a new 'ethos' (Kearney and Stapleton 1998, 178; Felle and Adshead 2009, 1).The Rainbow Coalition strengthened the scrutiny power of the Dáil and passed a new Ethics in Public Office Act 1995 mandating disclosure of business interests, while also reforming relationships between ministers and civil servants through what became the Public Service Act 1997 (Kearney and Stapleton 1998). The new openness extended to the ending of censorship in broadcasting relating to the Troubles (Adshead 2015). The 1990s, as one Labour leader put it, were a time when Ireland was 'coming out of a culture of secrecy' and 'there was a demand from the public and civil society for increased accountability' (Adshead et al. 2015, 165). Politically, the 'timing was fortuitous': McDonagh argues that FOI legislation would have been 'unlikely' to have been passed by its successor (2015, 48).

## The Act

The Act took two years between promise and implementation. The Labour Minister of State Eithne Fitzgerald, an FOI expert and long-time advocate, was in charge of the policy but, crucially, it had the supported of the Labour Deputy Prime Minister, meaning that it 'was owned by Dick Spring … leader of the second largest party in government'. This 'senior political commitment' proved crucial in persuading sceptics and providing time. There was a 'critical mass' of 'strong cross-party support, the readiness of departments to engage with change [and] the invaluable assistance of key officials'. The policy was aided by the wider 'programme of ongoing change' and 'by being part of a larger programme the impetus for FOI was enhanced and rewards for cultural opposition diminished' (Kearney and Stapleton 1998, 176–177). Outside government, although 'its introduction was preceded by much general discussion of the need for such legislation', there was an 'absence of detailed public debate on its proposed contents' and, unlike in the UK, with extensive discussion in parts of the press, there was a 'lack of detailed debate on the contents' (McDonagh 2015, 46).

Research began in 1994 into other FOI legislation, in parallel with bi-lateral discussions over concerns that, though 'time consuming', served to 'raise awareness' across government. Experts and evidence from elsewhere were used to allay fears and persuade. It was claimed there was 'remarkably broad support across departments for the fundamental principles of FOI', and anxieties were mainly over 'practical administrative issues', such as the timing or lead-in (Kearney and Stapleton 1998, 171). The Permanent Secretary to the Cabinet and officials within the Finance Ministry were apparently supportive of the policy (171). Nevertheless there was a long process of 'telling, selling and learning' that meant a 'daily struggle to ensure time was actually spent progressing the legislation' (171). The delay was 'partly explained by the complexity' (McDonagh 2015, 48). The 'nature of the legislation and its lack of congruence with existing culture … meant there were strong reservations' that went from 'outright opposition' that the law was 'unworkable' to 'assertions' that FOI was 'highly laudable but required far greater consideration'. Behind this was an ominous 'official silence' that was 'complemented by discreet efforts to build alliances against the measure' (Kearney and Stapleton 1998, 177). The Department of Justice was seen as one powerful force against it; the Bill was 'nearly lost' (Foley 2015, 191), and other departments played for time in the hope the government would fall before passing the legislation (McDonagh 2015).

In common with elsewhere, the final Act that emerged was a compromise, part of a process of persuasion that took 'days, weeks and, in one case, some months' (Kearney and Stapleton 1998, 178). A commitment to include whistle-blowing was dropped and protections for policy-making were strengthened. Perhaps most notably, the An Garda Síochána, the Irish police force, was excluded from FOI, making Ireland 'almost unique' in this respect (Dowling 2015, 72). In a parallel with the UK, the FOI Bill was the first Bill to be referred to a Parliamentary committee for scrutiny (McDonagh 2015). One TD (Teachta Dála, or member of the Dáil) described the Act as a 'grave disappointment' and a 'minimalist attempt' that would make 'very little practical difference', arguing that a 'much more radical approach is needed' (OIC 2008, 11). Nevertheless, the Act was generally subject to high expectations. The *Irish Times* suggested that 'it looks as though something seriously radical is about to happen' (Adshead et al. 2015, 163–164), and Senator Brendan Ryan spoke of FOI as having 'huge constitutional importance' and a 'magnificent revolutionary piece of legislation' symbolic of the 'political determination that administrative guile would not be allowed to undermine the spirit of openness' (OIC 2008, 11).

### Post-enactment: dismantling?

The Irish FOI Act was unusual in being a legacy law. It was passed in April 1997, just two months before the government fell and was replaced by a coalition of Fianna Fáil and Progressive Democrats, who took responsibility for FOI being rolled out. The new government spoke favourably of its inherited law and appeared broadly supportive, with the Prime Minister, reflecting the earlier government's rhetoric, praising it as a powerful means of strengthening citizens' rights (McDonagh 2003).

However, within eighteen months complaints began to surface. In 1999 a Civil Service Users' Network (CSUN) report highlighted abuse of the Act. In October of that year the Taoiseach Bertie Ahern criticised the 'major abusers' referring not to journalists but to 'members of the public and companies' whose use of the Act was 'very costly' and left government 'tied up in bureaucratic knots'. In the same week the Education Minister claimed that FOI had ended government 'brain storming' sessions (*Irish Times* 7/10/1999).

As a result, a High Level Review of FOI was conducted in 2002 by a group composed of the secretaries general of the departments of Enterprise, Trade and Employment, Foreign Affairs and Transport and the Secretary General (PSMD) of the Department of Finance. The resulting report of 2003 made clear that aspects of the law were inadequate, focusing on the protection of central decision-making and a potential chilling effect. The report concluded that 'a five year period of protection is not sufficient' for government and that premature release could 'seriously affect the functioning of Cabinet' (High Level Review 2003, 11). The 'early release of such records may inhibit officials from freely expressing views on particular issues, particularly views which depart radically from the "conventional line"' (14). Perhaps most controversially, the report recommended the introduction of an up-front fee for each request:

> The Group considers that an upfront fee is ultimately the only workable arrangement. The Group acknowledges that the introduction of a fee may not be viewed as an attractive measure; however, it would go to recognising that there is an administrative cost associated with FOI which in some cases can be significant and which is currently borne by taxpayers generally. A fee regime involving an upfront cost may also minimise so-called 'trawling' requests which have little or no public benefit. In the context

of wider Exchequer corrective measures, the rationalisation of the fee regime will also contribute to addressing the cost of the administrative burden of FOI. (17)

The following year the government introduced stronger categorical protection for documents, with a broad interpretation of what constituted meetings and correspondence, and a doubling of the delay on release of documents to ten years (Adshead and Felle 2015, xv). The public defence was that the closure period threatened to open up the delicate Northern Ireland peace process, despite there being a separate exemption (McDonagh 2003). Politicians may have had a pressing motivation as many of those in power had been in power five years before (Adshead 2015, 43). The government also introduced standard up-front fee of €15 per request, claiming that the average request cost €425 in 2003 and that fees would deter 'abuse' and recoup costs (O'Connor 2010, 6–7).

The changes were pushed through very speedily over opposition in 2003 as the government used its guillotine power and control to ensure a quick passage (Adshead and Felle 2015; MacCarthaigh 2005). Taoiseach Bertie Ahern assured the public that the 'main principles are not being changed' and that only a few 'technical areas' were being altered (OIC 2008, 13). There was little evidence that the changes to the exemptions were fully used by government (OIC 2004). However, the fees had a serious impact: according to the Information Commissioner the result was a 'dramatic' fall in non-personal requests of 75% in a single year, affecting use particularly by TDs and journalists (OIC 2004, 14l; OIC 2008). As of 2013 requests continued to present a 'tangible barrier' to ordinary requesters, and requests remained at half of their pre-fee level (O'Connor 2010, 8). O'Connor (2010) concluded that the fees recouped only 1.6% of the estimated cost and, given the relatively small number of non-personal requests to most bodies, were likely to cost more to administer than the income they generated. The effect on government culturally was as important. Behaviourally the changes also had a powerful influence, as 'the Civil Service took its cues from government, and the signal was clear: FOI was no longer important' (Adshead and Felle 2015, xvi).

### The restoration of 2014?
FOI represents a means of distancing an administration from the past while presenting a new tone (Adshead 2015). In 2011 a new Fine Gael–Labour coalition entered power with a commitment to strengthening and 'rebooting' FOI. The new government sought to draw a line under past practices following the 2008 economic crisis (Adshead 2015). The commitment chimed with a wider discussion of the failure of Ireland's scrutiny mechanisms to foresee the banking crash and the 'inability of Opposition Members of Parliament, or the media, to get access to documents that formed the basis for government decisions during the Celtic Tiger years' (Adshead and Felle 2015, xvi). FOI now appears a party-political issue as it is 'hard not to make a straightforward connection between the presence of the Labour party

in government and a commitment to FOI' (Adshead 2015, 44). For the coalitions in the 1990s and 2000s commitment to openness had been a mode of 'distinguishing themselves' from predecessors and a signal of a 'different style of government' (44). By contrast, Fianna Fáil, the dominant party for much of the twentieth century, preferred a more 'traditional way of governing' (44).

The new Taoiseach promised 'very open government' and argued that the 'the restoration and extension of FOI is central to the delivery of the Government's reform agenda to secure greater openness, transparency and accountability of public governance' (Kenny 2014). He argued that a new 'culture and practice of greater accountability and transparency are crucial' in rebuilding trust and reform (Kenny 2014). In an echo of the 1990s, new legislation to regulate lobbying and protect whistle-blowing was also promised alongside reform of the Irish Parliament. Kenny's push for political reform was further wrapped in the symbolism of Ireland's history: 'It is the best and only way to make our country what we want it to be as we face the centenary of 1916' (Kenny 2014).

The new FOI Act 2014 'restores the principles contained in the original law and places openness and transparency at the forefront of the operation of the legislation' (Adshead and Felle 2015, xvii). The new Act that emerged in 2014 reversed some (though not all) of the strengthened exemptions of 2002–03, leaving partially in place the exemptions for security, defence and international relations. After some initial reluctance and resistance, the government abolished up-front application fees for requesters. It also strengthened publication schemes and the Information Commissioner's powers and, perhaps most importantly, extended FOI to more than 100 new bodies including the Central Bank and NAMA, the Irish assets management agency, as well as non-public bodies in receipt of 'significant funding' (McDonagh 2015). The 2014 FOI Act now covered the police, though only for 'administrative records relating to human resources, finance or procurement matters', and offered a 'highly protective' exemption (McDonagh 2015, 147). In its new reformulation, the Act reversed the idea of coverage, meaning that the default presumption was that bodies were covered unless they were excluded (McDonagh 2015). It did not, however, cover the many 'half' public bodies across Ireland (Adshead et al. 2015).

### New Zealand: assault from within?

As Moe (2015) points out, vested interests can 'take action to bring change – even radical change' if institutions appear 'out of sync' with their contexts or there is evidence of policy 'drift' (298–299). Organisations may seek to take action that stops 'haemorrhaging' of support, legitimacy or capability, particularly when change is 'highly beneficial' (299) New Zealand offers just such a case, an exceptional story of information reform springing directly and accidentally from within. In the early 1980s a committee composed of the kind of officials normally opposed to openness pushed instead for a full and radical piece of legislation. According to Snell (2000) the 'New Zealand tale is one of informed insiders developing a model that was acceptable to the political and bureaucratic leadership' (578).

In common with other Westminster-style systems, information policy was previously one of protection. The Official Secrets Act of 1951, passed 'almost in a fit of post colonial absent-mindedness' (Keith 1989, 3), upheld a 'deeply engrained' culture of secrecy (Law Commission 2010, 24). By the 1960s there was 'low-level' popular pressure for change in New Zealand, primarily at a local level, over access to information concerning environmental issues, and in foreign affairs over the country's involvement in Vietnam (Snell 2000; Aitken 1998; Keith 1989). By the 1970s there was a noticeable drift towards change as Parliament and the courts sought greater scrutiny of government, with the National Party pressing for constitutional reform (Keith 1989).

The first attempt at FOI legislation was a Private Member's Bill in 1977 introduced by the Labour MP Richard Prebble (Aitken 1998). What became the New Zealand OIA was then the 'unintended legacy' of Prime Minister Robert Muldoon (Snell 2000, 583). It sprang from an 'unlikely source' in connection with a spying scandal (Keith 1989, 1). In the wake of a failed prosecution and public criticism of the intelligence services, Muldoon sought a review, which was stymied by classification under the Official Secrets Act (Gustafson 2000; Keith 1989). What began as a 'purely internal' review committee was widened into a more open group, while the committee's remit drifted outwards from classification to openness more generally (Keith 1984, 31; Keith 1989). Its deliberations 'carefully crafted a mechanism that would allow an evolution of bureaucratic and ministerial attitudes to the concept of open government' (Snell 2000, 579). Prime Minister Muldoon had 'commissioned a Committee on Official Information' and was unexpectedly 'presented with nascent freedom of information legislation' (583).

### The Danks Committee

Rather than the reforms being pushed by outsiders or a handful of champions, the committee meant that 'the reforms were sponsored and designed by officials operating deep within the traditional secretive workings of Westminster government' (Snell 2000, 584). Geoffrey Palmer, later Justice Minister and Prime Minister, who sat on it, later described the membership:

> Sir Alan Danks, the Chairperson, had had experience primarily as an academic economist ... Professor KJ Keith, then an outstanding academic lawyer ... The Deputy Secretary of Justice and law reformer par excellence, Jim Cameron ... Bryce Harland, an Assistant Secretary of Foreign Affairs and one of New Zealand's most distinguished diplomats ... The Chief Parliamentary Counsel, Walter Iles, the Secretary of Defence, Dennis McLean ... the Secretary of Cabinet, Mr PG Millen and Dr RM Williams, the Chair of the State Services Commission. (Palmer 2007)

They were 'some of the most able public servants of their generation' (Palmer 2007). Many of the senior officials and figures who mounted opposition in other regimes were, in New Zealand, part of the process of creation, the engine of reform. The fact that the heads of such departments as Defence were prepared to not only support but champion openness was a powerful signal to those who would seek to resist. As a result the committee 'was able to tailor a set of recommendations that would work', and the eventual report, titled 'Towards Open Government', was 'a document of high quality and considerable liberality' (Palmer 2007). It had the confidence to take action on its own, most notably by presenting the government with a draft legislation it had not asked for (Keith 1989).

The committee wrestled with how to create principles that would work across government and into the future (Keith 1984). While many early FOI regimes looked to the US FOIA, the committee focused on creating a different kind of legislation that would avoid what it saw as the adversarial and overly litigious regime (Snell 2000). As one member put it, the committee looked for 'a way of overcoming inertial resistance to making information more freely available, without causing a flood of litigation and adding to the burdens of the judiciary' (quoted in Snell 2000, 583). The architects 'focused on information and policy trends and tried to create an access regime that could respond to future developments and needs', and Snell argues that 'this difference in design beginnings was to prove critical' (2000, 584). There was, said one member, 'great difficulty in reaching final and acceptable views' (Keith 1989, 6). The committee's deliberations, perhaps by accident, took a calculated risk after it had 'wrestled for some months before coming up with a solution' (quoted in Snell 2000, 583). One member of the committee later reflected that 'some at least of the members might have been surprised if they could have foreseen that the outcome of their deliberations would be' (quoted in Snell 2000, 583).

The primary report began with a powerfully symbolic call for openness:

> The case for more openness in government is compelling. It rests on the democratic principles of encouraging participation in public affairs and ensuring the accountability of those in office; it also derives from concern for the interests of individuals. A no less important consideration is that the Government requires public understanding and support to get its policies carried out. This can come only from an informed public. (Committee on Official Information 1980, 13)

It went on to justify openness specifically in relation to New Zealand:

> New Zealand is a small country. The Government has a pervasive involvement in our everyday national life. This involvement is not only felt, but is also sought, by New Zealanders, who have tended to view successive governments as their agents, and have expected them to act as such.

It concluded that 'history and circumstances give New Zealanders special reason for wanting to know what their government is doing and why' (13).

In designing the OIA the committee had opted for a novel approach that would 'progressively' open up government: the Act later stated in section 4 that the purpose was to 'increase progressively the availability of official information to the people of New Zealand'. The committee felt 'it would be more fruitful in the New Zealand context to set in motion a process of opening up which, on the basis of a presumption of openness, would contribute and be responsive to changing attitudes and circumstances'. The OIA offered 'a process with a purpose' with an evolving framework. First, though this was more 'accidental than a calculated policy', the new law dealt with 'information' not documents; this meant, for example, that even unrecorded meetings could be asked to be recorded and released (Snell 2000, 585). Second, the essence of the design was also a presumption of openness. The report rejected the detailed exemptions or broadly drawn 'class' exclusions seen elsewhere, as 'these exemptions tend to be drafted in broad terms or they go into extensive detail which sometimes appears to reflect defensive attitudes' (Committee on Official Information1980, 20). The committee agonised over how to design workable but flexible exemptions (Keith 1989). No set exclusion, the report argued, could be 'properly and satisfactorily made all at one time by legislation', and so there would instead be a 'matrix of circumstances surrounding each request for information', including Cabinet documents, that were not subject to blanket exclusion (Snell 2000, 592). Withholding of information could be justified by reference to broadly defined interests: 'the interests of the country as a whole; the interests of individuals and organisations; and the interests of effective government and administration' (Danks 1980, 16). Third, an independent body, the Information Authority, 'would ensure that general progress towards the "larger aim" is appropriately monitored and reviewed' in conjunction with an ombudsman rather than the courts, where matters would inevitably become legalistic (Committee on Official Information 1980 and1981). The designers hoped that together these would create a dynamic law constantly moving towards openness:

> We were faced early in our work, with the choice of trying to design a once and for all static mechanism, with a complex set of exceptions, or a more flexible mechanism, operating by reference to principles and competing criteria that reflect a continuing shift away from a presumption of secrecy. We opted for a flexible process. (Committee on Official Information 1981, 21)

The OIA was a consciously 'gradualist approach' that created a 'sophisticated open-textured Act' which, almost uniquely for national legislation (Committee on Official Information 1981, 13) was 'not rules-based' (Palmer 2007). While other countries 'would tend to create a rigid system' the OIA offered a series of possibilities … capable of being moulded to an environment of changing attitudes and views' (Committee on Official Information 1981, 13).

> The whole report calls attention to a paradox. We have noted that in country after country the pursuit of improved access to official information, avowedly positive in

purpose, leads nevertheless to concentration on what information should be withheld or protected. Discussion develops a negative cast; attitudes become defensive. (5)

In persuading the government, the committee took care to address the by now typical concerns. On costs, the report pointed out that in modern government 'the cost of supplying information is already considerable' via Parliamentary questions. It then argued that 'the question of costs is ultimately one of priorities. If it is accepted that the Government has responsibility to keep the public informed of its activities, it will no doubt be recognised also that this aspect of its work must be given priority' (Committee on Official Information1980, 36). It ended with a more principled defence: 'Some of the positive outcomes of greater openness, such as better understanding of public policies, are not measurable in money terms. What price should be set on a better informed public, or a more outward looking Public Service? If greater openness enables Government to work more smoothly and effectively in the long run, a real gain in the efficient use of resources will be achieved' (36).

The report also set out to reassure politicians that, despite its innovative approach, constitutional protections remained in force: 'continuing protection as needs be for the free and frank exchange of views between Ministers and their colleagues, between Ministers and officials, or between other officers of the Government in the course of their duty'. This might only be 'short-term' but would protect the Cabinet (Committee on Official Information 1980, 18–19). So 'while working practices are changing, the convention of ministerial responsibility and the neutral public servant will remain the constitutional basis of the working relationship between ministers and officials (Committee on Official Information 1981, 37). It did, however, point out firmly the 'fact that the release of certain information may give rise to criticism or embarrassment of the government is not an adequate reason for withholding it from the public' (Committee on Official Information 1980, 18–19).

In a further dose of political realism, the report made an appeal to those working with the new law within and outside government: 'the will to change must inform the working of the system if it is to promote the evolution of attitudes and practice. This applies to all concerned – ministers, parliamentarians, officials, public interest groups, and the public media. But the initiative rests primarily with ministers and the public media' (Committee on Official Information 1980, 37). The report then ended where it began: 'The system … is designed specifically for New Zealand and its results will depend on the way the situation in this country develops. Our community is small, our affairs conducted within a comprehensibly human scale. The system we work in is well understood and able to absorb criticism because there is a national sense of its underlying integrity. Here, surely, lie grounds for hope that reform can be fruitful' (37).

*The passage*

The Danks Review was, outwardly, one of the least conflictual processes towards openness. Palmer (2007) argued that the process itself made the matter weighty and important: 'looking back it is hard to resist the conclusion that the development of the OIA was the biggest policy game in town at the time. It was a significant constitutional change' (3). He also reflected that it was rather smooth: 'it is not often matters of such importance and difficulty are accomplished so elegantly' (3).

This is not to say that the passage was wholly easy. The 'Treasury opposed the Bill at the Select Committee, no doubt with the permission of and on the instruction of the Minister of Finance who was also the Prime Minister, the Rt Hon Sir Robert Muldoon'. The Prime Minister of the day, Robert Muldoon, appeared less than enthusiastic. Although Muldoon 'was a strong believer in the battler, the little man, the ordinary citizen and his rights' he also famously dismissed the new legislation as a fad and a 'nine day wonder' (Shroff 2005, 1–2; Palmer 2007, 2). Palmer claims that much of the credit goes to one champion: 'then Minister of Justice and Attorney-General, the Honourable Jim McLay. He managed to achieve passage of the Bill in face of opposition from both his Prime Minister and the Treasury' (Palmer 2007, 2). The process was unusual in that the Bill, despite being government-sponsored, gave the opportunity for major amendments and departmental input to the committee (Keith 1984).

The Act was aided by a wider context of reform. The creation of the OIA interacted with a series of political changes that sought to 'restrain the power of government and achieve greater accountability' as well as strengthen minority rights (Aitken 1998, 118). It was part of a process beginning with the ombudsman in 1962, which was followed by reform of Parliamentary Select Committees in 1985, a Bill of Rights Act in 1990 and a Privacy Act in 1993, which ended with a change to the electoral law in 1996 (119). Further to this, in the early 1980s New Zealand embarked upon a series of radical New Public Management reforms (Lodge and Gill 2011). A stream of legislation, such as the Public Finance Act 1989 and the Fiscal Responsibility Act 1994, set objectives for performance and greater accountability (Aitken 1998, 118–119).

Politics and party competition also played a role as electoral pressure and, as Palmer put it, the 'proximities of elections and policies of the opposition' forced the hand of the government. The opposition Labour Party, one of whose members had championed FOI in 1977, pushed for FOI and was seeking 'to make it an election issue in 1981'. Instead, the government's proposals 'defused the issue' (Aitken 1998, 122).

As seen elsewhere, there was little public interest. Even by the time of the arrival of the legislation, there was no groundswell of enthusiasm, as one official recalled:

> the media were keen but sceptical; the public in so far as they were interested at all were mildly positive; Ministers were nervous but publicly accepting (under the 'guid-

ance' of the redoubtable Sir Robert Muldoon); and the civil service – trained and prepared to within an inch of its life – was largely resigned to the inevitable. (Shroff 2005, 3–4)

He went on to claim that 'there were a significant number of senior public servants, and, off the record, Ministers, who were totally unconvinced and became prophets of doom' (Shroff 2005, 4). The media too regarded it as a poor piece of legislation and, Snell argues, 'wildly misjudged' its effect (2000, 584). It is possible that media scepticism may also have helped 'sell' the policy to equally uncertain officials.

### The post-Act push

Jim McLay later reflected that the OIA 'fundamentally changed the relationship between a previously secretive government and those it governed' and quoted the Law Commission's conclusion that it was now 'central to New Zealand's constitutional arrangements' (2012, 172). The OIA underwent a series of changes and itself triggered further reform, gradually building additional laws and mechanisms. The law itself has been altered, generally in an expansive direction. The Act was extended to cover the newly reorganised state-owned enterprises in 1986 and hospital and school boards in 1987. In the same year the 'most significant change was to the ministerial veto. Changes were made to ensure that the veto was a Cabinet decision, not an individual ministerial decision, a move that 'effectively put a stop to the use of veto [as] the political cost was too high' (Palmer 2007; see also Aitken 1998). Palmer also instituted a twenty-day time limit in place of the vague 'as soon as practically possible'. The innovative 'Information Authority was very successful in this early work under the Act' until its automatic end five years into the Act.

The OIA was then built upon and developed. The law was then followed by equivalent Local Government Official Information and Meetings Act 1987 (LGOIMA), after a decision that local government required separate legislation (Law Commission 2010). The 1990 Bill of Rights further entrenched information rights, with clause 14 entrenching 'the right to freedom of expression, including the freedom to seek, receive, and impart information and opinions of any kind in any form', while the 1993 Privacy Act offered separate access to personal information (Law Commission 2010, 32).

### Conclusion

In Ireland and New Zealand FOI was pushed over decades by small groups, thrust centre stage by scandal and secured by politics. New Zealand, more by accident than by design, opted for a radical and different approach from within, in a series of unexpected turns. As Snell points out, the position, composition and process were key. The law was not 'forced' upon government either from without or by a small group of insiders but presented as a reasoned and powerfully argued step by the kind of figures who, in other regimes, opposed the law. In Ireland it was left as a 'legacy' to an incoming government.

In both cases parties played a leading role. In New Zealand party competition played a role in 'neutralising' opponents. In Ireland coalition politics helped FOI along in the wake of scandal. Yet in both cases the law was also aided by its context, as part of a wider process of making more powerful checks and creating a more accountable government as well as economic and institutional change focused on 'performance'. The Irish case also shows how the passage of FOI represents the beginning, not the end, of transparency conflict, delineating a new front rather than offering a clear-cut punctuation. Nor is it always a progression towards openness, as what opens up can always close.

# 10

# FOI and the remaking of politics

FOI regimes exist in a constant state of change and flux with conflicting pressures to expand and be dismantled. The dynamics and contradictions that form FOI laws are carried over into their implementation. The mobilisation and counter-mobilisation continue as resources, interpretation and support are contested over the fundamental questions of 'what', 'to whom', 'how' and 'when' (Barberis 2010, 122). However, reform attempts are uncertain and frequently short-lived.

## Remaking politics with FOI

Patashnik and Zelizer (2013) examine how 'policy breakthroughs can refashion the political context' and create new 'regimes' (1072). New policies can 'reorganize power relations' and 'redefine political conflict' while also promoting 'new configurations of rights' and 'political capacities' (Soss and Moynihan 2014, 327, 322). The 'struggle to remake politics does not end when reforms are enacted', as laws remain 'trial and error affairs' influenced by 'strategic preferences' to interaction with other policy 'and the resources of the existing environment' (Patashnik and Zelizer 2013, 1077).

Patashnik and Zelizer (2013) build on Pierson (1994) to argue that 'that the capacity of public policies to remake politics is contingent, conditional, and contested' (Patashnik and Zelizer 2013, 1071). Policy success or failure rests on a mixture of political or public support alongside less concrete factors such as whether it appears to 'work' and the feedback that flows back into the political system. Strong feedback can redistribute benefits, creating supportive communities and compelling actors to endorse a policy, while weak or non-existent feedback leads to fragile support and political neglect (Patashnik and Zelizer 2013).

Three effects can be used to assess the durability and potential effects of a policy and regime. The key factors are resource effects, interpretative effects and institutional supports:

- *Resource effects*: concerning the reallocation of benefits and how, and how quickly and 'deeply', policies reallocate them;
- *Interpretive effects*: not only ongoing assessment of the reforms but also conflict and 'battles over the narrative' as supporters and opponents use (and sometimes abuse) information and arguments to claim the policy is a success or failure. These narratives can then become 'truths' that feed back into the process;
- *Institutional supports*: whether the policy is receiving the appropriate level of co-operation from the institutions and mechanisms appointed to implement it. (Patashnik and Zelizer 2013)

It is a combination of the strength of these three factors that can determine the success or failure of a reform.

### FOI in place

Matland associated symbolic policy with 'a lack of implementation' and lack of 'substantive effect' (1995, 168). They are 'almost always about substantive failure', in part because of their symbolism and their tendency to be 'conflictual' with 'actors intensely involved' (169). Edelman argued that underneath the clear signal they can be 'repealed in effect by administrative policy, budgetary starvation or other little publicised means' (1985, 37).

FOI laws appear, at least in these cases, to be more substantive, and less obviously failures, than many symbolic laws. Nevertheless, they are fragile, contested and constantly in motion. They create a new policy regime framed from the interplay of 'design, types of administrative compliance and type of requests' that is further reshaped by legal rulings, reforms and changing political contexts (Snell 2006, 290). Ruijer and Meijer (2016) explain how such regimes are made up of a mix of formal and informal laws, rules and practices:

> Freedom of information legislation (FOI) is considered the backbone of transparency regimes ... However, transparency regimes are not just contained in rules. Arrangements and policies are also revealed through practices, symbols, and discourses ... rules, rationales and assumptions. (3)

These regimes, and FOI laws in particular, carry several unique features. First, they are primarily voteless, and no election would be 'won' through their strengthening, though they serve a symbolic purpose in certain circumstances and politicians use them for 'credit taking' and positioning (Moe 2015). Second, their symbolism makes the laws and policies difficult to reverse directly through abolition, so unhappy governments frequently seek less obvious or direct ways of altering them (Roberts 2012). Third, unlike many policies, transparency is frequently non-partisan and is, at least publicly, a principle supported by all parties, an effect greatly enhanced by the growing number of laws around the world and the large international transparency lobby (Birchall 2014).

While the 'failure' of FOI can be overstated, FOI regimes certainly bring uncertainty, struggle and conflict (Stubbs and Snell 2014; Piotrowski 2009). The trajectories that shaped the creation of the law follow through into its implementation and operation. The conventional portrait of FOI is of a policy moving in opposite directions: grudgingly implemented and then increasingly disliked by its political creators, while the press, courts and legislature press for greater openness (Fenster 2012b). Laws are consequently subject to constant conflict, attack and undermining through resource starvation or changes in their detail but are, over time, rebooted by the same triggers that initiated them: scandals, the arrival of new governments and technological change.

The feedback created by such systems is similarly unclear. Much use is personal, and much feedback is hidden or 'dispersed' (Fung and Weil 2010). FOI systems can be seen as creating a continuous series of minor ripples or individual cases driving relatively localised effects, with certain difficult, complex or, most importantly, politically sensitive or controversial releases suddenly 'punctuating' the entire system. The uneven pattern means that some areas or bodies or parts of a government may receive many requests and others may be left virtually untouched. The 'individualized' or 'atomized' nature may create sudden upsurges or 'punctuations' in 'political' exposures within an 'equilibrium' of quotidian requests (Terrill 2000; Yasseri et al. 2013).

### FOI laws over time

What is clear is that systems remain at the mercy of shifting political support and tides (Piotrowksi 2009). Snell characterises this process as a cycle of 'optimism, pessimism and revisionism' (2001, 343,350). The relatively short life-span of most FOI regimes means that the few detailed longitudinal analyses mostly focus on regional or local government. At Australian state level, laws have altered because of 'legislative changes, administrative compliance and a disappointing return on democratic dividends' (343). Roberts's (1998) analysis of more than a decade of regional Canadian access laws found them to be limited by outdated legislation, changes in state structures, particularly owing to outsourcing, and various levels of resistance and non-compliance. In South Africa Berliner (2015) concluded that local government openness was severely limited by poor resources and monitoring, though political competition acted as a spur to improvement. Erkkilä (2012) explained how Finland's century-long democratic ideal of publicity was reshaped in the 1990s towards a more economic framing of openness, with a consequent effect on the new laws, and how officials and politicians viewed information. Looking across a selection of transparency initiatives in developing countries, Kosack and Fung (2014) found that much depended on the 'action cycle' and whether information triggered a series of actions, whether users took 'short and long routes of accountability' and on 'the willingness of providers, policymakers, and politicians to make improvements' (75).

In their study of targeted transparency policies Fung et al. (2007) argued that 'transparency laws tend to degrade over time' as they typically impose 'costs upon a small group of disclosers in the hope of generating benefits for a large group', and so 'tend to remain trapped ... [in a] political dead end of dispersed benefits and concentrated costs' with 'poor prospects for improvement over time' (110). However, this 'natural' degradation cycle can be stopped by pressure from above or below. If those subject to it champion it, actors and 'entrepreneurial politicians' can create a 'dynamic that fractures the political coalition opposing transparency' and lend openness policies new energy (112). The naturally dispersed users of the information can also form what they call 'permanent user coalitions' that 'use new crises and problems to press for national debate and force re-examination and improvement of disclosure' (112). Later work found that 'reform based on transparency can face obstacles of collective action, political resistance, and long implementation chains' (Kosack and Fung 2014, 65).

### FOI and resource allocation: who benefits?

Resource allocation is central to the success or failure of a policy regime. The 'magnitude and timing of the resources received by constituent groups can shape whether a fragile policy begins to "take"' (Patashnik and Zelizer 2013, 1078). Compared with those of policies such as social welfare, the benefits that accrue from FOI are diffuse and personal, and FOI does not produce a large constituency of identifiable supporters among the public (Fung and Weil 2010). Instead it produces a core of users and, outside of this, a wider network of advocates in the media and across civil society, who act as a force for innovation and, more importantly, a bulwark against change.

#### Users of access laws

Users constitute a very small, self-selecting part of the population, with fewer than 1 in 1,000 people ever making a request (Hazell and Worthy 2010). Despite the immense symbolism of governments passing openness laws 'for the people', there is no general user (see Meijer et al. 2012 and Chapter 7 above). There are instead diverse users employing the laws in different ways for very different ends (Michener and Worthy 2015). As a general rule, they comprise a mixture of members of the public, businesses, NGOs and journalists, some of whom attract more attention than others (Michener and Worthy 2015). From the UK to India use is, above all, local. Requests are primarily targeted at local or regional level and driven by an overlapping mix of personal and political interest that makes any benefits largely hidden or personal. As White (2007) points out, this leads to apparently parallel systems with 'smoothly' running processes for 'niche' requests and 'turbulent' controversy for the more political (Snell 2006, 298).

What these requests actually mean, and what benefits and feedbacks accrue as a result, can vary. In some countries 'many non-personal [FOI] requests can disguise [their] true nature' (McDonagh 2010b, 82; see also Hazell 1989). In countries such as Australia and Ireland laws have been heavily used to obtain personal information where there was no separate privacy law (Paterson and McDonagh 2010; Hazell 1989). After 1974, a frequent complaint of the US FOI has been that it created a 'mini-industry' of lawyers and organisations making FOIs and reverse 'counter-FOIs' as a basis for litigation (Wald 1984, 665). Calland and Bentley (2013) characterise a spreading 'politicised use' in India connected to basic rights, curbing maladministration and, in some cases, life-or-death issues of access to resources: an RTI request in India is a 'weapon of last resort' for 'failed governance' (Raag/CES 2014, 51–52).

Measuring who benefits also implies that systems work as they should. However, the 'action chain' is long and uncertain (Kosack and Fung 2014). In any requesting system there is a chain of 'program logic' and 'many points at which the necessary sequence of events could break down' or where 'the policy design proves to be brittle' (Roberts 2015a, 4). Experiments using requests have been tried by the Open Society Justice Initiative (2006) to selected countries and Access Info Europe (2014) to the European Union. In countries as diverse as New Zealand, Mexico and Brazil responses have been found to be variable when tested (Price 2006; Lagunes 2006; Michener and Rodrigues 2015). An examination of village-level openness in England found low levels of response (John et al. 2015). A series of dual requests to schools and police forces in the US also found disappointing response rates and better answers from more legalistically worded requests (Cuillier 2010). This is not to say that the requests cannot make an impact: one experiment in India involving RTI requests to help process voting registration found that the use of a request 'results in dramatically faster processing times' and is 'almost as effective as bribery' and claimed that officials feared that non-compliance would hinder their career (Peisakhin 2012, 148). Nevertheless, success and smooth operation should not be assumed.

A further difficulty concerns who is using the laws. Reflecting broader patterns of participation, certain groups such as NGOs and journalists act as a 'vanguard' pushing the boundaries of the Act (Dunion 2011). In the UK users reflect the broader biases in political participation in terms of gender, education and background (Hazell et al. 2010). The only detailed, systematic research in India found requesters to be over 90% male, with few requests from women, the very poor or marginalised groups (Raag/NCPRI 2009, 8). Rural requesters made up only 14% of all requesters, despite representing 70% of India's population (Raag/CES 2014, 61). Consequently, RTI use is driven by proxies, primarily NGOs led by middle-class activists. Webb (2012) argues that in India this use by the educated middle class in 'brokerage and mediation' is exactly the situation that RTI, as a social leveller, was intended to avoid, and states that many of the 'opaque and informal conduits' that the RTI Act seeks to close are lifelines and 'essential to allow the urban poor to survive' (207).

Access and use can be changed through technology. As well as 'requester sites' developed in the UK, the RTI Act has led to the development of a national telephone helpline, video appeal hearings for remote locations and experiments with FOI requests via text (Calland and Bentley 2013; Roberts 2010). The US and elsewhere has also seen the development of crowdsourced requester forums, bringing together activists and journalists.

### Supporters

The new regime is supported by the same amalgam of civil society bodies that pushed for FOI, who continue to act as bulwarks against detrimental change and campaigners for reform. As seen in the cases here, the alliances stretch from national and local media to members of the legislature, opposition parties and frequently a broad swathe of civil liberties NGOs, now frequently joined by digital activists, hackers and champions of Open Data (Fenster 2012b).

It is unclear whether, or to what extent, the wider public is aware of legislation. A global survey in 2015 found fewer than 40% of those surveyed aware of their information rights, with a heavy bias towards developed countries, though the data contained some anomalies (World Justice Project 2015). To the extent that it is noticed, any legislation is likely to lead to disappointment when the symbolic rhetoric of access laws gives way to the difficult reality of its operation (Snell 2006). More than a decade after its passage, public knowledge of FOI in Australia appeared low (ALRC/ARC 1995). Indian research expressed concern at low levels of awareness, especially in rural areas and among marginalised groups, even though India is exceptional in having a television programme dedicated to RTI (Roberts 2010; Raag/NCPRI 2009; Raag/CES 2014).

Access to information legislation is likely to be noticed through an unusual event such as a scandal or a crisis. Only in India has RTI stimulated a political campaign that has, in the past few years, begun to gain a toehold within the political system itself. In 2013 a twenty-one-year-old RTI activist was elected head of a village on an anti-corruption ticket, the second such activist to be elected (*Times of India* 24/10/2013). In the elections to the state Delhi Congress in December 2013 the new Aam Admi Party, created and led by long-term RTI campaigners, governed briefly after it won twenty-eight seats out of a total of seventy. Though it performed disappointingly in the 2014 general election it again seized control of Delhi, winning sixty-seven of seventy seats in the State Assembly (*Wall Street Journal* 10/2/2015). More generally, FOI's beneficiaries are diffuse, though its wider support is vocal.

## The interpretation of FOI: who controls the narrative?

Policy is shaped not only by outcomes but also by interpretation. As a policy develops, it is subject to support, opposition and interpretation as 'supporters … seek to deepen the line of development set in motion by an inherited reform, while opponents, may seek to undermine it' (Patashnik and Zelizer 2013, 1072). One of the main conflictual dangers in any policy stems from politicians who 'become sceptical of the success or value' of a policy (1077).

The narrative and meaning of FOI are continuously fought over, as the 'empty signifier' is 'filled' by very different views (Stubbs and Snell 2014). There is frequently a 'struggle' or conflict over the policy and its value. Two sides struggle to control the narrative: Senior politicians and officials argue that FOI is either failed or counter-productive while advocates and supporters trumpet the benefits. The two sides frequently employ different language, with the critics pointing to practical deficiencies and the supporters emphasising the principles and symbolism.

### The sceptical narrative

'How many leaders have come into office determined to work for more open government, only to end by fretting over leaks, seeking new ways to classify documents and questioning the loyalty of outspoken subordinates?' (Bok 1986, 177). From Woodrow Wilson and Harold Wilson to Tony Blair and Barack Obama, disappointment and greater secrecy seem inevitable once in office. However, the powerful norms and democratic symbolism of the law make criticising the right to information politically risky. In 1982, Anthony Scalia, an Associate Justice of the US Supreme Court since the 1980s, set out the difficulties of attacking FOI laws and complained that 'public discussion of the Act displays a range of opinion extending from constructively-critical-but- respectful through admiring to enthralled'. FOI, he argued, was protected by a 'mutually reinforcing praise' and 'veneration' that can 'only be understood as the product of the extraordinary era that produced them' (15). As a result 'the executive branch generally limits its criticism to relatively narrow or technical aspects' (15).

Scalia then set out his own critique, famously describing FOI as 'the Taj Mahal of the Doctrine of Unanticipated Consequences, the Sistine Chapel of Cost-Benefit Analysis Ignored', and criticised the Act's 'foolish extravagances' in cost, that were almost 'incalculable' owing to the law being used by 'corporate lawyers' for fees (1982, 15, 17, 16). He concluded that once the 'fundamentally flawed premises … are accepted' then 'all efforts at even minor reform take on an Alice-in-Wonderland air', as FOI has become 'the ultimate guarantee of responsible government' meaning 'the sweeping aside of all other public and private interests at the mere invocation of the magical words "freedom of information"' (18). He ended by urging a rethink: 'The Act's defects cannot be cured as long as we are dominated by the obsession … that the first line of defence against an arbitrary executive is do-it-yourself oversight by the public and its surrogate, the press' (18).

Since Scalia's critique, a series of recurring tropes have appeared in an increasingly common set of public complaints by politicians. In a semi-acceptable sceptical narrative, senior politicians highlight the 'abuse' of FOI laws, their costs or their effects on how government functions. In 2012 Indian Prime Minister Singh spoke in terms very close to those of Tony Blair, emphasising misuse and claiming that 'there are concerns about frivolous and vexatious use of the Act in demanding information disclosure which cannot possibly serve any public purpose', as 'important legislation should not only be about criticising, ridiculing and running down public authorities' (*Times of India* 12/10/2012). His successor Narendra Modi asked rhetorically during his election campaign whether RTI has 'given something for your stomach to eat' or returned hidden 'black money' (NCPRI/CES 2014, 22).

Others have emphasised the resource costs of the new laws. The former Irish Taoiseach Brian Cowen described FOI as an 'expensive and time consuming aspect of government work' (O'Connor 2010, 3). Northern Ireland's then First Minister Ian Paisley combined abuse with costs when he complained that 'dealing with FOI requests takes up a considerable amount of staff time' and that 'on occasions, the requests are sent in by lazy journalists, who will not do any work, but who think that we should pay them and give them the information that they want' (OIC 2008, 9). As seen in the UK, a third line concerns the 'chilling effect' and impact of laws on government processes. Manmohan Singh repeated on a number of occasions that RTI 'could end up discouraging honest, well-meaning servants from giving full expression to their views' and should not 'adversely affect the deliberative processes in the government' (NCPRI/CES 2014, 22).

Each of these claims rests on, at root, a political perspective. Abuse does occur under all regimes, though what constitutes 'abuse' is subjective and somewhat political. In the UK small groups on both sides 'played games', and in New Zealand there was targeting of departments to slow down work (Hazell et al. 2010; White 2007). Yet these cases are rare. The media, the most frequent target of critics' ire, are a key player in any FOI regime, simply because of their power to spread FOI stories and role as a lynchpin of the coalitions defending FOI (Michener 2015b and 2015d).

In terms of resources, FOI introduces 'concentrated costs and dispersed benefits' (Fung et al. 2007, 117). Precise figures are hard to come by. Critics rarely contextualise the amount or seek to calculate any costs savings emerging from FOI requests through, for example, resources saved from cancellation of a policy (O'Connor 2010). Famously, the claims of costs triggered indirectly by US litigation launched by FOI were equivalent to the amount spent by the US military each year on marching bands (Wald 1984).

As Chapter 7 explained, evidentially any claim to a 'chilling' effect is unclear. Research must prove a negative, and mention of a 'chilling' may, by its very asking, trigger and frame a response (Prat 2006; Stasavage 2006; Stasavage 2007). The somewhat slender evidence elsewhere fits with that of the UK, namely that there is an occasional 'chilling' but one that is not systematic (Badgley et al. 2003;

Gilbert 2000). It appears that few requests aim for the decision-making process (see ALRC/ARC 1995; Hazell et al. 2010). One study in New Zealand found some changes in politically sensitive cases, and there is some evidence for an effect from Canada (White 2007; Roberts 2005). A study of the US Federal Reserve's meetings found greater reluctance in setting out arguments once meetings were opened up (Meade and Stasavage 2008). However, an early study of Australia, Canada and New Zealand discovered no change to ministerial advice or any 'post-it-note' culture but noted that this was a persistent myth (Hazell 1989; White 2007). In India there was 'little evidence' for any alterations to files or records (NCPRI 2009, 28).

To further complicate the issue, other research points to a positive, professionalising effect. The Australian Law Reform Commission found that FOI had helped 'discipline' communications and 'focused decision-makers' minds' (ALRC/ARC 1995, 13). In New Zealand, fifteen years of the OIA had 'improved the quality' of policy advice (Law Commission 1997, 5). Those within public bodies appear similarly uncertain: a survey of Irish local government found that 30% of local officials claimed a 'chilling' effect and just fewer than 50% denied it (McDonagh 2010a, 11). The argument also takes a rather particular view of what constitutes a document. The claims of a sudden 'switch' to working off paper pre-supposes a previously clear and concrete paper trail. Terrill (2000) points out how 'bargaining, deals and decisions are rarely made using paper' and how documents 'only record certain moments, but often not the reason they take the shape they do' (115). More importantly, the claim ignores the many other powerful forces acting upon records and conflates FOI with, for example, intricate systems of leaks or semi-authorised disclosures (Pozen 2013). Nevertheless the three lines of attack constitute the public or front-facing base of the sceptical narrative.

### Going off FOI

Aside from these concrete complaints, politicians frequently, if not invariably, 'go off' FOI in private because of a mix of annoyance and disappointment, though this is rarely stated.

Transparency is a disruptive instrument, springing surprises and the unexpected. Gordon Brown spoke of how 'Freedom of Information (FoI) can be inconvenient, at times frustrating and indeed embarrassing for governments' (BBC 25/10/2007). It can distract, highlight major and minor scandals and, in its ultimate 'disruptive' form in Canada, Australia and Ireland, lead to ministerial resignations (see Hazell et al. 2010). Politicians' complaints play into a wider set of claims in relation to the many and growing limitations that politicians feel there are on modern government, of which FOI is a part and a powerful symbol (see the Conclusion and also Heclo 1999).

The disillusion and annoyance may be reinforced by exactly how senior politicians and officials meet FOI in their work. Most people high up in an organisation see only a very small percentage of requests, and generally meet them in one of two ways, either via media stories or through their organisation. Internally, most senior officials and politicians are often notified of or copied into the 1 or 2% of particularly troublesome requests, sensitive cases or, worst of all, those involving them. The top of an organisation thus obtains a very selective, and very negative, view of what is being asked. In the UK, it is probable that the 2005 Labour Cabinet (many of whom were in the government that passed the Act) first thought about the Act seriously when a request asked for the Cabinet discussions over the legality of the invasion of Iraq. Two different sources detail Tony Blair's unhappiness at the release under FOI of the seemingly minor issue of who had visited the Prime Ministerial residence (Rawnsley 2010; Powell 2010).

Research in the UK appeared to bear this out. In 2016 a series of FOI requests made by the author to selected government departments and other bodies asked how many times senior politicians encountered the law between 1 June and 1 September 2015 (see Table 10.1). Most government departments appeared to involve ministers only when an MP made the request or for those cases involving section 36 of the Act in inherently sensitive areas concerning decision-making. Other bodies appeared to have rather different approaches. The Office of the Mayor of London claimed that the Mayor himself did not see requests, while the respec-

**Table 10.1** Details of all UK FOI requests signed off or seen by a minister (or equivalent) between 1 June and 1 September 2015

| Department or public body | System/procedure for notification |
| --- | --- |
| HM Treasury | Not known – only when section 36 engaged (over the protection of decision-making) |
| Ministry of Defence | Not known – only when section 36 engaged or an FOI request is made by an MP |
| Department of Culture, Media and Sport | Only when section 36 engaged – example of an FOI request over the return of the Elgin marbles |
| Department of Health | Only when section 36 engaged – example of an FOI request over complaints to the BBC over health coverage |
| National Assembly of Wales | Ministers 'sighted on all responses' but no formal guidance |
| Office of the First Minister and Deputy First Minister (Northern Irish Assembly) | Section 36 case over FOI discussion between Belfast and London |
| Mayor of London | No case in time period. Dealt with and seen on a 'case by case' basis according to 'perceived sensitivity' (dealt with by Deputy Mayor or mayoral staff) |

*Source*: Author's FOI requests.

tive ministers in the Welsh executive appeared to have sight of all requests in their portfolio area, though whether or not they are in fact seen is unclear. The Northern Irish executive cited only one request seen by the First Minister or Deputy First Minister relating, interestingly, to communications with London regarding the FOI Act. Across the bodies, any senior figure's view of FOI would be narrow and partial.

As well as annoyance, for those politicians who genuinely 'believed' in openness or its instrumental effects, there may be disappointment at the 'oversell' of passage – that the law would increase trust or bring efficiency (Hazell et al. 2010). This can give way to a sense that FOI is not being used by the 'right' users or in the correct way. Kreiss speaks of the 'stubborn persistence' among politicians of the belief that there exist 'atomistic, rational and general interest citizen[s]' (2015b, 2, 1). Schudson speaks of how some politicians harbour hope in an 'idealised good citizen', an assumption built around a public that can somehow be 'neutrally directed … to shared ends' (in Kreiss 2015b, 4).

## Supporting FOI

Against the sceptical narrative from within government are pitted the 'permanent user coalitions', a growing alliance of activists, journalists and politicians who are supportive of openness. They are frequently built around the pro-FOI groups like CFOI in the UK or NCPRI in India. These alliances stretch across the media and Parliament to often wide groups of NGOs and bodies such as trade unions. These diverse groups, whether users or not, support the principle of FOI and unite around the symbolism of the law. They block any attempts to amend legislation, portraying any 'dismantling' as an attack on democracy and entrenched 'rights' and draw on the moral and normative arguments connected to openness to question the government's motives for doing so, frequently alleging a desire for secrecy or to hide corruption (Fenster 2012b). Over time, FOI has become deeply rooted in a powerful narrative concerning its democratic importance or deliberative ideals, linked to concerns for the common good and public interest and a host of other basic rights to life or expression. The case is made more powerful as internationally the right to information moves closer to becoming a 'free standing moral' or legal right (Barberis 2010; McDonagh 2013).

These alliances can be and are quickly mobilised in defence of FOI and rapidly pull together publicity and attention, threatening to resist any change in the media, legislature and elsewhere. Detrimental changes to laws are fought in newspapers, in letter-writing campaigns and by recruiting members of legislatures to fight the passage. Most visibly in India, RTI advocates organised a wave of protests and sit-ins against a mooted change (Singh 2011).

The battle over interpretation is not a 'winnable' conflict but is symptomatic of the different perspectives, where even evidence is politicised and, to an extent, subjective. The conflict is unending, and any FOI law is marked by a continuous 'fighting on the borders' (Hazell et al. 2010).

## Institutional support for FOI

A third aspect of the longevity of any policy is the question of whether it is receiving the appropriate level of co-operation from the institutions and mechanisms appointed to implement it (Patashnik and Zelizer 2013, 1077). The surprise is, given political reactions, the level of principled support for FOI. The central fact of many of the laws studied is the level of bureaucratic support or acceptance:

> One of the truisms of FOI law reform is that it is brought in on a wave of government enthusiasm against public service scepticism yet the public service then learns to live with it at about the same pace that government antagonism grows. (McMillan 2002, 10)

Officials within organisations in New Zealand, the UK and US appear broadly supportive, or at least broadly acquiescent, towards FOI and co-operate with it, even if they find it troublesome to deal with in practice (Price 2006; Kimball 2012; Hazell et al. 2010).

This is more surprising given the host of common 'supply side problems', which stretch from 'benign problems, such as the ... lack of staff and equipment' to 'deliberate subversion' (Roberts 2015a, 4). Crucial to the success of any FOI law is the knowledge and availability of staff with the resources to deal with requests. Difficulties with administrative capacity or awareness can seriously undermine both the operation and any consequent benefits (Snell 2006; Roberts 2012). Once in place all laws often exhibit delay, lack of response and cumbersome and slow appeal systems (Hazell et al. 2010). New Zealand's 1997 and 2012 Law Commission reviews outlined the typical problems: 'tardiness' of response, the burden of low requests, resistance and poor coordination (Law Commission 2012). In Australia, for example, FOI systems have been 'starved' of resources and gridlocked in the 1980s and again in the early 2010s (Roberts 2012; Snell 2001). In India RTI has been seriously impeded by 'poor record management, inadequate budgets, [a] wrong mind set of civil servants, lack of human resources and lack of training and knowledge about the provisions of the Act' (Raag/NCPRI 2009, 27).

The question is whether organisations go further in actively resisting or sabotaging laws. Snell, drawing on Roberts, elaborated a series of degrees of response, from co-operation to neglect and outright adversarialism (2006). To enter the 'black box' of institutional reaction, it appears that exact responses are conditioned by the context, the persons involved and the issue at stake (Meijer 2014; Piotrowksi 2010; Welch 2012; Pasquier and Villeneuve 2007). Numerous studies have shown how departments or bodies react differently. Traditionally secretive or 'sensitive' bodies (such as defence, foreign affairs or interior ministries) find openness more challenging. There is evidence of varying institutional responses to FOI *within* single public bodies (Piotrowksi 2010; Welch 2012; Worthy 2013). Roberts (2005) identified a series of sophisticated strategies in Canada designed to minimise the fallout from sensitive or controversial requests. Authorities or departments that were already open dealt with FOI better than those who viewed it as an additional regulatory burden (Worthy 2013).

There may be a 'street-level' or 'frontline' difference in how or whether FOI works at different levels or across bodies (Gofen 2014; Wilson 2015). This may consist of simple 'divergence', 'sabotage' or even 'creative insubordination' (Gofen 2014, 474). The problem of 'tall mountains and the emperor far away' may exert an influence for those insulated from requests, publicity or central monitoring who may exhibit less awareness or compliance.

## FOI laws: dismantling, expansion or rebooting elsewhere

### Push-back and dismantling laws?

There have been few overt attempts to rescind FOI laws. The former New Zealand Prime Minister Geoffrey Palmer explained why:

> What would be the reaction if there was a serious proposal to repeal the Act and go back to the Official Secrets Act? Put in that way, the case in favour …is clearly unanswerable. There would be no political or public support a move to return to the way things were before the Act. It would be seen as undemocratic. I doubt that any political party that would be prepared even to propose it. (2007, 33)

Terrill quotes a Tasmanian politician explaining that no government would be 'stupid' enough to do so directly but could simply 'amend' a law into toothlessness (2000).

Laws can, however, be dismantled (see Chapter 7). The lowest level of such dismantling consists of 'negative signals', frequently taking the form of speeches, missives or signals against openness. As shown above, numerous politicians have criticised FOI. On a more formal level, in the US memoranda from Attorney Generals have come to be seen as a clear signal of how successive administrations viewed FOI. In 2001 a note from the Attorney General John Ashcroft, while committing to be 'fully compliant', also reminded officials of the need for 'efficient government' and to 'fully consider' protections, ending ominously with the statement that the Department of Justice would fully 'defend your decision' (Blanton 2006).

Laws can also be changed and amended. Fees for making requests have been a frequent source of change and a barometer of enthusiasm; in Ireland they have been introduced in 2003 and abolished in 2014 (see Chapter 9). Exemptions can be shifted, and more subtle ways can be found. Resources and costs are a key weakness. Australian governments starved FOI of resources in the 1980s, a pattern later emulated elsewhere from California to the Netherlands (Roberts 2012; Snell 2001). Claims of savings are often drivers for scaling back: in 2012 the Abbott government in Australia, intending originally to abolish the new post of Information Commissioner created in 2010 and citing financial savings, was blocked by the Senate. Instead the funding was cut, leaving the Commission in a legal limbo (Popple 2014).

A more stealthy approach is to simply neglect what needs to be done in order to sustain the operation or institutions of a regime, as in the case of Modhi's failure for a year to appoint a Chief Information Commissioner. The trend towards outsourcing, deregulation and delegation also creates holes in FOI coverage over time, as privatisation takes bodies out of legal reach (Roberts 2006). Simply not updating FOI regimes when new bodies or institutions such as independent schools or hospitals are made, can gradually widen FOI gaps. Other evasions can involve using private emails or hidden communications, as seen in the UK and US (Burgess 2015).

Other laws, amendments and legal orders can also be used to 'trim' or erode the reach of laws, often enabled by political contexts. In one of the most systematic and powerful moves against openness, the administration of George W. Bush made a series of sustained secrecy reforms in the aftermath of September 11, re-classifying millions of documents, using executive orders to restrict access to Presidential papers and sending out clearly restrictive memoranda (Roberts 2006). Australia's resource cuts were swiftly followed up with changes to the law limiting what parts of the Australian Parliament were subject to FOI. Japan in 2014 passed secrecy legislation that cut into its FOI, while the relaunched Danish FOI Act in 2013 added stronger protections for policy-making (*Huffington Post* 10/5/2014; Dahllhöf 2016).

Dismantling is easier said than done. The case of the UK shows a series of 'floated ideas', but few get far (see Chapter 7). The effect of lighter signals is mixed, and research by the National Security Archive found that successive memoranda had little effect on the operation of FOI (National Security Archive 2013; Roberts 2006). More overt attempts inevitably attract attention, and here the symbolic potency of FOI, combined with a powerful constituency, acts as a powerful impediment to both intent and action. When dismantling does take place, as in Ireland, it frequently 'clusters', with various changes enacted at once as the anti-FOI floodgates open.

The danger for political leaders is the damage such change can do to reputations. Between 2013 and 2014 the Japanese Prime Minister Shinzo Abe saw his personal support fall by 10% and an unprecedented fourteen-point drop in support for the government to 57% when he pushed a controversial state secrecy Bill (*Japan Times* 24/11/2013; Reuters 9/12/2013). In the same year in Canada, the Conservative Prime Minister Stephen Harper was damaged by perceptions concerning budget secrecy, with 69% of those polled viewing his government as 'too secretive' and 63% thinking the government had 'failed to live up' to be the promise of being 'open and transparent' (RCI 3/4/2013). Being caught evading FOI can be equally damaging. Perhaps the most high-profile example was that of Hillary Clinton, whose use of a private email server for apparently public, and classified, communications while Secretary of State came under intense media scrutiny. In October 2013 48% of voters questioned her honesty and 33% thought she had 'something to hide'. Between 2015 and 2016, following a series of investigations, the controversy continued to influence the views of at least some voters (Polling Report 2015). The 'clustering effect' of being seen as secretive followed when Clinton refused in 2016 to release transcripts of private speeches made to Wall Street hedge funds (Reuters 27/2/2016).

## Strengthening and expansion

Expanding FOI can be done through a similar series of graded moves. Politicians do speak in favour of FOI. One notable example is the UK Prime Minister Gordon Brown, who, in the first few months of his premiership, reversed the dismantling floated by Tony Blair and, in a speech redolent with symbolism, proposed extending the FOI and reducing the 'closure' period of archival records. Brown linked openness to a long struggle for freedoms and liberties in the UK:

> Because liberty cannot flourish in the darkness, our rights and freedoms are protected by the daylight of public scrutiny as much as by the decisions of Parliament or independent judges. So it is clear that to protect individual liberty we should have the freest possible flow of information between government and the people. (BBC 25/10/2007)

Gordon Brown's 2007 speech was, at least in part, intended to be a break with the 'control' of his predecessor, though an advisor claims that his archival reform was motived by a wish to 'open up' the royal family (McBride 2013). In opposition, his successor David Cameron pledged 'true Freedom of Information' through a greater use of Open Data and technology, and again in office promised a 'transparency revolution' with the aim of making 'in time … our government one of the most open and transparent in the world' (BBC 25/6/2009; Prime Minister's Office 29/5/2010). In the US memoranda have also signalled openness, with Clinton's Attorney General Reno reminding officials to comply with 'the letter and the spirit of FOI' and that the Act is the 'cornerstone of democracy' (National Security Archive 2013).

The 'flux' of legal and political alterations means laws can often 'creep' outwards. In India legal rulings made formerly public bodies subject to the RTI Act, and there was debate about extending the Act to cover the stock exchange (Roberts 2010). Between 2012 and 2013 there was a battle to open up both the Indian Cricket Board and political parties to RTI. Laws are often updated to cover new bodies, as occurred in New Zealand in 1987 (to cover hospital and education boards) and in the UK in 2010s (to cover examination boards and other bodies). They are also amended to change restrictive instruments within the law, as when New Zealand altered its veto power and time limits in 1987. In many jurisdictions the appeal system is also subject to change: the US created a new equivalent of an Information Commissioner in 2007, and Australia has repeatedly reshuffled its Commissioner since 2010.

The increasingly important interface with public and private bodies remains a grey area, with different laws adopting different approaches. The Nigerian and South African laws specifically cover private bodies. Other regimes have opted for various means of coverage: the UK has opted for contractual enforcement, and Ireland for coverage of any organisation receiving 'substantial' funds, while the Indian RTI law, partly as a compromise, took an innovative approach allowing access to any private information to which the Indian government had access as a result of other laws (Sharma 2015).

As well as FOI laws themselves, other legislation may support or strengthen FOI in an emerging ecosystem. The US FOIA of 1974 was accompanied by the Government in the Sunshine Act of 1976, mandating open meetings, and the Presidential Records Act and Ethics in Government Acts of 1978 (Roberts 2006). In India RTI was twinned with the National Rural Employment Guarantee Act 2005, designed to provide a minimum standard of employment for the rural poor, which itself mandated disclosure of payroll records as well as project documents (Shankar et al. 2011; Roberts 2010). In 2013 a new *Lokpal* or ombudsman was created to oversee government, triggered in part by the ongoing corruption campaign in India driven by RTI.

There may also be wider, less predictable triggers of change. In New Zealand, the switch from a first-past-the post electoral system to a MMP (mixed-member proportional) one was widely seen as having a decisive effect on the law. The former Prime Minister Geoffrey Palmer (2007) suggested that 'the operation of the OIA has been under greater pressure, and pressure from more points of view, under MMP than it was before'. The increased political competition introduced by proportional representation meant a greater use of OIA by MPs in Parliament. This became a 'major feature of the OIA landscape' as more parties used requests with a 'political purpose', with a knock-on effect on a number of constitutional conventions (Law Commission 2010, 10).

At the far end of the expansion is what can be seen as a decisive 're-boot' of legislation. As well as Ireland, which rebooted its legislation in 2014 (see Chapter 9), a number of countries have sought to decisively upgrade aged legislation. In Italy, the new Prime Minister promised, via tweet in 2012, a new FOI to replace the elderly Italian quasi-access law of the early 1990s, as part of a set of wider public administration reforms (Polisblog 2014). However, as of 2015 the new law remained in draft and was yet to arrive, despite strong Parliamentary and campaigning pressure. In 2009 the new Australian government, again distancing itself from the practices of its predecessor, launched what amounted to a substantial reboot altering the Act from a 'reactive' to a 'proactive' law (Popple 2014). The reforms included the abolition of up-front fees for requests and exemption certificates and the creation of a new Office of the Australian Information Commissioner that included both an Information Commissioner and an FOI commissioner (Australian Government 2013). These changes were curtailed by the successor government (Popple 2014).

Perhaps the most high-profile recent reboot was that of Barack Obama in 2009, which grew 'out of a rejection' of the Bush administration, what Obama called 'one of the most secretive, closed administrations in American history' (Coglianese 2009). For Obama the candidate, transparency worked as a 'political strategy', providing 'a major theme at the start of his administration' (Coglianese 2009, 539). Arguably, Obama believed in it as a principle but, more importantly, in the short term his support for it 'not only distances his administration from his unpopular predecessor's, but transparency sells well. Everyone seems to favour it, whether on the political left or the right' (539).

Obama's administration thus began with 'a radical break from the notoriously secrecy-oriented George W. Bush Administration' (Krotoszynski 2011, 460). His inaugural address promised that 'transparency and the rule of law will be the touchstones of this presidency', and on the first day two open government memoranda and an open government directive were issued, as well as a rescinding of the Ashcroft memorandum and a reversal of his predecessor's restrictions on access to Presidential Archives (Ellington 2013, 133). Obama's memorandum dealt with openness in ringing terms:

> A democracy requires accountability, and accountability requires transparency. As Justice Louis Brandeis wrote, 'sunlight is said to be the best of disinfectants.' In our democracy, the Freedom of Information Act (FOIA), which encourages accountability through transparency, is the most prominent expression of a profound national commitment to ensuring an open Government. The Freedom of Information Act should be administered with a clear presumption: In the face of doubt, openness prevails. All agencies should adopt a presumption in favor of disclosure ... to usher in a new era of open Government. (White House 2009)

Obama's reforms were more than simply a reboot. FOI was combined with new online experiments in Open Data, including a Federal spending tracker (Recovery. gov), a coordinating Transparency Board and website and other symbolic moves such as the opening up of White House visitors' log book (Peled 2011). In December of 2009, Obama's Executive Order 13,526 revised the Federal government's system of classifying information (Krotoszynski 2011, 460).

However, expansionary promises and public support for openness bring dangers of disappointment and backfire. Obama's reforms appear a case in point. Coglianese (2009) wrote of how 'in the medium to long term, though, the political calculus does not work out so clearly in Obama's strategic favour'. The promises 'raised public expectations that are ... difficult to meet' and made Obama 'vulnerable to charges of hypocrisy by the right' (539). One study argued that by 2011 Obama's reforms were 'more theoretical than real' and were quickly undermined (Krotoszynski 2011, 466). His Open Data reforms were blocked by 'passive-aggressive' resistance and a lack of co-operation amid silos and inter-departmental battles, while his FOI changes appeared to have little effect (Peled 2011; National

Security Archive 2013; National Security Archive 2014). Ellington (2013) concluded that Obama's declassification, particularly his December 2009 Executive Order, made serious moves forward but that his use of state secrecy privileges and his later aggressive pursuit of leak suspects, which 'went beyond anything seriously contemplated by even the very opaque Bush administration', undermined his symbolic claims (144). In 2016 the US House of Representatives Committee on Oversight and Government Reform declared that FOIA under Obama was 'broken'. The law was characterised by delays, abuse of exemptions and, perhaps most damning, the political involvement of the White House in blocking requests. There had developed a 'culture of unresponsiveness', and the committee accused the 'executive of adopting an unlawful presumption in favour of secrecy' (Committee on Oversight and Government Reform 2016, 6).

There is political risk not only in reversing openness. Promises of transparency often come back to haunt politicians, and there is an ever-present danger that anyone promising or championing openness will, at some point, be hoisted by their own petard. As well as his repeated commitment to transparency generally, David Cameron made a very high-profile bid to tackle tax evasion through Beneficial Ownership, and spoke out repeatedly against tax havens, not once but three times: in his speech at the Open Government Partnership summit in 2013, in his letter to all British Overseas Territories and Crown Dependencies in 2014 and his berating of tax havens again in 2015 (Worthy 2015b). In 2016 the mega-leak of the so-called Panama Papers showed how Cameron had benefited from his father's offshore tax arrangements. The charge opened him up to charges of hypocrisy and double standards, leading to calls for his resignation. Polling found that his ratings slipped sharply (YouGov 8/4/2016). David Cameron, in a bid to stave off damage, became the first UK Prime Minister to publish his tax returns, something he had promised to do in 2012. He was followed by a slew of other party leaders and pressure for all MPs to follow suit.

### Conclusion: the transparency and accountability ecosystem

FOI regimes are dynamic and fluid. Once enacted they are supported, opposed and fought over by the same groups that battled over their passage. The battle takes place in various venues, from courts to the media and legislature, while underneath flows of requests push laws in new directions. The very process of operation, from unpredictable use to rulings, gives them an independent, chaotic momentum, particularly as technology brings innovation, newer ways of making FOI work and parallel channels of openness. The battle is also fought out on a symbolic level as sceptics' claims of concrete difficulties clash with the symbolic claims for democracy. Supporters draw on FOI's powerful narrative, and entrenched support in the media and legislature is often, but not always, sufficient to halt all but the most determined, or clever, changes.

Access to information regimes have helped to create a new landscape and sit in 'enabling environments' (see Scrollini 2013). Kreimer (2008) describes an 'ecology of transparency' composed of 'countervailing mechanisms of control' and a 'network of other structural checks' (1016):

> to the extent that FOIA has functioned as an effective check, it has been a part of an ecology of transparency that includes the permanent infrastructure of federal civil servants with integrity, internal watchdogs, reasonably open opportunities to publish and share information, and a set of civil society actors capable of pursuing prolonged campaigns for disclosure. (1017)

Fenster (2016) maps theses differing 'laws, institutions, and technologies':

> most prominently, in the legal rights and administrative obligations that FOI and related laws have created [but also] through civil society organizations ... by deploying information technologies that make government data widely available and usable through open source platforms; and through vigilante leaking of massive caches of government documents, as perpetrated most famously by WikiLeaks and Edward Snowden. (276)

Schudson (2010) points out how there is an ever-growing network of 'political observatories' within this ecosystem, all gathering information, made up of a mixture of citizen bloggers, NGOs and independent auditors (2010).

As Table 10.2 shows, transparency laws sit on a spectrum of instruments, a more or less interlocking landscape of new and old tools of openness and accountability (Fung et al. 2007). These include targeted sector-specific or body-specific laws covering areas from financial products to food labelling, whistle-blowing laws and leaks all the way to the 'radical transparency' or 'vigilantism' of WikiLeaks (see Fenster 2012a; Roberts 2012).

Together, these bodies mix formal and informal 'monitory' bodies and various pieces of 'old' and 'new' technology (see Schudson 2015; Keane 2009; Edgerton

**Table 10.2** The transparency and accountability ecosystem in the UK

| Instrument | Definition | UK examples |
|---|---|---|
| Laws and regulations | Access laws, either general or sector-specific 'targeted laws', whistle-blowing laws | FOI Act, environmental information regulations, public data re-use laws, Local Government Audit Act 2011, Local Government Transparency Code 2015 |
| Innovations and technology | Open Data sites, leak platforms, Alavateli sites, e-petition sites | Whatdotheyknow.com, data.gov or data.gov.uk, WikiLeaks, Panama Papers |
| Monitory bodies | Formal or informal watchdogs | IPSA, the Tax Payers' Alliance, the Bureau of Investigative Journalism |

2011). The new ecosystem is chaotic but also highly responsive and co-evolutionary, with rules and bodies interacting, creating alliances or leading to new innovations, as seen with crowd-funded 'requesting' sites like Muck Rock in the US or Right to Know in Ireland. The boundaries between and legality of each of these instruments is ever shifting and changing, with grey areas where plants become leaks and legal frameworks are dissolved or bypassed (Pozen 2013; Fenster 2012a).

This new environment carries the same 'democratic, participatory and rights orientated ethos' that gave birth to FOI itself (Schudson 2013a, 3). These new watchdogs draw on low-cost tools including access to information laws, broader open government policies and targeted transparency (Fung 2013, 189). Some of the new innovations, such as Open Data, broadly follow the path and pattern of FOI as structured means of accessing government information and data. However, layered atop are more dynamic and less controlled instruments, from social media to mass leaks, that often take a more 'hybrid form' (Birchall 2014, 84). FOI is now part of this diverse armoury, which can be used by potential 'veto wielders' to exercise 'counter-democratic control' (Schudson 2015).

The new ecosystem may also bring new forms of political activity, from 'e-expression' to Statactivism, the use of 'mobilization of statistics' to drive action (Gibson and Cantijoch 2013; Bruno et al. 2014). It is set to continue changing as new technology offers new ways of bringing transparency and citizen control. For example, the development of Distributed Ledger Technology, known as 'Blockchain', potentially offers more decentralised, democratic and participatory ways of storing data and managing information (Wright and De Filippi 2015). The UK government's Chief Scientist urged it to take advantage of the new transparency potential of this technology (Government Office for Science 2016). The ecosystem forms part of a new political information cycle that is gradually supplementing the mainstream media, offering new participants avenues into influencing politics built around principles of 'availability, proportionality, accessibility, and actionability' (Chadwick 2013; Fung 2013, 191).

The hybrid of formal and informal oversight bodies is creating a 'permanent' and 'continuous' oversight of government (Schudson 2015, 237). Various terms have been mooted for this new form, from 'monitory' democracy to 'counter-availing' power, though it also resembles Bentham's 'system of distrust' and a kind of *terosocracy* of continual fluid watching or surveillance (Keane 2009; Schudson 2015; Deleuze 1992; Edgerton 2011). Whether such activity is positive or negative remains a matter of some dispute, as does the question of whether such action merely 'monitors' government or becomes a true locus of 'counter-availing' democratic power.

This new environment offers important lessons for the limitations of openness: the 'radical transparency' of WikiLeaks and Edward Snowden challenges the 'balance' with formal transparency systems but also the claims of transformative change (Birchall 2014; Fenster 2012a; Roberts 2012). The failure of WikiLeaks to kick-start change showed how the 'simple logic' of 'radical transparency can be defeated' and demonstrated the need for information to exist in the right context (Roberts 2012). Yet the radical transparency itself exposes the often hidden values within the universalising transparency project and offers an alternative to the 'technocratic' and 'de-politicised' mainstream conception (Birchall 2014).

FOI now sits within a very different 'political information cycle' from that of even a decade ago. On the one hand this could potentially open up the political environment to new actors and groups, or greatly empower those already present (Chadwick 2013; Scrollini 2013). On the other it begs the question of whether transparency can have a 'transformative potential' on a 'public too dispersed' and in an 'information environment too saturated' (Fenster 2012a, 807).

# Conclusion:
# why do governments pass FOI laws?

FOI 'may be the constitutional development of the Twentieth Century – what the franchise was to the Nineteenth' (Keith 1984, 31). Yet how do these voteless laws come to be? Amid all the competing pressures, there is no substantial part of the electorate clamouring for them, while few reforms succeed in potentially threatening so many bodies at once. For any budding politician, FOI appears to be the ultimate self-denying, if not self-damaging, ordinance.

The symbolic power and force surrounding FOI places it onto the agenda and makes it hard to obviously back down from. Once committed, politicians fear the damage to their promises and moral capital, and are reluctant to oppose them outright. However, FOI's resonance alone is not enough to overcome the institutional barriers and obstacles, and the policies are fought over at the level of detail and, frequently, diluted. Behind closed doors, compromises and manoeuvres carry weakened laws to the statute book.

## Why do governments pass FOI laws?

The passage and operation of FOI has been likened to a 'kind of morality play' (Wald 1984, 649). There is frequently both willingness and a pressure towards transparency as laws emerge from a volatile mix of principle, politics and symbolism (Michener 2015c).

Numerous actors have, at least some of the time and to some extent, genuinely believed in transparency as a political ideal. Transparency laws, at least in theory, offer a politician a whole range of potential beneficial effects. Some are abstract and symbolic, positioning an actor as a champion, a believer in democracy, or offering them a 'badge' of progressive values. FOI can be a form of political insurance, either binding together coalitions as an inter-party 'fire alarm' or, more long-term, ensuring access to information in the future (Michener 2015b; Berliner 2014). There is also, as seen with Tony Blair, an almost irresistible political advantage in using openness to damage an opponent. These different 'high' and 'low' motivations often, and conveniently, co-exist.

The political pressures are also numerous (Berliner 2014). At the outset pressure is frequently gradual and slow-moving, but it gathers energy and momentum as the media, campaigners and the legislature join forces. FOI is sometimes 'presented' to a government by court rulings, draft legislation or civil society campaigns. An unintended 'drift' towards openness can provide powerful moments for building the case, as scandals over secrecy erode the case for information control. As seen in India and the UK, the piecemeal build-up of openness through targeted or local legislation can gradually strengthen the case for FOI from the bottom upwards, offering advocates institutional 'gaps' for leverage.

Given the lack of electoral interest, a number of other institutions supply the momentum and act as 'proxy' forces for the public interest. Foremost is what is often a steadily growing network of coalitions that develop a reach across civil society. The organisations are frequently built around a core FOI group (such as CFOI or NCPRI) and then extend across the national and local media and civil rights groups to lawyers, advocates, artists and trade unions. Political parties are also vital players and strong supporters. Parties view FOI as an issue of principle but also come to self-identify with the policy and what it means. FOI may be a result of partisan politics, when competition pressures actors to neutralise any advantage (Berliner 2015). Legislatures as a whole become motors of reform, sites of cross-party alliances expressed through formal bodies such as committees or draft legislation. Though frequently blamed by politicians, parts of the official machine can initiate calls for FOI, as seen in Ireland, India and the UK. As seen with other openness legislation, the motives for supporting are as varied as for opposing it. Transparency legislation can be used to build alliance or 'lock in' governments to favoured policy or to get credit internationally (David-Barrett and Okamura 2016).

Beyond these considerations of principle and politics are a series of symbolic motives (Michener 2011). FOI has a symbolic potency that sends important signals of a government's intent: the ideal and idea of 'Freedom of Information' or 'Right to Information' carries a powerful series of messages. As the policy has spread around the world it has become 'the dramatically satisfying answer to every crisis and question about the state' (Fenster 2015, 151).

First, it symbolises radical change. At its most fundamental, FOI is about the redistribution of power over one of the most fundamental and fought-over resources in politics. It symbolises a popular transfer of sovereignty of power and influence from an elite to the populace. The radical aura of 'levelling' and 'equality' still clings to it, and it remains a 'threat' to old 'elites' and a potent promise to voters to open up bureaucracies and hand political control to the 'people'. Allowing citizens to 'see' and 'understand' what is done in their name offers a profoundly empowering narrative.

Second, FOI carries a powerful moral force. It is frequently presented as a 'recalibration' of relations between government and governed, an offer to enhance accountability, popular participation and public trust (Fenster 2012b). It signals to the populace that a government is willing to be observed and challenged, and, in doing so, implies that there is 'nothing to hide' and no malign intentions or corrupt motive. The idea of trust is a bonding idea, as government trusts the populace with the power.

Third, FOI offers a modernising symbol of an 'open' society. An FOI law brings new democratic freedoms, as a 'deepening' of democracy, and bringing of rights 'up to date', especially as FOI is now closely bound up in the language of basic human rights (Birkinshaw 2006; McDonagh 2013).

Together these three components make for a strong 'narrative identity' and a 'distinctive position' (Carter and Jacobs 2014, 138). Few politicians can ignore or resist the political credibility that can be gained from being seen to 'empower the public' and 'open up' government (Berliner 2014; Lemov 2011). Responding to a scandal with the 'radicalism' and 'morality' of FOI can potentially turn a political crisis or problem into an advantage, satisfying party members and the media that a solution has been found (Birchall 2014). In India the government willingly embraced the symbolic narrative as a means of appearing different from previous governments and responsive to grassroots demands (Sharma 2015).

Most FOI laws gain added symbolism and energy from their context. Some governments appear born to openness, others assume it, and some have it thrust upon them. Laws are frequently passed amid periods of change and challenge, originating, as Roberts (2015b) argues, as a 'long term reaction' against 'executive power' (6). FOI frequently appears as part of a parcel of redistributing and re-orientating power, as with Whitlam's transformative programme, Johnson's Great Society agenda or Blair's radical constitutional reform. It may also serve, as in Ireland, as a legacy of a reformist government, a final parting gift to empower the public (Michener 2011). These conducive contexts lend any law even greater symbolism as part of a 'greater reform' and 'empowerment'. They also lends the policy momentum and profile, making FOI appear to be an idea whose 'time has come'.

### Symbolism and moral capital

The symbolic power of FOI places it on the agenda of a government and, once the process is begun, makes backing away difficult. It proves infectious, at least among the small coalitions pushing for it. It mobilises, energises and spreads among those key groups bound to support it, especially as it is suffused with democratic norms (Fenster 2012b). The concept is elastic and malleable enough to hold varied groups together, from businesses to NGOs and across ideological divides (Stubbs and Snell 2014). Parties and leaderships come to feel that the symbolism is part of a self-image of a radical, moral and modernising force. This is especially salient when the government (or at least the leader) is new.

As well as acting as a propellant towards reform, FOI also works as barrier to retreat. The promise of FOI, bound up in self-image and frequently involving public or manifesto promises, makes wholesale retreat difficult. Superficially, this should not be so. Governments reneging on a commitment to FOI would be unlikely to sustain any lasting electoral damage. Though politicians from the US and Australia have behaved as if it did, the direct electoral consequences of any outright rejection of FOI appear to be slight or non-existent (Lemov 2011).

However, the significance of the symbolism lies in the losing or gaining of 'moral capital' (Birchall 2014; Michener 2009). Kane (2001) argues that this capital constitutes a 'moral grounding' for a politician, part of the 'fundamental values' that the public use to 'judge the agent or institution to be both faithful and effective' and a 'quantum of respect and approval' (10). The idea of 'moral capital has genuine legitimising effects' as it can be of 'great political benefit to the receiver' and serves to 'mobilise' and 'disarm the opposition' and can help in 'creating and exploiting political opportunities that otherwise would not exist' (10–11). Promising FOI bolsters the moral capital of a politician by demonstrating their faithfulness and honesty, their trust in the public and their support for democratic values. As seen with Blair and Obama, it also carries an 'anti-establishment' aura, with the added value of cross-sectional and cross-party appeal (Hood 2010; Kane 2001).

So while the loss of FOI may not be immediately dangerous, the erosion would push the advantages into reverse. Dropping or resisting FOI could make a reformist government or leader appear anti-democratic and distrusted, and could equate to a loss of moral capital. Any backing down would disappoint and raise suspicions as to why and, almost inevitably, what there is to hide, and could create a dangerous narrative about betrayal of people, principle or 'radical' intent. A government's or leader's trust and faithfulness would be eroded, and with it their capacity to make powerful moral arguments, especially if linked to the 'betrayal' of a particular promise. This symbolic betrayal could then have real political consequences. The rejection of FOI would be likely to become a recurrent trope and line of attack for opponents, as well as a policy 'gift' to other political parties. Over time, secrecy scandals, leaks or exposes would be connected to the 'lack' or 'loss' of FOI. This could become a draining 'negative spiral' of lost trust and eroded legitimacy.

However, symbolism alone is not enough. When FOI moves from campaign to formulation the process itself exerts a powerful pressure, as FOI becomes less about symbolic meaning and more about negotiation, manoeuvre and compromise. A complex choreography takes place to reconcile differences, with key actors internally divided and torn between (a few) enthusiastic champions battling ambivalence, ignorance and dislike. The time needed to push proposals forward is the same time in which doubts grow, opposition coalesces and windows close. The detail and complexity of creating legislation are often used for delay, opposition and weakening. Trapped within institutions and processes, these laws, as Terrill points out, are shaped and defined by their opposition, partly because of the lack of a wider, counter-availing public force (2000).

## How does FOI survive?

So how does FOI survive? One answer is that it does not always do so. Laws have been frozen, dropped, lost amid committees or left in a legal void (Michener 2011). For most governments, however, the symbolism is enough to cut off lines of retreat and cause veto players to hesitate (Berliner 2010). FOI policy is frequently left hanging in a delicate position as 'windows' of opportunity appear to close (Michener 2011).

At this point, various actors may take the strain and 'pick up the policy'. The 'saviours' come in many guises and can often be found in 'history's supporting cast' (Schudson 2015, 267). Snell's 'White Knights' are frequently Cabinet ministers with the authority, weight and prestige to carry laws. They can also be hidden persuaders with the ear of the powerful, such as press secretaries or advisors or even powerful outsiders who are not part of government, such as Sonia Gandhi. Perhaps the most common group are the reluctant champions or grudging advocates, actors who push the policy out of duty, obligation or fear of worse consequences (Snell 2000; Snell 2001). Jack Straw is perhaps a perfect exemplar of a particular kind of believer in a 'moderate' law, with the skills to push a Bill through the legislature. Other influential actors have a role in not stopping a law, as veto players who do not act (Berliner 2010). Lyndon Johnson stands out as the ultimate example; his negative actions, against his own political instincts, 'saved' the 1966 FOI Act.

Survival hinges frequently on strengthening protections for government and weakening the power and scope of the law. Recurrent bargaining takes place over executive veto powers and the strength of particular exemptions, particularly over policy-making, all the way to tailor-made exclusions of convenience. The battles are long and complex as the policy evolves within the system; the UK lost and regained and then revised its veto, while the Indian RTI twice lost and regained its state-level coverage. Perhaps symptomatic of the level of threat that FOI presents, among sceptics FOI is frequently seen or portrayed as a threat to entire political systems: FOI was potentially unconstitutional in the US and undermined the Westminster model in Australia and the UK. The Indian RTI's coverage of state and regional bodies hinged, at certain points, on whether the central government could constitutionally and legally legislate for them.

The newly softened proposals often then face a further battle in the legislature. Parliaments and legislatures try to use the symbolism of FOI to warn, oppose or reboot flagging laws, from the Moss committee's long eleven years to the forensic work of the Indian, Australian and UK committees. Legislative pressure often, however, concerns what is possible. FOI supporters in the legislature, caught between the desire to strengthen weak legislation and the fear of losing it entirely, frequently settle for something on the statute book.

Passing an FOI law is very much the end of the beginning. The force, extent and operation of the law remain malleable and uncertain. As a law primarily powered by use and political support, FOI creates a dynamic and ever-changing regime, self-perpetuating and sometimes expanding. Users, in particular the 'vanguard' campaigners and media, push the boundaries, test the edges and force legal rulings (Dunion 2011). No law stands still, as politicians, appeal bodies or courts shape the force and extent of the law, for good or ill. The meaning and extent of transparency are continuously contested and challenged (Fenster 2015).

### The case of the UK

Britain's FOI Act is an exemplar of these processes. The legislation took many years, with a succession of governments seeking to do anything but pass a law, despite a growing and increasingly organised campaign. Transparency spread incrementally across local government level as part of a gradual 'guerrilla' campaign (Wilson 2011).

In its first burst of activity between 1996 and 1998, New Labour's experience seemed to run against the grain. The FOI radicals pursued a vision of the reform as a radical redistribution of power. The hiatus and confusion of New Labour's arrival in power were brief but just long enough to push the paper through. Opponents were either distracted or unwilling and unable to fight. What began as an ambitious attempt to see what could be got through became a powerful signal and strong, if raw, policy proposal. The White Paper was a rapidly constructed set of 'guiding principles', pushed out in six months and published to widespread applause and surprise. This brief time gave opposition little time to fight back and, before the paper was published, nothing to fight against. Politically and procedurally, the paper was 'forced' through among inattention.

Normal service then resumed as political gravity, entropy and process conspired to work against the radical proposals. As the government reconsidered what openness could mean the disorientation faded. The process of creating the draft law took almost twice as long, more than ten months of hard grind, negotiation and close legislating. Doubts filtered into the small group of key actors just as the context shifted and the process entered a more difficult, detailed stage.

The two policies at each stage had remarkably similar effects. Neither the White Paper nor the draft Bill were a finished policy. Both were more 'trial balloons' or 'guiding principles' than finished products. Behind the unpolished nature and 'maximum' or 'minimum' intent was the same strategy: to see what could be got through into law, both sides perhaps following Keynes's famous dictum that 'when the final result is expected to be a compromise, it is often prudent to start from an extreme position'. Nevertheless, each policy went too far, exceeding opponents' fears and then acting to galvanise and motivate opponents, becoming a pivot for resistance and change: the White Paper from within parts of government and the draft Bill from without. What emerged was a complex and unpredictable compromise.

The question, looking back, is how can the same government, composed of the same actors, push such different policies and visions in so brief a time? The isolated nature of FOI and its electoral insulation meant decisions were relegated to a limited handful of people deep inside government. It was, in one sense, the attitudinal changes among a very limited group that caused the move (Dunleavy 2009).

Those instrumental in the reversal later argued that the government was naive or in thrall to the 'positive' narrative pitched to them from outside. Straw claimed that CFOI had been 'extremely active' and that ministers had 'become word perfect in the mantra of change' while not foreseeing 'counter-balancing arguments' that would 'hit us in government' (2012, 275). Campaign bodies virtually controlled the process through Clark and doubters were unwilling or too distracted to put up resistance (aside from Straw himself). Blair argued similarly that FOI was, in an ambiguous phrase, developed 'with care but without foresight' (2011, 127). His government legislated 'in the first throes of power'; writing a decade later, Blair claimed that he 'quakes at the imbecility of it' and asked where the warnings from the officials were when he needed them (516).

These justifications offer some explanation as to what happened behind closed doors. The new government was indeed inexperienced, and to an extent naive and somewhat distracted, particularly in the early radical phase. Yet FOI had been a manifesto commitment since 1974, before CFOI or its predecessor, and was supported by a powerful part of the Labour Party for decades and, it appeared, the Prime Minister. Nor was it really a 'first throes of power' issue: the White Paper was produced very rapidly but the preparation of the draft Bill drifted over eighteen months and paralleled a larger shift towards preserving executive power.

It needed only a few key actors shifting positions to change these ideas: it took Irvine's influence to decline, Straw to take control and Blair to change his mind. The sceptics, led by the 'reluctant champion' Straw, saw FOI as, at best, a promise that was, in numerous ways, threatening and potentially damaging to government, the official machine and its communications. Consequently, the new law would be a de-politicised, or at least 'diverted', instrument towards services and an entrenching, not radically re-altering, of rights. FOI was, crucially, part of a rip tide of a re-asserting executive power.

The process did not end in the Cabinet committee. A cross-party coalition of FOI supporters fought to move FOI back towards its original vision. Parliament wrung a series of compromises over the Information Commissioner, the veto and the scope of the Act, in the face of executive dominance and concern that the Bill would be lost.

In the UK, the symbolism undoubtedly placed FOI on the government agenda. It also worked to cut off the retreat: the government, and Blair in particular, felt they could not back down as they had been so clearly committed. The appeal of FOI's radicalism, the promise and its fit to the self-image of the Labour Party pushed the government onwards while the counter-accusation of betrayal, with its political consequences, made the sceptics hesitate. The government grudgingly passed a Bill that it hoped would create a rather different sort of FOI. However, legislating to allow questioning and scrutiny is always likely to generate the unexpected. What FOI reveals, how it works and who it benefits always prove different from expectations.

## Where is FOI now?

Supporters and critics agree that FOI is an important piece of legislation, though whether it is democratic may be a more open question. FOI has become a 'symbol' of dysfunction within the political system to some or a means of solving it to others.

To some critics FOI has become a negative symbol, symptomatic of a system in which there is too much of the 'wrong kind' of democracy and too little of the 'right' (Flinders 2015b, 191). Drawing on Heclo (1999), it has been argued that a certain kind of openness has damaged democracy: 'politics is more open and inclusive than ever. News about politics and government endlessly cascades from the media, and public opinion is incessantly sounded and courted', and yet the electorate 'seem more and more alienated from the political process' (62). This 'insistence on greater exposure ... in the political environment' is rooted in the most sustained and comprehensive effort at ethics reform and public disclosure in American history took place' (65). This included both formal openness via 'publicly recorded votes, open committee meetings ... televised debates, new freedom of information laws, mandating public disclosure and public hearings' as well as 'informal openness' through media exposes and 'interpretive reporting', worsened by increasing extreme activists and a wealth of 'political technologies' claiming to constantly sample 'public opinion' (65). The consequence is productive and counter-productive:

> Obviously, the new openness is both good and bad. It offers access to voices that would not otherwise be heard, and it encourages exposure of political failures and wrongdoing. But it also promotes grandstanding, needless disputation, and endless delay. Perhaps worst of all, it creates in the American public a pervasive sense of contentiousness, mistrust, and even outright viciousness. (Heclo 1999, 65)

This in turn impacts upon the populace:

> Moreover, [citizens] today are informed more rapidly about more subjects than ever before. But the complexity of public problems usually gets lost in the dramatic factoids

and disconnected commentaries. Instead of knowledge about public affairs, [they] acquire a superficial knowingness. (65)

The argument runs that FOI is one of a suite of tools creating a 'hyper-democracy', where new ways of continuous monitoring are used not by the public but by 'elites' or non-representative groups. Rather than increasing public understanding, its abuse serves to oversimplify a complex reality and create too much openness and too little knowledge (Heclo 1999). In a 'low trust high blame' environment like the UK FOI becomes a 'gotcha tool' for shock exposure (Fung and Weil 2010). It is perhaps symbolic of an 'Amazonian politics' whereby citizens have a 'retail relationship with government' (Flinders 2015a, 8). Birchall (2014) has taken this further, arguing that FOI provides an excuse for transparency of a very particular kind, and that the universalising support hides very particular conceptions of the neo-liberal state and society. Transparency 'depoliticizes what are essentially political decisions', which are 'presented as a technical rather than political settlement' (2014, 78). Discussion itself serves a political purpose, as 'although we do not yet live in transparent times, we do live in an age of transparency advocacy' (78).

Alternatively, FOI may represent a means of closing a gap and ending a deep dissonance within British politics (Richards and Smith 2015). FOI is one powerful new weapon for a growing 'anti-establishment' upsurge challenging a political system that is essentially 'elitist, power hoarding and majoritarian' (Flinders 2015b, 191). Against successive waves of 'bottom-up insurgencies' that hold transparency and accountability as their bedrock, political elites cling to a tradition that 'prioritise[s] strong government over accountability and participation' in a winner-takes-all, voter-targeting system that breeds disillusionment, 'imposition and disunity' (Richards and Smith 2015, 45). However, this old 'arena' and its traditional 'uni-dimensional' processes now faces the 'information challenges of the digital age', from FOI to social media and Open Data. This battery of new weapons has forced more 'complex relationships' and 'new time horizons'. The 'hyper-democratic problems' are less a failure of 'openness' than a failure of elites to respond properly to the politics of a new age (48–49). FOI suits a new 'postmaterial political culture' of 'citizen initiated campaigning', movement-like party structures and individualised political interaction (see Chadwick and Stromer-Galley 2016). FOI fits with the new individual, fluid type of politics but the political system has simply failed to keep up.

The image for both these views is that given, later in his career, by Donald Rumsfeld, of Gulliver tied down by Lilliputians or a Leviathan restrained (see Roberts 2006). Modern government is subject to a vast, somewhat chaotic and disorderly range of accountability instruments. FOI, as a high-profile and particularly noticeable one, has come to symbolise whether, how and to what extent government should be restrained and by whom.

## Beyond FOI

What both these views also agree upon is that FOI is now caught within the slip-stream of a wider drive towards transparency. FOI is very much an analogue legal-istic instrument, designed in the 1960s and updated in the 1990s and early 2000s, in a world of digital transparency driven by experiment and evolution, composed of new 'social layers' and networked modes conceiving information and data (Levine 2012).

In the UK, FOI has sat since the Labour government of Gordon Brown within a powerful drive towards Open Data, which David Cameron promised to boost to bring 'true freedom of Information' (BBC 25/6/2009). This has included expanding the data portal data.gov.uk, publication of central and local government spending and online crime maps, moving to experiments in deliberative forums. Since joining the Open Government Partnership in 2011, the UK government has pushed further in opening up the police, NHS (courting controversy over patient privacy) and the private sector, through publication of data on Beneficial Ownership and extractive transparency. Devolved bodies in Scotland and Northern Ireland as well as the Houses of Parliament have pushed their own separate agendas (Worthy 2015b). It is unclear to what extent the policies have worked, and there has been disappoint-ment over the performance of some of the more sophisticated instruments (Moss and Coleman 2014; Worthy 2015a)

The technology of publication overlaps with the legal right to open up (Yu and Robinson 2012). Indeed in 2012 the Cabinet Office Minister spoke of wishing to make 'Freedom of Information redundant, by pushing out so much [open] data that people won't have to ask for it' (Informationage.com 4/7/2012). The Open Data discourse carries over and magnifies some of the assumptions within FOI: that information is neutral and that the public wish to be, and should be, auditors (Birchall 2014). Beyond this, the idea remains 'deeply ambiguous' as it 'blur[es] the distinction between the technology of Open Data and the politics of Open Government' and is often underpinned by a technological determinism (Yu and Robinson 2012, 181). The discussion is dangerous in that it purposely overlaps and obscures basic, but fundamental differences between offering chosen data via codes (in Open Data) and creating an evolving, legally enforceable right (as with FOI).

FOI is also now operating within a new information ecosystem or 'ecology' (Kreimer 2008). The question for the future is how or whether these differing components can fit together or whether 'philosophical difference may correlate with a critical difference in political effects' (Fung 2013, 190). The practical behav-ioural effects may clash with the broad democratic hopes or views of government: whether it is a protector from corporate exploitation or itself the source of secrecy. The 'radical transparency' may serve to 'subvert or at least interrupt dominant attitudes toward disclosure's limited and prescribed role in the political sphere'

(Birchall 2014, 85). New means may no longer 'subscribe to the well-behaved, containable, regulatory, seemingly apolitical and neutral manifestation of transparency' (Birchall 2014, 84). How these new instruments fit, and their effects, may determine whether the new ecosystems will bring 'sunlight' or 'confusion' (Schudson 2015, 259).

# References

Access Info Europe (2014) *AsktheEU.org: Transparency Report 2011–2013 Council of Europe.* www.access-info.org/documents/Access_Docs/Advancing/Council_of_Europe/council_report_2014_05_16.pdf (last accessed 24 November 2014).

Ackerman, J. M., and Sandoval-Ballesteros, I. E. (2006) 'The Global Explosion of Freedom of Information Laws'. *The Administrative Law Review*, 58 (1): 85–130.

Act Now (2015) 'Open the Floodgates! Water Companies Subject to EIR'. https://act-nowtraining.wordpress.com/2015/03/06/open-the-floodgates-water-companies-subject-to-eir/ (last accessed 2 November 2015).

Adshead, M. (2015) 'Two Steps Forward and One Step Back: Political Culture and FOI', in M. Adshead and T. Felle (eds) *Ireland and the Freedom of Information Act.* Manchester: Manchester University Press, pp. 32–52.

Adshead, M., and Felle, T. (2015) 'Introduction', in M. Adshead and T. Felle (eds) *Ireland and the Freedom of Information Act.* Manchester: Manchester University Press, pp. 1–6.

Adshead, M., Felle, T., and O'Connor, N. (2015) 'Conclusion', in M. Adshead and T. Felle (eds) *Ireland and the Freedom of Information Act.* Manchester: Manchester University Press, pp. 163–182.

Aitken, J. (1998) 'Open Government in New Zealand'. in A. McDonald and G. Terrill (eds) *Open Government? Freedom of Information and Privacy.* London: Macmillan, pp. 117–142.

ALRC/ARC (Australian Law Reform Commission and Administrative Review Council Committee) (1995) *Open Government: A Review of the Federal Freedom of Information Act 1982.* Canberra: AGPS.

Applebaum, A. (2003) *Gulag: A History.* New York: Doubleday Books.

Archibald, S. (1979) 'The Freedom of Information Act Revisited'. *Public Administration Review*, 39 (4): 311–318.

Archibald, S. (1993) 'The Early Years of the Freedom of Information Act, 1955 to 1974'. *PS: Political Science and Politics*, 26 (4): 726–731.

Ashdown, P. (2002) *The Ashdown Diaries*, volume 2: *1997–1999*. London: Penguin Books.

Austin, R. (2000) 'Freedom of Information: The Constitutional Impact', in J. Jowell and D. Oliver (eds) *The Changing Constitution*, 4th edn. Oxford: Oxford University Press, pp. 319–328.

Austin, R. (2004) 'The Freedom of Information Act 2000 – A Sheep in Wolf's Clothing?', in J. Jowell and D. Oliver (eds) *The Changing Constitution*, 5th edn. Oxford: Oxford University Press, pp. 401–415.

Austin, R. (2007) 'The Freedom of Information Act 2000: A Sheep in Wolf's Clothing?', in J. Jowell and D. Oliver (eds) *The Changing Constitution*, 6th edn. Oxford: Oxford University Press, pp. 387–406.

Australian Government (2013) *Review of the Freedom of Information Act 1982 and Australian Information Commissioner Act 2010*. Canberra: Australian Government.

Badgley, K., Dixon, M., and Dozois, P. (2003) 'In Search of the Chill: Access to Information and Record-Keeping in the Government of Canada'. *Archavia*, 55. http://journals.sfu.ca/archivar/index.php/archivaria/issue/view/414 (last accessed 24 November 2014).

Bailur, S., and Longley, T. (2014) *The Impact of Online Freedom of Information Tools: What is the Evidence?* London: MySociety.

Barberis, P. (2010) 'The Morality of Open Government', in R. A. Chapman and M. Hunt (eds) *Freedom of Information: Local Government and Accountability*. London: Ashgate Publishing Ltd, pp. 121–135.

Bauhr, M., and Grimes, M. (2014) 'Indignation or Resignation: The Implications of Transparency for Societal Accountability'. *Governance*, 27 (2): 291–320.

Bayne, P. (1993). 'Freedom of Information'. *Australian Journal of Administrative Law*, 51 (1): 197–226.

BBC (7/12/1983) 'Lecture 5: Opening up Government'. www.bbc.co.uk/programmes/pooh2cpb; transcript, http://downloads.bbc.co.uk/rmhttp/radio4/transcripts/1983_reith5.pdf (last accessed 15 October 2015).

BBC (4/1/2005) 'Openness Law Reveals Papers'. www.news.bbc.co.uk/1/hi/uk/4143415.htm (last accessed 5 October 2014).

BBC (25/10/2007) 'In Full: Brown's Speech on Liberty'. http://news.bbc.co.uk/1/hi/uk_politics/7062237.stm (last accessed 25 August 2015).

BBC (25/6/2009) 'Cameron's Data Speech in Full'. http://news.bbc.co.uk/1/hi/uk_politics/8119047.stm (last accessed 2 November 2016).

BBC (11/3/2011) 'Lord Clark: No Apology over Freedom of Information Act'. www.bbc.co.uk/news/uk-politics-12705923 (last accessed 12 January 2016).

BBC (7/3/2012) 'Cameron's Dividing Line on Access to Information'. www.bbc.co.uk/news/uk-politics-17286328 (last accessed 24 November 2014).

BBC (3/10/2012) 'Walberswick Parish Councillors Quit over FOI Requests'. www.bbc.co.uk/news/uk-england-suffolk-19804046 (last accessed 5 October 2014).

BBC (6/2/2013) 'Walberswick Parish Council Apologies Issued and Elections Pending'. www.bbc.co.uk/news/uk-england-suffolk-21340522 (last accessed 5 October 2014).

BBC (1/11/2014) 'How the Civil Service Objected to Kinnock's FOI Plans'. http://news.bbc.co.uk/1/shared/bsp/hi/pdfs/foipolicy.pdf (last accessed 2 November 2015).

Beetham, D., Ngan, P. and Weir, S. (2001) 'Democratic Audit: Labour's Record So Far'. *Parliamentary Affairs*, 54 (2): 376–390.

*Belfast Telegraph* (10/7/2015) 'We Must Fight Watering Down of Freedom of Information Act'.

Benn, T. (1974) *Speeches*. Nottingham: Spokesman Books.

Benn, T. (1990) *Conflicts of Interests: Diaries 1977–1980*, London: Hutchinson.

Bennett, C. J. (1997) 'Understanding Ripple Effects: The Cross-National Adoption of Policy Instruments for Bureaucratic Accountability'. *Governance*, 10 (3): 213–233.

Berliner, D. (2010) 'Veto Players, Democracy, and the Diffusion of Freedom of Information Laws'. http://papers.ssrn.com/abstract=1643291 (last accessed 11 May 2015).

Berliner, D. (2013) 'Follow Your Neighbour? Regional Emulation and the Design of Transparency Policies'. KFG Working Papers. http://ideas.repec.org/p/erp/kfgxxx/poo55.html (accessed 11 May 2015).

Berliner, D. (2014) 'The Political Origins of Transparency'. *The Journal of Politics*, 76 (2): 479–491.

Berliner, D. (2015) 'Sunlight or Window Dressing? Local Government Compliance with South Africa's Promotion of Access to Information Act'. Fourth Global Conference on Transparency Research, Lugano, Switzerland, 4–6 June.

Bhattacharjea, A. (2005) 'From Freedom to Right', in *Speaking Truth to Power: A Symposium on People's Right to Information*. www.india-seminar.com/2005/551/551%20ajit%20bhattacharjea.htm (last accessed 7 September 2015).

Birchall, C. (2014) 'Radical Transparency?'. *Cultural Studies – Critical Methodologies*, 14 (1): 77–88.

Birkinshaw, P. (1998) 'An "All Singin' and All Dancin'" Affair: The New Labour Government's Proposals for Freedom of Information'. *Public Law*, 2: 176-189.

Birkinshaw, P. (2001) *Freedom of Information: The Law, the Practice and the Ideal*, 3rd edn. London: Butterworths.

Birkinshaw, P. (2006) 'Freedom of Information and Openness: Fundamental Human Rights?'. *Administrative Law Review*, 58 (1): 177–218.

Birkinshaw, P., and Parkin, A. (1999) 'Freedom of Information', in R. Blackburn and R. Plant (eds) *Constitutional Reform: Labour's Constitutional Reform Agenda*. London and New York: Longman, pp. 193–202.

Birkinshaw, P., and Parry, N. (1999) 'The End of the Beginning? The Freedom of Information Bill 1999'. *Journal of Law and Society*, 26 (4): 538–554.

*Birmingham Post* (25/5/1999) 'Freedom Bill Deeply Flawed'.

*Birmingham Post* (29/10/2015) 'A Tax on Journalism: New Campaign to Keep Vital Freedom of Information Act Free for All'.

Blair, T. (1996) 'Speech by the Rt. Hon. Tony Blair MP, Leader of the Labour Party', June 1996. Transcript of a tape). www.cfoi.org.uk/blairawards.html (last accessed 7 January 2016).

Blair, T. (1998) *The Third Way: New Politics for the New Century*. Fabian Society Pamphlet 588. London: Fabian Society.

Blair, T. (2011) *A Journey*. London: Hutchinson.

Blanton, T. (2002) 'The World's Right to Know'. *Foreign Policy*, 131: 50–58.

Blanton, T. (2006) 'Freedom of Information at 40 LBJ Refused Ceremony, Undercut Bill with Signing Statement'. http://nsarchive.gwu.edu/NSAEBB/NSAEBB194/ (last accessed 6 September 2015).

Bogdanor, V. (2003) *The British Constitution in the Twentieth Century*. Oxford: Oxford University Press.

Bogdanor, V. (2009) *The New British Constitution*. London: Bloomsbury Publishing.

Bogdanor, V. (2010) 'An Era of Constitutional Reform'. *The Political Quarterly*, 81 (1): S53–S64.

Bok, S. (1986) *Secrets: Concealment and Revelation*. Oxford: Oxford University Press.

Bok, S. (1991) 'Reassessing Sartre'. *The Harvard Review of Philosophy*, 1 (1): 48–58.

Boyne, G. A., James, O., John, P., and Petrovsky, N. (2009) 'Democracy and Government Performance: Holding Incumbents Accountable in English Local Governments'. *The Journal of Politics*, 71 (4): 1273–1284.

Brazier, R. (1998) *Constitutional Reform: Reshaping the British Political System*. Oxford: Oxford University Press.

Bromley, C., Curtice, J., and Seyd, B. (2001) 'Political Engagement, Trust and Constitutional Reform', in A. Park, J. Curtice, K. Thomson, L. Jarvis, and C. Bromley (eds) *British Social Attitudes: The 18th Report – Public Policy, Social Ties*. London: Sage, pp. 199–225.

Bromley, C., Seyd, B., and Curtice, J. (2002) *Has Constitutional Reform 'Reconnected' Voters with Government?* London: UCL.

Brooke, H. (2005) *Your Right to Know: How to Use the Freedom of Information Act and Other Access Laws*. London: Pluto Press.

Bruno, I., Didier, E., and Vitale, T. (2014) 'Statactivism: Forms of Action between Disclosure and Affirmation'. *Partecipazione e conflitto: The Open Journal of Sociopolitical Studies*, 7 (2): 198–220.

Brysk, A. (1995) '"Hearts and Minds": Bringing Symbolic Politics Back In'. *Polity*, 27 (4): 559–585.

Burch, M., and Holliday, I. (1996) *The British Cabinet System*. London: Prentice Hall.

Burgess, M. (2015) *Freedom of Information: A Practical Guide for UK Journalists*. London: Routledge.

Cabinet Office (1969) *Information and the Public Interest* (Cmnd 4089). London: HMSO.

Cabinet Office (White Paper) (1993) *Open Government* (Cmnd 2290). London: HMSO.

Cabinet Office (1997a) *Code of Practice on Access to Government Information*, 2nd edn. www. CFOI.org.uk/coptext.html (last accessed 14 February 2006).

Cabinet Office (1997b) *Your Right to Know: The Government's Proposals for a Freedom of Information Act* (Cmnd 3818). London: TSO.

Cabinet Office (2012) *Open Data: Unleashing the Potential*. London: TSO.

Cabinet Office (2013) *Open Government Partnership UK National Action Plan 2013 to 2015*. London: TSO.

Cabinet Office (2016) *Written Statement to Parliament: Open and Transparent Government*. https://www.gov.uk/government/speeches/open-and-transparent-government (last accessed 4 April 2016).

Cain, B., Fabbrini, S., and Egan, P. (2003) 'Towards More Open Democracies: The Expansion of FOI Laws', in B. E. Cain, R. J. Dalton, and S.E. Scarrow (eds) *Democracy Transformed? Expanding Political Opportunities in Advanced Industrial Democracies*. Oxford: Oxford University Press, pp. 115– 139.

Calland, R., and Bentley, K. (2013) 'The Impact and Effectiveness of Transparency and Accountability Initiatives: Freedom of Information'. *Development Policy Review*, 31 (S1): S69–S87.

Campbell, A. (2011) *Diaries, volume 2: Power and the People*. London: Random House.

Campbell, J. (2014) *Roy Jenkins*. London: Random House.

*Canberra Times* (21/3/2015) 'Australia's Prime Ministers: By Their Fruits Shall You Know Them'. /www.canberratimes.com.au/comment/australias-prime-ministers-by-their-fruits-shall-you-know-them-20150320-1m4b78#ixzz3i26yNZSt (last accessed 4 January 2016).

Caro, R. A. (2002) *The Years of Lyndon Johnson: Master of the Senate*. New York: Alfred A. Knopf Incorporated.

Caro, R. A. (2012) *The Years of Lyndon Johnson: The Passage of Power*. New York: Alfred A. Knopf Incorporated.

Carter, N., and Jacobs, M. (2014) 'Explaining Radical Policy Change: The Case of Climate Change and Energy Policy under the British Labour Government 2006–10'. *Public Administration*, 92 (1): 125–141.

Castells, M. (2013) *Communication Power*. Oxford: Oxford University Press.

CFOI (1984a) *Secrets Newspaper [No. 2]*. https://www.cfoi.org.uk/2009/12/secrets-news paper-1984-1993/ (last accessed 23 November 2015).

CFOI (1984b) *Secrets Newspaper [No. 3]*. https://www.cfoi.org.uk/2009/12/secrets-news paper-1984-1993/ (last accessed 23 November 2015).

CFOI (1992) *A Guide to the Right to Know Bill*. www.cfoi.org.uk/rtk7pguide.html (last accessed 12 March 2006).

CFOI (1993) *Government Blocks the Bill*. www.cfoi.org.uk/rtklead.html (last accessed 4 February 2007).

CFOI (1995) *The Campaign's View on the Operation of the Open Government Code*. https://www.cfoi.org.uk/1995/03/the-campaigns-views-on-the-operation-of-the-open-govern ment-code-of-practice/ (last accessed 21 June 2016).

CFOI (1998a) *Conference on the Freedom of Information White Paper*. www.cfoi.org/pdf/wpconference.pdf (last accessed 4 November 2006).

CFOI (1998b) *Speech by the Lord Chancellor, Lord Irvine of Lairg, to the Campaign for Freedom of Information 1997 Awards*. www.CFOI.org.uk/irvineawards.htm (last accessed 4 November 2006).

CFOI (1999) 'Press Release: "Deeply Disappointing" Information Bill "weaker than the Conservatives' Code"'. www.cfoi.org.uk/draftBill240599pr.html (last accessed 4 November 2006).

CFOI (2000a) 'FOI Bill: Report Stage Briefing'. https://www.cfoi.org.uk/2000/11/foi-Bill-report-stage-briefing/. (last accessed 4 November 2006).

CFOI (2000b) 'Research Paper: Labour's Commitments to Freedom of Information'. www.cfoi.org.uk/labcmits.htm (last accessed 23 November 2006).

CFOI (2015) 'FOI and Policy Advice'. https://www.cfoi.org.uk/2015/07/foi-and-policy-advice/ (last accessed 23 November 2015).

Chadwick, A. (2013) *The Hybrid Media System: Politics and Power*. Oxford: Oxford University Press.

Chadwick, A., and Stromer-Galley, J. (2016) 'Digital Media, Power, and Democracy in Parties and Election Campaigns: Party Decline or Party Renewal?' *International Journal of Press/Politics*, 21 (3): 283-293.

Chambers, S. (2004) 'Behind Closed Doors: Publicity, Secrecy, and the Quality of Deliberation'. *Journal of Political Philosophy*, 12 (4), 389-410.

Chandler, J. (2010) 'Freedom of Information and Participation: Comparing Central and Local Government', in R. A. Chapman and M. Hunt (eds) *Freedom of Information: Local Government and Accountability*. London: Ashgate Publishing Ltd, pp. 103–112.

Chapman, R., and Hunt, M. (2010) *Freedom of Information: Local Government and Accountability*. London: Ashgate Publishing Ltd.

Chapman, R. A., and Hunt, M. (eds) (1987) *Open Government*. New York: Croom Helm.

Cherry, M., and McMenemy, D. (2013) 'Freedom of Information and "Vexatious" Requests: The Case of Scottish Local Government', *Government Information Quarterly*, 30 (3): 257–266.

*Civil Service World* (2/11/2015) 'Freedom of Information: Civil Servants would Support Charging for Requests, CSW Study Finds'.

Clarke, P. (2004) *Hope and Glory: Britain 1900–2000*. London: Penguin Books.

Cobb, R. W., and Elder, Charles. (1973) 'The Political Uses of Symbolism'. *American Politics Quarterly*, 1 (3): 305–338.

Cockerell, M., Hennessy, P., and Walker, D. (1984) *Sources Close to the Prime Minister*. London and Basingstoke: Macmillan.

Coglianese, C. (2009) 'The Transparency President? The Obama Administration and Open Government'. *Governance*, 22 (4): 529–544.

Colquhoun, A. (2010) *The Cost of Freedom of Information*. London: Constitution Unit.

Committee on Official Information (Danks) (1980) *Towards Open Government: General Report*, volume 1. Wellington: Government Printer.

Committee on Official Information (Danks) (1981) *Towards Open Government: Supplementary Report*. Wellington: Government Printer.

Committee on Oversight and Government Reform (U.S. House of Representatives) (2016) *FOIA is Broken: A Report*. Washington, DC: Congress.

*Congressional Record* (20/11/1974) House, 'Freedom of Information Amendments – Veto Message', col. 36622.

*Congressional Record* (21/11/1974) Senate, 'Freedom of Information Veto', col. 36865.

Constitution Unit (2001) 'Freedom of Information: The History of the Legislation'. www.ucl.ac.uk/constitution-unit/foidp/history-legislation/foi- Act-2000.html (last accessed 12 August 2015).

Cornford, J. (1982) 'The Right to Know Secrets', in A. May and K. Rowan (eds) *Inside Information: British Government and the Media*. London: Constable and Company, pp. 33–36.

Costas, J., and Grey, C. (2014) 'Bringing Secrecy into the Open: Towards a Theorization of the Social Processes of Organizational Secrecy'. *Organization Studies*, 35 (1): 1423–1447.

Cowley, P. (2000) 'Can Sheep Bark? British Labour MPs and the Modification of Government Policy'. European Consortium for Political Research, Workshop on Parliamentary Control of the Executive, Copenhagen, Denmark, 14-19 April. https://ecpr.eu/Filestore/PaperProposal/96b47f45-2d11-4011-9941-b68df10dce01.pdf (last accessed 7 July 2016).

Cowley, P. (2002) *Revolts and Rebellions*. London: Politicos.

Cowley, P. (2005) *The Rebels: How Blair Mislaid his Majority*. London: Politicos.

Crewe, I., and King, A. (1995) *SDP: The Birth, Life and Death of the Social Democratic Party*. Oxford: Oxford University Press.

Crossman, R. (1972) *Inside View: Three Lectures on Prime Ministerial Government*. London: Cape.

Cuillier, D. (2010) 'Honey vs. Vinegar: Testing Compliance-Gaining Theories in the Context of Freedom of Information Laws'. *Communication Law and Policy*, 15 (3): 203–229.

Curtice, J. (2010) 'Rebuilding the Bonds of Trust and Confidence? Labour's Constitutional Reform Programme', *The Political Quarterly*, 81 (1): S65–S77.

Curtis, L. J. (1983). 'Freedom of Information in Australia'. *Federal Law Review*, 5 (1): 5–26.

Dahllöf, S. (2016) 'Danish Pro-Access Majority Refrains from Using Power', 4 May 2016. www.freedominfo.org/2016/05/danish-pro-access-majority-refrains-from-using-power/ (last accessed 31 July 2016).

*Daily Mail* (25/5/1999) 'A Depressing Damp Squib of a Bill'.

*Daily Mail* (27/5/1999) 'X and the Right to Know Nothing'.

*Daily Mail* (25/9/2015) 'He Would, Wouldn't He? Sir Cover Up Attacks Law'.

*Daily Mail* (30/10/2015) 'Minister for Hypocrisy: Chris Grayling said Reporters "Misused" Freedom Law but Crowed as Stories Shamed Labour'.

*Daily Mail* (13/11/2015) 'Scandals That Would Never Have Been Exposed'.

*Daily Mail* (14/11/2015) 'How Whitehall Spends £289 Million of YOUR Cash on Propaganda and Marketing ... but Just £5.6 Million of Freedom Law it Now Claims is "Too Expensive"'.

*Daily Mail* (7/12/2015) 'How Right to Know Law has Saved Taxpayers Cash: Public Sector Waste Revealed by Threatened Freedom of Information Act'.

*Daily Mail* (10/12/2015) 'Freedom of Information Act MUST be Protected, says Daily Mail Editor'.

*Daily Mail* (11/12/2015) 'The Great Public Backlash over Bid to Curb Freedom of Information Law'.

*Daily Telegraph* (9/12/2015) 'It's Our Right to Know'.

*Daily Telegraph* (17/12/2015) 'It's Our Right to Know What Government is Up To'.

Dallek, R. (2005) *Lyndon B. Johnson: Portrait of a President*. Oxford: Oxford University Press.

Darch, C. (2013) 'Statistics, Indicators and Access to Information in African Countries', in Fatima Diallo and Richard Calland (eds) (2013) *Access to Information in Africa: Law, Culture and Practice*, volume 1. Leiden: Brill, pp. 109–127.

Darch, C., and Underwood, P. G. (2005) 'Freedom of Information Legislation, State Compliance and the Discourse of Knowledge: The South African Experience'. *The International Information & Library Review*, 37(2): 77–86.

Darch, C., and Underwood, P. G. (2010) *Freedom of Information in the Developing World: Demand, Compliance and Democratic Behaviours*. Oxford: Chandos.

David-Barrett, E., and Okamura, K. (2016) 'Norm Diffusion and Reputation: The Rise of the Extractive Industries Transparency Initiative'. *Governance*, 29 (2): 227-246.

Davis, K. C. (1967) 'The Information Act: A Preliminary Analysis'. *The University of Chicago Law Review*, 34 (4): 761–816.

de Fine Licht, J. (2014a) 'Policy Area as a Potential Moderator of Transparency Effects: An Experiment'. *Public Administration Review*, 74 (3): 361–371.

de Fine Licht, J. (2014b) 'Transparency Actually: How Transparency Affects Public Perceptions of Political Decision-Making'. *European Political Science Review*, 6 (2): 309–330.

Deleuze, G. (1992) 'Postscript on the Societies of Control'. *October*, 59, 3-7.

Denver, D. (1998) 'The Government that Could Do No Right', in A. King et al., *New Labour Triumphs: Britain and the Polls*. Chatham, NJ: Chatham House Publishers, pp. 15-48.

Deutscher, I. (1970) *The Prophet Armed: Trotsky, 1879–1921*. Oxford: Oxford University Press.

Diamond, P. (2011) 'Beyond the Westminster Model'. *Renewal*, 19 (1): 64–74.

Donoughue, B. (2005) *Downing Street Diary: With Harold Wilson in Number Ten*. London: Jonathan Cape.

Dorey, P. (2008) *The Labour Party and Constitutional Reform: A History of Constitutional Conservatism*. London: Palgrave Macmillan.

Dowling, R. (2015) 'Freedom of Information and Policing: Still a Very Secret Service', in M. Adshead and T. Felle (eds) *Ireland and the Freedom of Information Act*. Manchester: Manchester University Press, pp. 68–85.

Doyle, J. (1997) 'Freedom of Information: Lessons from the International Experience'. *Administration*, 44 (1): 64–82.

Draper, D. (1997) *Blair's Hundred Days*. London: Faber and Faber.

Dunion, K. (2011) *Freedom of Information in Scotland in Practice*. Dundee: Dundee University Press.

Dunleavy, P. (2009) 'Assessing how Far Charter 88 and the Constitutional Reform Coalition Influenced Voting System Reform in Britain'. *Parliamentary Affairs*, 62 (4): 618–644.

Dunleavy, P., Margetts, H., Smith, T., and Weir, S. (2001) 'Constitutional Reform, New Labour in Power and Public Trust in Government'. *Parliamentary Affairs*, 54 (3): 405–424.

Dunleavy, P., Weir, S., and Subrahmanyam, G. (1995) 'Public Response and Constitutional Significance'. *Parliamentary Affairs*, 48 (4): 602–616.

*Economist* (4/7/1998) 'Britain: Cobwebs: Freedom of Information'.

Edelman, M. J. (1985) *The Symbolic Uses of Politics*. Urbana and Chicago: University of Illinois Press.

Edgerton, D. (2011) *Shock of the Old: Technology and Global History since 1900*. London: Profile Books.

Egan, D. (1999) *Derry Irvine: Politically Incorrect?* Edinburgh: Mainstream Publishing Ltd.

Eisenstein, E. L. (2005) *The Printing Revolution in Early Modern Europe*. Cambridge: Cambridge University Press.

Ellington, T. C. (2013) 'The Most Transparent Administration in History? An Assessment of Official Secrecy in the Obama Administration's First Term'. *Public Integrity*, 15 (2): 133–148.

Elliott, M. (2015) 'A Tangled Constitutional Web: The Black-Spider Memos and the British Constitution's Relational Architecture'. University of Cambridge Faculty of Law Research Paper No. 34/2015. http://ssrn.com/abstract=2621451 (last accessed 17 March 2016).

Emerson, T. I. (1976) 'Legal Foundations of the Right to Know'. *Washington University Law Quarterly*, 1 (1): 1–24.

Erkkilä, T. (2012). *Government Transparency: Impacts and Unintended Consequences*. London: Palgrave Macmillan.

Evans, M. (2003) *Constitution-Making and the Labour Party*. Palgrave Macmillan: London.

Evans, M. (2008) 'New Labour and the Rise of the New Constitutionalism', in M. Beech and S. Lee (eds) *Ten Years of New Labour*. London: Palgrave Macmillan, pp. 68–88.

*Evening Standard* (5/4/2000) '60 MPs to Rebel over the Information Bill'.

Ewing, K. D., and Gearty, C., A. (1990) *Freedom under Thatcher: Civil Liberties in Modern Britain*. Oxford: Oxford Paperbacks.

Feinberg, L. E. (2001) 'Mr. Justice Brandeis and the Creation of the Federal Register'. *Public Administration Review*, 61 (3): 359–370.

Felle, T., and Adshead, M. L. (2009) 'Democracy and the Right to Know: 10 Years of Freedom of Information in Ireland'. University of Limerick Politics and Public Administration Working Paper 4. http://ssrn.com/abstract=1682504 (last accessed 17 March 2016).

Fenster, M. (2012a) 'Disclosure's Effects: WikiLeaks and Transparency'. *Iowa Law Review*, 97: 753-807.

Fenster, M. (2012b) 'The Transparency Fix: Advocating Legal Rights and their Alternatives in the Pursuit of a Visible State'. *University of Pittsburgh Law Review*, 73 (3). http://ssrn. com/abstract=1918154 (last accessed 15 December 2015).

Fenster, M. (2015) 'Transparency in Search of a Theory'. *European Journal of Social Theory*, 18 (2), 150–167.

Fenster, M. (2016) 'The Informational Ombudsman: Fixing Open Government by Institutional Design', in I. Bouhadana, W. Gilles and R. K. Weaver (eds) *Freedom of Information and Governmental Transparency in an Open Government Era*. Paris: Les Éditions IMODEV, pp. 275–297.

Fischer, L (1991) *The Life of Mahatma Gandhi*. London: Vintage.

Fitzgerald, E. (1996) 'Freedom of Information: Building A New Culture of Openness', in R. Lohan, M. Conrad, K. Hannigan and J. Jackson (eds) *For the Record: Data Archives, Electronic Records, Access to Information*. Dublin: Institute of Public Administration, pp. 8–13.

Flinders, M. (2000) 'The Politics of Accountability: A Case Study of Freedom of Information Legislation in the United Kingdom'. *The Political Quarterly*, 71 (3): 422–435.

Flinders, M. (2009a) 'Charter 88, New Labour and Constitutional Anomie', *Parliamentary Affairs*, 62 (4): 645–662.

Flinders, M. (2009b) *Democratic Drift: Majoritarian Modification and Democratic Anomie in the United Kingdom*. Oxford: Oxford University Press.

Flinders, M. (2010) 'Constitutional Anomie'. *Government and Opposition*, 44 (4): 383–409.

Flinders, M. (2015a) 'The General Rejection? Political Disengagement, Disaffected Democrats and 'Doing Politics' Differently'. *Parliamentary Affairs*, 68 (suppl. 1): 241–254.

Flinders, M. (2015b) 'The Problem with Democracy'. *Parliamentary Affairs*, 69 (1): 181–203.

Foley, M. (1999) *The Politics of the British Constitution*. Manchester: Manchester University Press.

Foley, M. (2015) 'Keeping the State's Secrets: Ireland's Road from "Official" Secrets to Freedom of Information', Dublin Institute of Technology Paper 30, pp. 186-194. http:// arrow.dit.ie/aaschmedbk/30 (last accessed 13 October 2015).

Ford, G. (1973) 'Gerald R. Ford's Remarks upon Taking the Oath of Office as President'. www.fordlibrarymuseum.gov/library/speeches/740001.asp (last accessed 6 September 2015).

Fox, R. (2012) 'Disgruntled, Disillusioned and Disengaged: Public Attitudes to Politics in Britain' Today'. *Parliamentary Affairs*, 65 (4): 877–887.

Franks, S., and Vandermark, A. (1995) 'Televising Parliament: Five Years On'. *Parliamentary Affairs*, 48 (1): 57–71.

Fraser, M., and Simons, M. (2010) *Malcolm Fraser: The Political Memoirs*. Melbourne: The Miegunyah Press.

Fung, A. (2013) 'Infotopia: Unleashing the Power of Democratic Transparency'. *Politics and Society*, 41 (2): 183–212.

Fung, A., and Weil, D. (2010) 'Open Government, Open Society', in T. Lathrop and L. Ruma (eds) *Collaboration, Transparency, and Participation in Practice*, New York: O'Reilly Media, pp. 105–114.

Fung, A., Graham, M., and Weil, D. (2007) *Full Disclosure: The Perils and Promise of Transparency*. Cambridge: Cambridge University Press.

Gaddis, J. L. (2005) *The Cold War*. London; Penguin Books.

Gallup (2006) 'Gerald Ford Retrospective'. www.gallup.com/poll/23995/gerald-ford-retro spective.aspx (last accessed 13 October 2015).

Ganz, G. (1999) 'European Parliamentary Elections Act 1999: The Constitutional Issues'. *Amicus Curiae*, 1 (18): 4–8.

Gibson, R., and Cantijoch, M. (2013) 'Conceptualizing and Measuring Participation in the Age of the Internet: Is Online Political Engagement Really Different to Offline?' *The Journal of Politics*, 75 (3): 701–716.

Gilbert, J. (2000) 'Access Denied: The *Access to Information Act* and its Effect on Public Records Creators'. *Archivaria*, 49. http://journals.sfu.ca/archivar/index.php/archiv aria/issue/view/426 (last accessed 13 October 2015).

*Glasgow Herald* (25/5/1999) 'Cry for Greater Freedom of Scottish Information: Dewar Challenged to Better Westminster Bill'.

Gofen, A. (2014) 'Mind the Gap: Dimensions and Influence of Street-level Divergence'. *Journal of Public Administration Research and Theory*, 24 (2): 473–493.

Government Office for Science (2016) *Distributed Ledger Technology: Beyond Block Chain: A Report by the UK Government Chief Scientific Adviser*. London: TSO.

Grimmelikhuijsen, S. (2009) 'Do Transparent Government Agencies Strengthen Trust?' *Information Polity*, 14 (3): 173–186.

Grimmelikhuijsen, S. (2012) 'Linking Transparency, Knowledge and Citizen Trust in Government: An Experiment'. *International Review of Administrative Sciences*, 78 (1): 50–73.

Grimmelikhuijsen, S. G., and Meijer, A. J. (2014) 'The Effects of Transparency on the Perceived Trustworthiness of a Government Organization: Evidence from an Online Experiment'. *Journal of Public Administration Research and Theory*, 24 (1): 137–157.

*Guardian* (24/4/1999) 'Behind Closed Doors: Freedom of Information must be a Priority'.

*Guardian* (22/5/1999) 'Straw Weakens Secrecy Bill'.

*Guardian* (25/5/1999a) 'Abysmal Handiwork'.

*Guardian* (25/5/1999b) 'Fury at "Deeply Flawed" Secrecy Bill'.

*Guardian* (25/5/1999c) 'Straw Puts Key State Secrets Off Limits'.

*Guardian* (21/6/ 1999a) 'How Ministers Line Up'.

*Guardian* (21/6/1999b) 'Pressure Mounts Over Public Right to Know'.

*Guardian* (22/6/1999) 'It was Blair who Sabotaged Freedom of Information'.

*Guardian* (24/6/1999) 'Tidal Wave of Support Surges On'.

*Guardian* (24/8/1999) 'New Labour is the Most Radical Option in Town'.

*Guardian* (29/9/1999) 'It is Dangerous for my Party to Close Down Debate'.

*Guardian* (11/10/1999) 'Climbdown on Secrecy'.

*Guardian* (21/10/1999) 'Backbenchers Urge Rethink on Secrecy'.

*Guardian* (3/4/2000) 'Ministers "On the Ropes" over Freedom of Information Bill'.

*Guardian* (4/4/2000) 'Poodles or Politicians: Now is the Time to Decide'.

*Guardian* (7/4/2000) 'Rebel Applauds "Somersault"'.

*Guardian* (29/9/2000) 'Bills Logjam Delays New Parliament'.

*Guardian* (14/11/2000) 'See the Lib Dem Approach: Compliant, Abject, Half-Baked'.

*Guardian* (17/11/2000) 'More Information on Lib-Dem Sell Out'.

*Guardian* (28/11/2000) 'Straw Cuts Short Secrecy Debate'.

*Guardian* (26/10/2001) 'Blair Seeks to Delay Access to Whitehall Information'

*Guardian* (1/9/2010) 'World Exclusive Tony Blair Interview'.

*Guardian* (29/10/2015) 'Freedom of Information Act Misused by Media to Create Stories, Says Grayling'.

*Guardian* (30/10/2015) 'Freedom of Information Act: 103 Stories that Prove Chris Grayling Wrong'.

*Guardian* (9/11/2015) 'Government's FoI Review Threatens to damage Democracy, Says PA'.

Gundersen, K. (2008) 'Freedom of Information', in P. Facey, B. Rigby and A. Runswick (eds) *Unlocking Democracy: 20 Years of Charter 88*. London: Politico's, pp. 224–243.

Gusfield, J. R. (1967) 'Moral Passage: The Symbolic Process in Public Designations of Deviance'. *Social Problems*, 15 (2): 175–188.

Gusfield, J. R. (1968) 'On Legislating Morals: The Symbolic Process of Designating Deviance'. *California Law Review*, 56 (1): 54–73.

Gustafson, B. (2000). *His Way: A Biography of Robert Muldoon*. Auckland: Auckland University Press.

Hacker, J. S., and Pierson, P. (2014). 'After the "Master Theory": Downs, Schattschneider, and the Rebirth of Policy-Focused Analysis'. www.maxpo.eu/Downloads/Paper_Pierson.pdf (last accessed 12 June 2016).

Hamilton, N. (2011). *American Caesars: Lives of the US Presidents, from Franklin D. Roosevelt to George W. Bush*. London: Random House.

Hansard HC 4 April 2000, Vol 347, Col. 843.

Hansard HC 4 April 2000, Vol 347, Col. 921–922.

Hansard HC 4 April 2000, Vol 347, Col. 922.

Hansard HC 4 April 2000, Vol 347, Col. 995–996.

Hansard HC 4 April 2000, Vol 347, Col. 998.

Hansard HC 4 April 2000, Vol 347, Col. 998–999.

Hansard HC 5 April 2000, Vol 347, Col. 1004.

Hansard HC 5 April 2000, Vol 347, Col. 1012.

Hansard HC 5 April 2000, Vol 347, Col. 1015.

Hansard HC 5 April 2000, Vol 347, Col. 1018.

Hansard HC 5 April 2000, Vol 347, Col. 1027–1029.

Hansard HC 5 April 2000, Vol 347, Col. 1030-1031.

Hansard HC 27 November 2000, Vol 357, Col. 666.

Hansard HC 27 November 2000, Vol 357, Col. 670.

Hansard HC 27 November 2000, Vol 357, Col. 706.

Hansard HC 27 November 2000, Vol 357, Col. 743.

Hansard HC 23 June 2015, Vol 597, Col. 752.

Hansard HL 4 April 2000, Vol 611, Col. 828.

Hansard Corpus (2016) 'British Parliament (Hansard) 1803-2005'. www.hansard-corpus. org/ (last accessed 12 June 2016).

Hansard Society (2010) *Audit of Political Engagement 7: The 2010 Report with a Focus on MPs and Parliament*. London: Hansard Society.

Hart, J. (1995) 'President Clinton and the Politics of Symbolism: Cutting the White House Staff'. *Political Science Quarterly*, 110 (3), 385-403.

Hay, C., and Wincott, D. (1998) 'Structure, Agency and Historical Institutionalism'. *Political Studies*, 46 (5): 951–957.

Hayes, J. (2009) *A Shock to the System: Journalism, Government and the Freedom of Information Act 2000*. https://reutersinstitute.politics.ox.ac.uk/fileadmin/documents/Publications/ Hayes_A_Shock_to_the_System.pdf (last accessed 12 November 2014).

Hazell, R. (1989) 'Freedom of Information in Australia, Canada and New Zealand'. *Public Administration*, 67 (2): 189–210.

Hazell, R. (1997a) *Constitutional Reform and the New Labour Government*. CIPFA/Times Lecture. www.ucl.ac.uk/spp/publications/unit-publications/14.pdf (last accessed 12 November 2015).

Hazell, R. (1997b) 'Introducing Freedom of Information'. Constitution Unit, London. www. ucl.ac.uk/spp/publications/unit-publications/9.pdf (last accessed 10 October 2015).

Hazell, R. (1998) *Commentary on the Freedom of Information White Paper*. London: Constitution Unit.

Hazell, R. (1999) *Commentary on the Draft Freedom of Information Bill*. London: Constitution Unit.

Hazell, R., and Worthy, B. (2010) 'Assessing the Performance of FOI in Different Countries'. *Government Information Quarterly*, 27 (4): 352–359.

Hazell, R., Bourke, G., and Worthy, B. (2012) 'Open House? Freedom of Information and its Impact on the UK Parliament'. *Public Administration*, 90 (4): 901–921.

Hazell, R., Worthy, B., and Glover, M. (2010) *The Impact of the Freedom of Information Act on Central Government in the UK*. London: Palgrave.

Heald, D. (2012) 'Why is Transparency about Public Expenditure so Elusive?' *International Review of Administrative Sciences*, 78 (1): 30–49.

Heclo, H. (1999) 'Hyperdemocracy'. *The Wilson Quarterly*, 23 (1), 62-71.

Hennessy, P. (1995) *The Hidden Wiring: Unearthing the British Constitution*. London: Gollancz.

Hennessy, P. (1998a) 'The Blair Style of Government: A Historical Perspective and Interim Audit'. *Government and Opposition*, 33 (1): 3–20.

Hennessy, P. (1998b) 'Re-Engineering the State in Flight: A Year in the Life of the British Constitution'. Lloyds TSB Forum, London.

Hennessy, P. (2001) *The Prime Minister: The Office and its Holders since 1945*. London: Palgrave Macmillan.

Hennessy, P. (2003a) 'The Long March? Whitehall and Open Government since 1945', in

S. Platten (ed.) *Open Government: What do we Need to Know?* Norwich: Canterbury Press, pp. 20–37.

Hennessy, P. (2003b) *Whitehall*, 2nd edn. London: Pimlico.

High Level Review (2003) *Report of the High Level Review Group on the FOI Act.* Dublin: Department of the Taoiseach. www.taoiseach.gov.ie/eng/Publications/Publications_Archive/Publications_for_2003/hlrgReportOnFOI.pdf (last accessed 12 October 2015).

Hill, C. (1991) *The World Turned Upside Down: Radical Ideas during the English Revolution.* London: Penguin Books.

Hillebrandt, M. Z., Curtin, D., and Meijer, A. (2014) 'Transparency in the EU Council of Ministers: An Institutional Analysis'. *European Law Journal*, 20 (1): 1–20.

HL 97 (Ad Hoc House of Lords Committee on FOI Bill) (1999a) *Minutes of Evidence: Professor Peter Hennessy.* Sessional papers 1998–99. London: HMSO.

HL 97 (Ad Hoc House of Lords Committee on FOI Bill) (1999b) *Report on the Draft Freedom of Information Bill.* London: HMSO.

Home Office (1978) *Reform of Section 2 of the Official Secrets Act 1911.* Commons Paper 7285. London: HMSO.

Home Office (1999) *Freedom of Information: Consultation on the Draft Legislation.* London: TSO.

Hood, C. (2006) 'Transparency in Historical Perspective', in C. Hood and D. Heald (eds) *Transparency: The Key to Better Governance?* (*Proceedings of the British Academy*, 135). Oxford: Oxford University Press, pp. 3–23.

Hood, C. (2007) 'What Happens when Transparency Meets Blame-Avoidance?', *Public Management Review*, 9 (2): 191–210.

Hood, C. (2010) 'Accountability and Transparency: Siamese Twins, Matching Parts, Awkward Couple?' *West European Politics*, 33 (5): 989–1009.

Hooper, D. (1988) *Official Secrets: Use and Abuse of the Act.* London: Cornet Books.

House of Commons (1998) *Early Day Motion 1589: Freedom of Information.* www.parliament.uk/edm/1997-98/1589 (last accessed 21 September 2015).

House of Commons (1999) *Early Day Motion 901, 19.10.1999.* www.parliament.uk/edm/1998-99/901 (last accessed 21 September 2015).

House of Commons Library (1997) *The Code of Practice on Access to Official Information.* House of Commons Library Research Paper 97/69. London: TSO.

House of Commons Library (1999) *The Freedom of Information Bill.* London: TSO.

House of Commons Library (2000) *The Freedom of Information Bill – Lords Amendments Bill HL 129 of 1999–2000.* London: TSO.

House of Commons Library (2004) *Collective Responsibility of Ministers.* London: TSO.

House of Commons Library (2014) *FoI and Ministerial Vetoes.* London: TSO.

House of Commons Library (2015) *Political Party Funding: Controversies and Reform.* Commons Briefing Paper SN07152 London: TSO.

House of Commons Library (2016) *Freedom of Information: Changing the Law?* Commons Briefing Paper SN07400 London: TSO.

*Huffington Post* (10/5/2014) 'Japan Wrongly Blames U.S. For Repressive Japanese Secrecy Law'.

ICO (Information Commissioner's Office) (2014) *Annual Track.* https://ico.org.uk/

media/about-the-ico/documents/1043485/annual-track-september-2014-individuals. pdf (last accessed 1 November 2015).

ICO (Information Commissioner's Office) (2015) *Working Effectively: Lessons from 10 Years of the Freedom of Information Act.* https://ico.org.uk/about-the-ico/news-and-events/ news-and-blogs/2015/10/working-effectively-lessons-from-10-years-of-the-freedom-of-information-act/ (last accessed 1 November 2015).

*Independent* (31/8/1997) 'Leading Article: A Chance to Open the Files'.

*Independent* (26/7/1998) 'No More Secrets Please!'

*Independent* (7/8/1998) 'Secrecy should Have No Part in a Modern Democracy'.

*Independent* (13/9/1998) 'The Vice of Secrecy at No 10'.

*Independent* (24/9/1998) 'Ashdown Warns Blair "not to betray voters"'.

*Independent* (28/9/1998) 'Labour Renege on Open Government: The Blair Government is a Bastion of Secrecy, No Different, if not More Sinister, than the Tories'.

*Independent* (5/2/1999) 'Access to Secrets will be Diluted'.

*Independent* (13/5/1999) 'Bill will Force Police to Give Information'.

*Independent* (24/5/1999) 'Will Jack Straw Go All the Way for True Freedom of Information?'

*Independent* (30/4/1999) 'Parliament Open Government-Information Bill More Radical than Expected'.

*Independent* (25/5/1999a) 'Anger at Feeble Secrecy Bill'.

*Independent* (25/5/1999b) 'Democracy is Poorly Served by this Disappointing Bill'.

*Independent* (25/5/1999c) 'Good Government Needs Scrutiny and Challenge'.

*Independent* (25/5/1999d) 'Information Bill Attacked as Toothless'.

*Independent* (27/9/1999) 'We've Seen the Caution, Mr Blair, Now Where is the Radicalism?'

*Independent* (11/11/2000) 'Straw Placates Peers with Stronger Freedom of Information Bill'.

*Independent* (15/3/2000) 'Ministers Face Backlash over Plans to Introduce Cabinet Government for Local Councils'.

*Independent* (7/4/2000) 'FOI is Ours by Right, Mr Straw, Not at Your Discretion'.

*Independent* (17/4/2000) 'Livingstone will Ban All Lobbying Firms from Greater London Authority'.

Independent Commission on Freedom of Information (2015) *Independent Commission on Freedom of Information: Call for Evidence.* London: TSO.

Independent Commission on Freedom of Information (2016a). *Independent Commission on Freedom of Information Oral Evidence Session: 20 January 2016 Transcript.* London: TSO.

Independent Commission on Freedom of Information (2016b) *Independent Commission on Freedom of Information Report.* London: TSO.

Informationage.com (4/7/2012) 'Francis Maude: "I'd Like to Make FOI Redundant"'. www.information-age.com/technology/information-management/2111138/francis-maude%3A-%22id-like-to-make-foi-redundant%22 (last accessed 20 November 2015).

Informationrightsandwrongs.com (8/11/2015) 'The First Time Parliament Heard the Term Freedom of Information'. https://informationrightsandwrongs.com/2015/11/08/ the-first-time-parliament-heard-the-term-freedom-of-information/ (last accessed 20 November 2015).

Institute for Government (2015a) 'FOIA Fighters: How Departments Dealt with Freedom of Information Requests in the First Quarter of the New Government', 25 September 2015. www.instituteforgovernment.org.uk/blog/12423/foia-fighters-how-departments-

dealt-with-freedom-of-information-requests-in-the-first-quarter-of-the-new-govern
ment/(last accessed 1 November 2015).

Institute for Government (2015b) *The Role of a Modern Cabinet Secretary.* www.institute
forgovernment.org.uk/events/role-modern-cabinet-secretary-conversation-sir-jeremy-
heywood (last accessed 21 September 2015).

Institute for Government (2015c) 'Under FOIA: Departments' Responses to Freedom of
Information Requests'. www.instituteforgovernment.org.uk/blog/10006/under-foia-
departments-responses-to-freedom-of-information-requests/ (last accessed 1 November
2015).

IPSOS/Mori (1991) *State of the Nation Survey 1991.* https://www.ipsos-mori.com/research
publications/researcharchive/2746/State-of-the-Nation-Survey-1991.aspx (last accessed
2 August 2016).

IPSOS/Mori (1995) *State of the Nation Survey 1995.* https://www.ipsos-mori.com/research
publications/researcharchive/2753/State-of-the-Nation-Survey-1995.aspx (last accessed
2 August 2016).

Ipsos/MORI (2013) *Public Awareness of Freedom of Information (FOI).* https://www.ipsos-
mori.com/researchpublications/researcharchive/3286/Public-awareness-of-Freedom-
of-Information-FOI.aspx (last accessed 1 November 2015).

Ipsos/MORI (2015) 'Politicians Trusted Less than Estate Agents, Bankers and
Journalists', 15 January 2015. https://www.ipsos-mori.com/researchpublications/
researcharchive/3504/Politicians-trusted-less-than-estate-agents-bankers-and-journali
sts.aspx(last accessed 1 November 2015).

*Irish Times* (7/10/1999) 'Information Act is being Abused Says Taoiseach'.

Jacobs, A. M., and Weaver, R. K. (2015) 'When Policies Undo Themselves: Self-Undermining
Feedback as a Source of Policy Change'. *Governance*, 28 (4): 441–457.

James, O., and Moseley, A. (2014) 'Does Performance Information about Public Services
Affect Citizens' Perceptions, Satisfaction, and Voice Behaviour? Field Experiments with
Absolute and Relative Performance Information'. *Public Administration*, 92 (2): 493–511.

*Japan Times* (24/11/2013) 'Cabinet's Approval Rating Falls to 57.9%'.

Jenkins, R., and Goetz, A. M. (1999) 'Accounts and Accountability: Theoretical Implications
of the Right-to-Information Movement in India'. *Third World Quarterly*, 20 (3):
603–622.

John, G. (2009) *Relations that Divide and Unite: A Study of FOI Legislation and Transparency
in Scotland.* PhD thesis, University of St Andrews, http://hdl.handle.net/10023/751 (last
accessed 2 July 2015).

John, P. (1999) 'Ideas and Interests; Agendas and Implementation: An Evolutionary
Explanation of Policy Change in British Local Government Finance'. *The British Journal
of Politics & International Relations*, 1 (1): 39–62.

John, P. (2014) 'The Great Survivor: The Persistence and Resilience of English Local
Government'. *Local Government Studies*, 40 (5): 687–704.

John, P., Worthy, B., and Vanonni, M. (2015) 'Parish Pump Transparency?' Paper, European
Consortium for Political Research, Montreal.

*The Journal* (Newcastle, UK) (29/5/1999) 'Straw Brings Down the Shutters on Clark's
Legacy'.

Judge, D. (1993) *The Parliamentary State.* London: Sage.

Justice Committee (2012a) *Letter from Rt Hon Tony Blair to Rt Hon Sir Alan Beith MP, Chair, Justice Committee, re: Post-Legislative Scrutiny of the Freedom of Information Act 2000, Dated July 2012.* www.publications.parliament.uk/pa/cm201213/cmselect/cmjust/96/tb01.htm (last accessed 1 November 2015).

Justice Committee (2012b) *Minutes of Evidence HC 96 – ii: Lord Hennessy of Nympsfield and Lord O'Donnell of Clapham.* www.publications.parliament.uk/pa/cm201213/cmselect/cmjust/96/120327.htm (last accessed 1 November 2015).

Justice Committee (2012c) *Minutes of Evidence HC 96 – ii: Jack Straw.* www.publications.parliament.uk/pa/cm201213/cmselect/cmjust/96/120417.htm (last accessed 1 November 2015).

Justice Committee (House of Commons) (2012d) *Post-Legislative Scrutiny of the Freedom of Information Act 2000*, volumes 1 and 2 (HC 96 –i). London: TSO.

Kane, J. (2001). *The Politics of Moral Capital.* Cambridge: Cambridge University Press.

Keane, C. (2008) 'Don't Ask, Don't Tell Secrets – their Use and Abuse in Organizations'. *Journal of Management Inquiry*, 17 (2): 107–110.

Keane, J. (1995) *Tom Paine: A Political Life.* London: Bloomsbury.

Keane, J. (2009) *The Life and Death of Democracy.* London: Simon and Schuster.

Keane, J. (2011) 'Democracy in the Age of Google, Facebook and Wikileaks'. www.johnkeane.net/wp-content/uploads/2011/03/democracy-in-the-age-of-google.pdf (last accessed 20 July 2016).

Kearney, G., and Stapleton, A. (1998) 'The Development of Freedom of Information Legislation in Ireland', in A. McDonald and G. Terrill (eds) *Open Government? Freedom of Information and Privacy.* London. Macmillan, pp. 167–179.

Keith, K. J. (1984) 'The Official Information Act 1982', in R. Gregory (ed.) *The Official Information Act: A Beginning.* New Zealand Institute of Public Administration, Wellington, pp. 31–45. http://ssrn.com/abstract=2340833 (last accessed 10 May 2016).

Keith, K. J. (1989) 'Seminar on the Official Information Act 1982'. Wellington: Institute of Policy Studies.

Kellner, P., and Crowther-Hunt, L. (1981) *The Civil Servants: An Inquiry into Britain's Ruling Class.* London: Macdonald Futura Publishers.

Kennedy, G. (1978) *Advocates of Openness: The Freedom of Information Movement.* PhD thesis, University of Missouri, Columbia.

Kenny, E. (2014) 'Speech by the Taoiseach, Mr. Enda Kenny TD, at the 15th Annual Philip Monahan Memorial Lecture, Friday, 31st January'. www.taoiseach.gov.ie/eng/News/Taoiseach's_Speeches/Speech_by_the_Taoiseach_Mr_Enda_Kenny_TD_at_the_15th_Annual_Philip_Monahan_Memorial_Lecture_Friday_31st_January_2014.html (last accessed 19 October 2015).

Kimball, M. B. (2012) 'Shining the Light from the Inside: Access Professionals' Perceptions of Government Transparency'. *Communication Law and Policy*, 17 (3): 299–328.

King, A. (1976) 'Modes of Executive-Legislative Relations: Great Britain, France, and West Germany'. *Legislative Studies Quarterly*, 1 (1): 11–36.

King, A. (1998) 'Why Labour Won – at Last', in A. King et al., *New Labour Triumphs: Britain at the Polls.* Chatham, NJ: Chatham House Publishers, pp. 177–207.

King, A. (2009) *The British Constitution.* Oxford: Oxford University Press.

King, A. (2015) *Who Governs Britain?* London: Penguin UK.

King, G., Pan, J., and Roberts, M. E. (2014) 'Reverse-Engineering Censorship in China: Randomized Experimentation and Participant Observation'. *Science*, 345. doi:10.1126/science.1251722.

Kingdon, J. (1984) *Agendas, Alternatives, and Public Policies*. Boston: Little, Brown.

Klug, F. (2010). 'New Labour and the Distribution of Power: Constitutional Reform, Human Rights and Civil Liberties'. *The Political Quarterly*, 81 (1): S78–S95.

Knill, C., Schulze, K., and Tosun, J. (2012) 'Regulatory Policy Outputs and Impacts: Exploring a Complex Relationship'. *Regulation & Governance*, 6 (4): 427–444.

Knill, C., Tosun, J., and Bauer, M. W. (2009) 'Neglected Faces of Europeanization: The Differential Impact of the EU on the Dismantling and Expansion of Domestic Policies'. *Public Administration*, 87 (3): 519–537.

Kosack, S., and Fung, A. (2014) 'Does Transparency Improve Governance?' *Annual Review of Political Science*, 17 (1): 65–87.

Kreimer, S. F. (2008) 'The Freedom of Information Act and the Ecology of Transparency'. *University of Pennsylvania Journal of Constitutional Law*, 10 (5): 1011–1079.

Kreiss, D. (2015a) 'The Networked Democratic Spectator'. *Social Media + Society*, 1 (1). doi: 2056305115578876.

Kreiss, D. (2015b). 'The Problem of Citizens: E-Democracy for Actually Existing Democracy'. *Social Media + Society*, 1 (2). doi: 2056305115616151.

Krotoszynski, R. J., Jr (2011) 'Transparency, Accountability, and Competency: An Essay on the Obama Administration, Google Government, and the Difficulties of Securing Effective Governance'. *University of Miami Law Review*, 65: 449-482. http://ssrn.com/abstract=2169055 (last accessed 11 October 2011).

Kuklinski, J. H., Quirk, P. J., Jerit, J., Schwieder, D., and Rich, R. F. (2000) 'Misinformation and the Currency of Democratic Citizenship'. *Journal of Politics*, 62 (3): 790–816.

Labour Party (1989) *Final Report of Labour's Policy Review for the 1990s: Meet the Challenge, Make the Change: A New Agenda for the 1990s*. London: Labour Party.

Lagunes, Paul (2006) 'Irregular Transparency? An Experiment Involving Mexico's Freedom of Information Law'. http://ssrn.com/abstract=1398025 (last accessed 5 May 2016).

Law Commission (New Zealand) (1997) *Review of the Official Information Act 1982* (R40). Wellington: Law Commission.

Law Commission (New Zealand) (2010) *The Public's Right to Know: A Review of the Official Information Act 1982 and Parts 1–6 of the Local Government Official Information and Meetings Act 1987*. Wellington: Law Commission.

Law Commission (New Zealand) (2012) *The Public's Right to Know: Review of the Official Information Legislation*. Wellington: Law Commission.

Leigh, D. (1980) *The Frontiers of Secrecy: Closed Government in Britain*. London: Junction Books.

Lemov, M. R. (2011) *People's Warrior: John Moss and the Fight for Freedom of Information and Consumer Rights*. Plymouth: Rowman & Littlefield.

Levine, D. S. (2012) 'The Social Layer of Freedom of Information Law'. *North Carolina Law Review*, 90: 101-142.

Lipsey, D. (2011) 'A Very Peculiar Revolution: Britain's Politics and Constitution, 1970–2011'. *The Political Quarterly*, 82 (3):341–354.

Lodge, M., and Gill, D. (2011) 'Toward a New Era of Administrative Reform? The Myth of Post-NPM in New Zealand'. *Governance*, 24 (1): 141–166.

Lopez, D., et al. (2002) 'Veto Battle 30 Years Ago Set Freedom of Information Norms: Scalia, Rumsfeld, Cheney Opposed Open Government Bill Congress Overrode President Ford's Veto of Court Review'. National Security Archive Electronic Briefing Book No. 142. http://nsarchive.gwu.edu/NSAEBB/NSAEBB142/ (last accessed 6 September 2015).

MacCarthaigh, M. (2005) *Accountability in Irish Parliamentary Politics*. Belfast: Institute of Public Administration.

Major, J. (2000) *John Major: The Autobiography*. London: HarperCollins UK.

Major, J. (2003) 'Afterword', in S. Platten (ed.) *Open Government: What Do We Need to Know?* Norwich: Canterbury Press, pp. 72–79.

Mandelson, P. (2010) *The Third Man: Life at the Heart of New Labour*. London: HarperCollins UK.

Manninen, J. (2006) 'Anders Chydenius and the Origins of World's First Freedom of Information Act', in J. Manninen (ed.) *The World's First Freedom of Information Act: Anders Chydenius' Legacy Today*. Kokkola, Finland: Anders Chydenius Foundation, pp. 18–56.

Margetts, H. (2006) 'E-Government in Britain – a Decade On'. *Parliamentary Affairs*, 59 (2): 250–265.

Margetts, H. (2011) 'The Internet and Transparency'. *The Political Quarterly*, 82 (4): 518–521.

Marquand, D. (1999a) 'Populism or Pluralism? New Labour and the Constitution'. www.ucl.ac.uk/spp/publications/unit-publications/46.pdf (last accessed 12 October 2015).

Marquand, D. (1999b) *The Progressive Dilemma*. London: Phoenix.

Marvel, J. D. (2016). 'Unconscious Bias in Citizens' Evaluations of Public Sector Performance'. *Journal of Public Administration Research and Theory*, 26 (1): 143–158.

Mathur, K. (2002) 'Good Governance and Pursuit of Transparency in Administration: The Indian Efforts', in P. Sahni and U. Murdury (eds) *Governance for Development: Issues and Strategies*. New Delhi: Prentice Hall, pp. 48–56.

Matland, R. E. (1995) 'Synthesizing the Implementation Literature: The Ambiguity-Conflict Model of Policy Implementation'. *Journal of Public Administration Research and Theory*, 5 (2): 145–174.

Matthews, F. (2015) 'Inaction and Reaction – Coalition Government and Constitutional Reform in the UK'. *British Politics*, 10 (3): 308–334.

McBride, D. (2013) *Power Trip: A Decade of Policy, Plots and Spin*. London: Biteback.

McClean, T. (2011) 'Not with a Bang but a Whimper: The Politics of Accountability and Open Data in the UK'. Paper, American Political Science Association, Annual Meeting. http://ssrn.com/abstract=1899790 (last accessed 20 July 2016).

McConnell, A., and 't Hart, P. (2014) 'Public Policy as Inaction: The Politics of Doing Nothing'. http://ssrn.com/abstract=2500010 (last accessed 5 May 2016).

McDonagh, M. (2003) *Freedom of Information in Ireland: Five Years On*. Report commissioned by the National Security Archive. www.freedominfo.org/2003/09/report-freedom-of-information-in-ireland-five-years-on/ (last accessed 20 November 2015).

McDonagh, M. (2010a) 'Access to Local Government Information in Ireland: Attitudes of Decision-Makers'. *Open Government: A Journal on Freedom of Information*, 6 (6): 1–20.

McDonagh, M. (2010b) 'The Impact of Freedom of Information on Irish Local Government', in R. Chapman and M. Hunt (eds) *Freedom of Information: Local Government and Accountability*. London: Ashgate Publishing Ltd, pp. 70-93.

McDonagh, M. (2013) 'The Right to Information in International Human Rights Law'. *Human Rights Law Review*, 13 (1): 25–55.

McDonagh, M. (2015) *Freedom of Information Law in Ireland*, 3rd edn. Dublin: Thomson Round Hall.

McDonald, A., and Hazell, R. (2007) 'What Happened Next: Constitutional Change under New Labour', in A. McDonald (ed.) *Reinventing Britain: Constitutional Change under New Labour*. Berkeley, Los Angeles and London: University of California Press, pp. 3–31.

McLay, J. (2012) '1984 and All That: Opening Address to the Empower NZ Workshop'. *New Zealand Journal of Public and International Law*, 10 (2): 167–187.

McMillan, J. (1977) 'Freedom of Information in Australia: Issue Closed'. *Federal Law Review*, 8: 379–434.

McMillan, J. (2002) 'Twenty Years of Open Government – What have we Learnt?' Inaugural Professorial Address to the Australian National University, 4 March 2002.

McNair, B. (2004) 'PR Must Die: Spin, Anti-Spin and Political Public Relations in the UK', 1997–2004. *Journalism Studies*, 5 (3): 325–338.

Meade, E. E., and Stasavage, D. (2008) 'Publicity of Debate and the Incentive to Dissent: Evidence from the US Federal Reserve'. *The Economic Journal*, 118 (2): 695-717.

Meijer, A. (2013) 'Understanding the Complex Dynamics of Transparency'. *Public Administration Review*, 73 (3), 429-439.

Meijer, A. (2014) 'Transparency', in M. Bovens, R. E. Goodin, and T. Schillemans (eds) *The Oxford Handbook of Public Accountability*. Oxford: Oxford University Press, pp. 507–524.

Meijer, A., Curtin, D., and Hillebrandt, M. (2012) 'Open Government: Connecting Vision and Voice'. *International Review of Administrative Sciences*, 78 (1): 10–29.

Meijer, A., 't Hart, P., and Worthy, B. (2015) 'Assessing Government Transparency: An Interpretive Framework'. *Administration & Society*. doi: 0095399715598341.

Michael, J. (1982) *The Politics of Secrecy: Closed Government in Britain*. Bury St Edmunds: Penguin.

Michener, G. (2009) 'The Surrender of Secrecy? Explaining the Strength of Transparency and Access to Information Laws'. Paper, American Political Science Association, Toronto Meeting. http://ssrn.com/abstract=1449170 (last accessed 10 March 2016).

Michener, G. (2011) 'FOI Laws Around the World'. *Journal of Democracy*, 22 (2): 145–159.

Michener, G. (2015a) 'Assessing Freedom of Information in Latin America a Decade Later: Illuminating a Transparency Causal Mechanism'. *Latin American Politics and Society*, 57 (3): 77–99.

Michener, G. (2015b) 'How Cabinet Size and Legislative Control Shape the Strength of Transparency Laws'. *Governance*, 28 (1): 77–94.

Michener, G. (2015c) 'Policy Evaluation via Composite Indexes: Qualitative Lessons from International Transparency Policy Indexes'. *World Development*, 74 (1): 184–196.

Michener, G. (2015d) *Why Policymakers Commit to Transparency: Legitimacy, Insurance, Monitoring and the Importance of the News Media as Mediator*. Global Initiative for Fiscal Transparency. www.fiscaltransparency.net/eng/resource_open_public.php?IdToOpen =20150702109 (last accessed 2 November 2015).

Michener, G., and Rodrigues, K. (2015) '"Who Wants to Know?" Assessing Discrimination in Transparency and Freedom of Information Regimes'. Fourth Global Conference on Transparency Research, Lugano, Switzerland, 4–6 June.

Michener, G., and Worthy, B. (2015) 'The Information-Gathering Matrix: A Framework for Conceptualizing the Use of Freedom of Information Laws'. *Administration & Society*. doi: 0095399715590825.

Milton, J. (1979) *Selected Prose*. London: Penguin.

Ministry of Justice (2010) *Information Rights Tracker Survey: Key Wave 14 Results*. https://www.gov.uk/government/uploads/system/uploads/attachment_data/file/217865/foi-tracker-survey-wave-14.pdf (last accessed 1 November 2015).

Ministry of Justice (2011) *Memorandum to the Justice Select Committee*. London: TSO.

Missen, A. (1984) 'Freedom of Information – the Australian Experience Lecture to the Campaign for Freedom of Information at the House of Commons, Westminster, 17th July 1984'. https://www.cfoi.org.uk/1984/07/freedom-of-information-the-australian-experience/ (last accessed 7 November 2015).

Moe, T. M. (2015) 'Vested Interests and Political Institutions'. *Political Science Quarterly*, 130 (2), 277–318.

Moloney, K. (2001) 'The Rise and Fall of Spin: Changes of Fashion in the Presentation of UK Politics'. *Journal of Public Affairs*, 1 (2): 124–135.

Moon, J. (1984) 'Freedom of Information Act: A Fundamental Contradiction', *The American University Law Review*, 34: 1157–1189.

Moore, C. (2013) *Margaret Thatcher: The Authorized Biography*, volume 1: *Not for Turning*. London: Penguin UK.

Moore, C. (2015) *Margaret Thatcher: The Authorized Biography*, volume 2: *Everything She Wants*. London: Penguin UK.

Morgan, K. O. (2001) *Britain since 1945: The People's Peace*. Oxford: Oxford University Press.

Morgan, K. O. (2013) 'The Left and Constitutional Reform: Gladstone to Miliband'. *The Political Quarterly*, 84 (1): 71–79.

Moss, G., and Coleman, S. (2014) 'Deliberative Manoeuvres in the Digital Darkness: e-Democracy Policy in the UK'. *The British Journal of Politics and International Relations*, 16 (3): 410-427.

Muck Rock (2016) 'Requester's Voice: Campaign for Freedom of Information's Maurice Frankel', 11 March 2016. https://www.muckrock.com/news/archives/2016/mar/11/requesters-voice-campaign-freedom-informations-mau/ (last accessed 20 March 2015).

Mullin, C. (2011) *A Walk-On Part: Diaries 1994–1999*. London: Profile Books.

National Centre for Social Research (2015) *British Social Attitudes Data*. www.bsa-data.natcen.ac.uk/ (last accessed 20 February 2016).

National Security Archive (2013) *Freedom of Information Regulations: Still Outdated, Still Undermining Openness*. http://nsarchive.gwu.edu/NSAEBB/NSAEBB417/ (last accessed 2 November 2015).

National Security Archive (2014) *Half of Federal Agencies Still Use Outdated Freedom of Information Regulations*. http://nsarchive.gwu.edu/NSAEBB/NSAEBB460/ (last accessed 2 November 2015).

Norton, P. (2013) *Parliament in British Politics*, 2nd edn. London: Palgrave Macmillan.

Norris, P. (1998). 'The Battle for the Campaign Agenda', in A. King et al., *New Labour Triumphs: Britain at the Polls* Chatham, NJ: Chatham House Publishers, pp. 113–144.

*Northern Echo* (16/2/2016) 'We Need to Shine a Light on our Masters'.

Nyhan, B., and Reifler, J. (2010) 'When Corrections Fail: The Persistence of Political Misperceptions'. *Political Behavior*, 32 (2): 303–330.

Nyhan, B., and Reifler, J. (2015) 'Displacing Misinformation about Events: An Experimental Test of Causal Corrections'. *Journal of Experimental Political Science*, 2 (1): 81–93.

Oborne, P. and Walters, S. (2004) *Alastair Campbell*. London: Aurum Press Ltd.

O'Connor, N. (2010) *An Economic Argument for Stronger Freedom of Information Laws in Ireland*. Think Tank for Action on Social Change Discussion Paper. www.tascnet.ie/upload/file/An%20Economic%20Argument.pdfOffice of the Information Commissioner (OIC) (2004) *Review of the Operation of the Freedom of Information (Amendment) Act 2003*. www.oic.gov.ie/en/Publications/Special-Reports/Investigations-Compliance/Review-of-the-Operation-of-FOI2003/Up-front-Fees.html (last accessed 2 November 2014).

Office of the Information Commissioner (OIC) (2008) *Freedom of Information: The First Decade*. Dublin: OIC.

O'Neill, O. (2006) 'Transparency and the Ethics of Communication', in C. Hood and D. Heald (eds) *Transparency: The Key to Better Governance?* Oxford: Oxford University Press, 75–91.

Open Society Justice Initiative (2006) *Transparency and Silence: A Study of Access to Information in 14 Countries*. Oxford: Oxford University Press.

*Oxford Mail* (16/11/2015) 'FOI: We Have a Right to Know How all Public Money is Spent'.

Pakanati, R. (2011) 'Window of Opportunity: Pre-Legislative Scrutiny and the Right to Information Act in India'. http://ssrn.com/abstract=2576158 (last accessed 15 May 2016).

Palmer, G. (2007) 'A Hard Look at the New Zealand Experience with the Official Information Act after 25 Years'. Paper, International Conference of Information Commissioners, Wellington. www.lawcom.govt.nz/ (last accessed 2 November 2015).

PASC (Public Administration Select Committee) (1998a) *Minutes of Evidence: Lord Irvine of Lairg and Sarah Tydesdale*. www.publications.Parliament.uk/pa/con199798/comselect/cmpubadm/398-v/398v01.htm (last accessed 2 November 2015).

PASC (1998b) *Minutes of Evidence: Rt Hon David Clark MP and Mr. Charles Ramsden*. www.publications.Parliament.uk/pa/con199798/comselect/cmpubadm/398-ii/398ii01.htm (last accessed 2 November 2015).

PASC) (1998c) *Third Report: Your Right to Know: The Government's Proposals for a Freedom of Information Act*, volume1 (HC 398-1). www.publications.Parliament.uk/pa/con199798/comselect/cmpubadm/39802.htm (last accessed 2 November 2015).

PASC (1999a) *Freedom of Information Draft Bill: The Committee's Response to the Home Office Reply*. www.publications.Parliament.uk /pa/cm199899/cmselect/cmpubadm/83.htm (last accessed 2 November 2015).

PASC (1999b) *Government Response to the Third Report on the Freedom of Information Bill*. www.publications.Parliament.uk/pa/cm199899/cmselect/cmpubadm/570/9072101.htm (last accessed 2 November 2015).

PASC (1999c) *Minutes of Evidence: Mark Fisher MP* www.publications.Parliament.uk/pa/cm199899/cmselect/cmpubadm/570/90622a01.htm (last accessed 2 November 2015).

PASC (1999d) *Minutes of Evidence: The Rt. Hon Jack Straw MP, Lee Hughes and Timothy*

*Middleton* (first hearing). www.publications.Parliament.uk/pa/cm199899/cmselect/cmpubadm/570/90622a01.htm (last accessed 2 November 2015).

PASC (1999e) *Minutes of Evidence: The Rt. Hon Jack Straw MP, Lee Hughes and Timothy Middleton* (second hearing). www.publications.Parliament.uk/pa/cm199899/cmselect/cmpubadm/570/90622a01.htm (last accessed 2 November 2015).

PASC (1999f) *Third Report: The Draft Freedom of Information Bill.* www.publications.Parliament.uk/pa/cm199899/cmselect/cmpubadm/570/57002.htm (last accessed 2 November 2015).

PASC (2002) *Minutes of Evidence Sir Richard Wilson GCB, Secretary of the Cabinet and Head of the Home Civil Service, 14 March 2002.*www.publications.parliament.uk/pa/cm200102/cmselect/cmpubadm/303/2031401.htm (last accessed 2 November 2015).

Pasquier, M., and Villeneuve, J.-P. (2007) 'Organizational Barriers to Transparency: A Typology and Analysis of Organizational Behaviour Tending to Prevent or Restrict Access to Information'. *International Review of Administrative Sciences*, 73 (1): 147–162.

Patashnik, E. M., and Zelizer, J. E. (2013) 'The Struggle to Remake Politics: Liberal Reform and the Limits of Policy Feedback in the Contemporary American State'. *Perspectives on Politics*, 11 (4): 1071–1087.

Paterson, M., and McDonagh, M. (2010) 'Freedom of Information: Taking Account of the Circumstances of Individual Applicants'. Monash University Faculty of Law Legal Studies Research Paper No. 2010/60. http://ssrn.com/abstract=1960306 (last accessed 8 March 2016).

Patterson, J. T. (1996) *Grand Expectations: The United States, 1945–1974*. Oxford: Oxford University Press.

Pattie, C., and Johnston, R. (2012) 'The Electoral Impact of the UK 2009 MPs' Expenses Scandal'. *Political Studies*, 60 (4): 730–750.

Paxman, J. (2003) *The Political Animal: An Anatomy*. London: Penguin Ltd.

PCA (Parliamentary Commissioner for Administration) (2005) *Access to Official Information: Monitoring the Non-Statutory Code of Practice 1994–2005*. www.official-documents.co.uk/document/hc0506/hc00/0059/0059.pdf (last accessed 16 May 2006).

Peisakhin, L. (2012) 'Transparency and Corruption: Evidence from India'. *Journal of Law and Economics*, 55 (1): 129–149.

Peled, A. (2011) 'When Transparency and Collaboration Collide: The USA Open data Program'. *Journal of the American Society for Information Science and Technology*, 62 (11): 2085–2094.

Peled, R., and Rabin, Y. (2010) 'The Constitutional Right to Information'. *Columbia Human Rights Law Review*, 42 (2). http://ssrn.com/abstract=1706606 (last accessed 6 November 2015).

Peters, B. G., Pierre, J., and King, D. S. (2005) 'The Politics of Path Dependency: Political Conflict in Historical Institutionalism'. *Journal of Politics*, 67 (4): 1275–1300.

Pierson, P. (1994) *Dismantling the Welfare State? Reagan, Thatcher and the Politics of Retrenchment*. Cambridge: Cambridge University Press.

Pierson, P. (1996) 'The New Politics of the Welfare State'. *World Politics*, 48 (2): 143-179.

Pierson, P. (2000) 'Increasing Returns, Path Dependence, and the Study of Politics'. *American Political Science Review*, 94 (2): 251–267.

Pierson, P. (2015) 'Power and Path Dependence', in J. Mahoney and K. Thelen (eds)

*Advances in Comparative-Historical Analysis*. Cambridge: Cambridge University Press, pp. 123–147.

Piotrowksi, S. J. (2009) 'Is Transparency Sustainable?' *Public Administration Review*, 69 (2): 359–361.

Piotrowksi, S. J. (2010) 'The Operationalization of Municipal Transparency: Primary Administrative Functions and Intervening Factors'. *Transparencia y Privacidad*, 1. www.transparenciayprivacidad.org.mx/numero_1/articulos_1_in.html (last accessed 12 November 2015).

Polisblog (2014) 'Che fine ha fatto il FOIA promesso da Matteo Renzi?' www.polisblog.it/post/256806/che-fine-ha-fatto-il-foia-promesso-da-matteo-renzi-da-digit14-la-domanda-al-premier (last accessed 12 November 2015).

Polling Report (2015) 'BC News/Wall Street Journal Poll', 15-18 October 2015. www.pollingreport.com/hrc.htm (last accessed 12 May 2016).

Ponting, Clive (1986) *Whitehall: Tragedy and Farce*. London: Sphere Books.

Popper, K. R. (2002) *Conjectures and Refutations: The Growth of Scientific Knowledge*. London: Psychology Press.

Popple, J. (2014) 'The OAIC FOI Experiment'. *AIAL Forum*, 78: 31–43. http://ssrn.com/abstract=2542101 (last accessed 5 May 2016).

Powell, J. (2010) *The New Machiavelli: How to Wield Power in the Modern World*. London: Random House.

Pozen, D. (2013) 'The Leaky Leviathan: Why the Government Condemns and Condones Unlawful Disclosures of Information'. *Harvard Law Review*, 127: 512–635. http://ssrn.com/abstract=2223703 (last accessed 14 March 2016).

Prat, A. (2005) 'The Wrong Kind of Transparency', *American Economic Review*, 95 (3): 862-877.

Price, S. (2006) 'The Official Information Act: A Window on Government or Curtains Drawn?' New Zealand Centre for Public Law Occasional Paper. www.medialawjournal.co.nz/downloads/OP_Price.pdf (last accessed 20 March 2016).

Prime Minister's Office (29/5/2010) 'PM's Podcast on Transparency'.

Pupillo, T. D. (1993) 'Changing Weather Forecast: Government in the Sunshine in the 1990's: An Analysis of State Sunshine Laws', *Washington University Law Quarterly*, 71: 1165–1187.

Raag/CES (Right to Information Assessment and Analysis Group and Centre for Equity Studies) (2014) *Peoples' Monitoring of the RTI Regime in India 2011–13*. New Delhi: NCPRI.

Raag/NCPRI (Right to Information Assessment and Analysis Group and National Campaign for People's Right to Information) (2009) *Safeguarding the Right to Information – Report of the People's RTI Assessment 2008*. New Delhi: NCPRI.

Radio Canada International (3/4/2013) 'New Poll is Bad News for the Harper Government'.

Rawnsley, A. (2000) *Servants of the People: The Inside Story of New Labour*. London: Hamish Hamilton Ltd.

Rawnsley, A. (2010) *The End of the Party*. London: Penguin UK.

Rees, M. (1987) 'The Parameters of Politics', in R. Chapman and M. Hunt (eds) *Open Government*. New York: Croom Helm, pp. 31–38.

Rentoul, J. (2001) *Tony Blair: Prime Minister*. London: Warner Books.

Reuters (9/12/2013) 'Japan PM Abe's Ratings Slide after State Secrets Act'.

Reuters (27/2/2016) 'Clinton Deflects Calls to Release Wall Street Speech Transcripts'.

*R (Evans) v Attorney General* (2015) UKSC 21. https://www.supremecourt.uk/cases/docs/uksc-2014-0137-press-summary.pdf (last accessed 1 November 2015).

Richards, D., and Smith, M. J. (2015) 'In Defence of British Politics against the British Political Tradition'. *The Political Quarterly*, 86 (1): 41–51.

Richter, P., and Wilson, R. (2013) '"It's the Tip of the Iceberg": The Hidden Tensions between Theory, Policy and Practice in the Management of Freedom of Information in English Local Government Bodies – Evidence from a Regional Study'. *Public Money & Management*, 33 (3): 177–184.

Richards, D., Blunkett, D., and Mathers, H. (2008) 'Old and New Labour Narratives of Whitehall: Radicals, Reactionaries and Defenders of the Westminster Model'. *The Political Quarterly*, 79 (4): 488-498.

Riddell, P. (2005) *The Unfulfilled Prime Minister: Tony Blair's Quest for a Legacy*. London: Politico's.

Roberts, A. (1998) 'Limited Access: Assessing the Health of Canada's Freedom of Information Laws'. http://ssrn.com/abstract=2091495 (last accessed 13 July 2016).

Roberts, A. S. (2005) 'Spin Control and Freedom of Information: Lessons for the United Kingdom from Canada'. *Public Administration*, 83 (1): 1–23.

Roberts, A. S. (2006) *Blacked Out: Government Secrecy in the Information Age*. Cambridge: Cambridge University Press.

Roberts, A. S. (2010) 'A Great and Revolutionary Law? The First Four Years of India's Right to Information Act'. *Public Administration Review*, 70 (6): 925–933.

Roberts, A. S. (2012) '"Transparency in Troubled Times": Tenth World Conference of the International Ombudsman Institute; Suffolk University Law School Research Paper 12-35.

Roberts, A. S. (2015a) *Promoting Fiscal Openness*. http://ssrn.com/abstract=2608967 (last accessed 14 July 2016).

Roberts, A. S. (2015b) 'Too Much Transparency? How Critics of Openness Misunderstand Administrative Development'. Fourth Global Conference on Transparency Research, Lugano, Switzerland, 4–6 June. http://ssrn.com/abstract=2601356 (last accessed 5 December 2015).

Robertson, K. G. (1982) *Public Secrets: A Study in the Development of Government Secrecy*. London: Macmillan Press.

Robertson, K. G. (1999) *Secrecy and Open Government: Why Governments Want You to Know*. London: Macmillan Press.

Rogers, A. (1997) *Secrecy and Power in the British State: A History of the Official Secrets Act*. London: Pluto Press.

Rowat, D. C. (ed.) (1979) *Administrative Secrecy in Developed Countries*. London: Macmillan.

Ruijer E., and Meijer, A. (2016) 'National Transparency Regimes: Rules or Principles? A Comparative Analysis of the United States and The Netherlands' *International Journal of Public Administration*, 39 (11): 895-908 .

Russell, M. (2013) *The Contemporary House of Lords: Westminster Bicameralism Revived*. Oxford: Oxford University Press.

Russell, M., and Cowley, P. (2015) 'The Policy Power of the Westminster Parliament: The "Parliamentary State" and the Empirical Evidence'. *Governance*, 29 (1): 121–137.

Russell, M., and Sciara, M. (2008) 'The Policy Impact of Defeats in the House of Lords'. *The British Journal of Politics & International Relations*, 10 (4): 571–589.

Sanders, D. (1998) 'The New Electoral Battleground', in A. King et al., *New Labour Triumphs: Britain at the Polls*. Chatham, NJ: Chatham House Publishers, pp. 209–248.

Scalia, A. (1982) 'The Freedom of Information Act has no Clothes'. *Regulation*, 6: 14–19.

Scammell, M. (2001) 'The Media and Media Management', in A. Seldon (ed.) *The Blair Effect*. St Ives: Little, Brown and Co., pp. 509–534.

Schudson, M. (2010) 'Political Observatories, Databases & News in the Emerging Ecology of Public Information'. *Daedalus*, 139 (2): 100–109.

Schudson, M. (2013a) 'Origins of the Freedom of Information Act in the United States', in N. Bowles, J. T. Hamilton and D. Levy (eds) *Transparency in Politics and the Media: Accountability and Open Government*. Oxford: I. B. Tauris, pp. 1–19.

Schudson, M. (2013b) "Reluctant Stewards: Journalism in a Democratic Society'. *Daedalus*, 142 (2): 159–176.

Schudson, M. (2015) *The Rise of the Right to Know: Politics and the Culture of Transparency, 1945–1975*. Cambridge, MA: Harvard University Press.

Scottish Information Commissioner (2015) *2014/2015 Annual Report*. www.itspublicknowl edge.info/home/SICReports/AnnualReport201415.aspx (last accessed 1 November 2015).

Scrollini, F. A. (2013) 'Transparency Arenas: A Framework'. http://ssrn.com/abstract= 2352003 (last accessed 5 March 2016).

Seldon, A. (1997) *Major: A Political Life*. London: Phoenix.

Seldon, A. (2001) 'The Net Blair Effect', in A. Seldon (ed.) *The Blair Effect: The Blair Government 1997–2001*. St Ives: Little, Brown and Co., pp. 593–601.

Seldon, A. (2004) *Blair*. London: Phoenix.

Shankar, S., Gaiha, R., and Jha, R. (2011) 'Information, Access and Targeting: The National Rural Employment Guarantee Scheme in India'. *Oxford Development Studies*, 39 (1): 69–95.

Sharma, P. (2015) *Democracy and Transparency in the Indian State: The Making of the Right to Information Act*. London: Routledge.

Shepherd, E., Stevenson, A., and Flinn, A. (2011) 'Records Management in English Local Government: The Effect of Freedom of Information'. *Records Management Journal*, 21 (2): 122–134.

Shroffs, M. (2005) 'The Official Information Act and Privacy: New Zealand's Story'. Paper, Freedom of Information Live, London. www.privacy.org.nz/assets/Files/67725421.pdf.

Simmel, G. (1906) 'The Sociology of Secrecy and of Secret Societies'. *The American Journal of Sociology*, 11 (4): 441–498.

Singh, S. (2005) 'The Notion of Transparency', in 'Speaking Truth to Power: A Symposium on People's Right to Information'. www.india-seminar.com/2005/551/551%20 shekhar%20singh.htm (last accessed 7 September 2015).

Singh, S. (2007) 'India: Grassroots Initiatives', in A. Florini (ed.) *The Right to Know: Transparency for an Open World*. New York: Columbia University Press, pp. 19–54.

Singh, S. (2011) 'The Genesis and Evolution of the Right to Information Regime in India', in

S. Singh et al. (eds) *Transparent Governance in South Asia.* Delhi: The Indian Institute of Public Administration. www.iipa.org.in/www/iipalibrary/transparentgovernance.iipali brary.in/index.html (last accessed 7 September 2015).

Smookler, J. (2006) 'Making a Difference? The Effectiveness of Pre-Legislative Scrutiny'. *Parliamentary Affairs,* 59 (3): 522–535.

Snell, R. (2000) The Kiwi Paradox: A Comparison of Freedom of Information in Australia and New Zealand. *Federal Law Review,* 28 (3): 575-616.

Snell, R. (2001) 'Freedom of Information: The Experience of the Australian States – an Epiphany'. *Federal Law Review,* 29 (3): 343-358.

Snell, R. (2002) 'FoI and the Delivery of Diminishing Returns, or How Spin-Doctors and Journalists have Mistreated a Volatile Reform'. *The Drawing Board: An Australian Review of Public Affairs,* 3 (2): 187-207.

Snell, R. (2006) 'Freedom of Information Practices'. *Agenda,* 13 (4): 291–307.

Soss, J., and Moynihan, D. P. (2014) 'Policy Feedback and the Politics of Administration'. *Public Administration Review,* 74 (3): 320–332.

Spence, K. (2010) *Volunteering Information? The Use of Freedom of Information Laws by the Third Sector in Scotland: Survey Findings.* Glasgow: University of Strathclyde.

Spence, M. (1973) 'Job Market Signaling'. *The Quarterly Journal of Economics,* 87 (3): 355-374.

Spence, M. (2002) 'Signaling in Retrospect and the Informational Structure of Markets'. *The American Economic Review,* 92 (3): 434-459.

SSCCLA (Senate Standing Committee on Constitutional and Legal Affairs) (1978) *Freedom of Information, Report by the Senate Standing Committee on Constitutional and Legal Affairs on the Freedom of Information Bill 1978, and Aspects of the Archives Bill 1978.* Canberra: AGPS.

Stasavage, D. (2006) 'Does Transparency Make a Difference? The Example of the European Council of Ministers'. *Proceedings of the British Academy.* http://as.nyu.edu/docs/ IO/5395/transparency.pdf (last accessed 12 June 2016).

Stasavage, D. (2007) 'Polarization and Publicity: Rethinking the Benefits of Deliberative Democracy'. *Journal of Politics,* 69 (1): 59–72.

Stiglitz, J. (1999) 'On Liberty, the Right to Know, and Public Discourse: Transparency in Public Life'. Amnesty International Lecture, 27 January 1999. www.internationalbudget. org/wp-content/uploads/On-Liberty-the-Right-to-Know-and-Public-Discourse-The-Role-of-Transparency-in-Public-Life.pdf (last accessed 18 June 2016).

Stiglitz, J. (2002) *Transparency in Government: The Right to Tell.* Washington DC: World Bank.

Stolz, B. (1999) 'Congress, Symbolic Politics and the Evolution of 1994 "Violence Against Women Act"'. *Criminal Justice Policy Review,* 10 (3): 401–427.

Stolz, B. (2007) 'Interpreting the US Human Trafficking Debate through the Lens of Symbolic Politics'. *Law & Policy,* 29 (3): 311–338.

Straw, J. (1999a) 'Rights and Responsibilities in the New Democracy'. Constitution Unit Annual Lecture 1999, 27 October 1999. https://www.ucl.ac.uk/spp/publications/unit-publications/53.pdf (last accessed 12 September 2015).

Straw, J. (1999b) Speech by the Rt Hon. Jack Straw MP, Home Secretary, at the Campaign for Freedom of Information's annual awards ceremony, 7 June 1999. https://www.cfoi. org.uk/1999/06/speech-by-the-rt-hon-jack-straw-mp-home-secretary-at-the-campaign-for-freedom-of-informations-annual-awards-ceremony-7-june-1999/ (last accessed 12 September 2015).

Straw, J. (2010) 'New Labour, Constitutional Change and Representative Democracy'. *Parliamentary Affairs*, 63 (2): 356–368.

Straw, J. (2012) *Last Man Standing*. London: Macmillan.

Stubbs, R. (2008) 'Freedom of Information and Democracy in Australia and Beyond'. *Australian Journal of Political Science*, 43 (4): 667–684.

Stubbs, R., and Snell, R. (2014) 'Pluralism in FOI Law Reform: Comparative Analysis of China, Mexico and India'. *The University of Tasmania Law Review*, 33 (1): 141–164.

*Sun* (21/1/2016) 'FOI Class Act'.

*Sun* (14/2/2016) 'Britain has Sinister Cover-Up Fetish … We Must Fight It'.

*Sun* (14/4/2016) 'Sick Mo Gets a Whipping'.

Taylor, J., and Burt, E. (2010) 'How do Public Bodies Respond to Freedom of Information Legislation? Administration, Modernisation and Democratisation'. *Policy & Politics*, 38 (1): 119–134.

Terrill, G. (2000) *Secrecy and Openness: The Federal Government from Menzies to Whitlam and Beyond*. Melbourne: Melbourne University Press.

Thatcher, M. (1995) *The Path to Power*. London: Macmillan.

Theakston, K. (1992) *The Labour Party and Whitehall*. London: Routledge.

Theakston, K. (2005) 'Prime Ministers and the Constitution: Attlee to Blair'. *Parliamentary Affairs*, 58 (1): 17-37.

Theakston, K. (2006) 'Whitehall and Reform', in P. Dorey (ed.) *The Labour Governments*. London: Routledge, pp. 147–168.

Thelen, K. (1999) 'Historical Institutionalism in Comparative Politics'. *Annual Review of Political Science*, 2 (1): 369-404.

*Thetford, Brandon and Watton Times* (13/1/2016) 'Suffolk County Council Dodging Paper Trail with Meetings'.

Thorpe, D. R. (2003) *Eden: The Life and Times of Anthony Eden First Earl of Avon, 1897–1977*. London: Random House.

*Times* (14/5/1999) 'Straw Wins Changes to Information Bill'.

*Times* (25/5/1999) 'The Need to Know'.

*Times* (5/4/2000) 'Mournful Ghost: A Labour Manifesto Pledge that has Been Quietly Strangled'.

*Times* (28/3/2015) '24 Hours with David Cameron'.

*Times* (8/12/2015) 'Greater Secrecy "will put Britain back in Dark Ages"'.

*Times of India* (12/10/2012) 'RTI should be Circumscribed if it Encroaches on Privacy: PM Manmohan Singh'.

*Times of India* (24/10/2013) '21 Year Old RTI Activist Chosen as Sarpanch'.

Turner, A. W. (2013) *A Classless Society: Britain in the 1990s*. London: Aurum Press.

Van de Walle, S., Van Roosbroek, S., and Bouckaert, G. (2008) 'Trust in the Public Sector: Is There Any Evidence for a Long-Term Decline?' *International Review of Administrative Sciences*, 74 (1): 47–64.

Vattimo, G. (1992) *The Transparent Society*. Cambridge: Polity Press.

Vincent, D. (1998) *The Culture of Secrecy 1832–1997*. Oxford: Oxford University Press.

Vivyan, N., Wagner, M., and Tarlov, J. (2012) 'Representative Misconduct, Voter Perceptions and Accountability: Evidence from the 2009 House of Commons Expenses Scandal'. *Electoral Studies*, 31 (4): 750–763.

Wagner, M., Tarlov, J., and Vivyan, N. (2014) 'Partisan Bias in Opinion Formation on Episodes of Political Controversy: Evidence from Great Britain'. *Political Studies*, 62 (1): 136–158.

Wald, P. M. (1984) 'Freedom of Information Act: A Short Case Study in the Perils and Paybacks of Legislating Democratic Values'. *The Emory Law Journal*, 33: 649-679.

Waller, P., Morris, R., Simpson, D., and Hazell, R. (2009) *Understanding the Formulation and Development of Government Policy in the Context of FOI*. London: Constitution Unit.

*Wall Street Journal* (10/2/2015) 'Dehli Elections Aam Aadni Party Sweeps to Victory'.

Webb, M. (2012) 'Activating Citizens, Remaking Brokerage: Transparency Activism, Ethical Scenes, and the Urban Poor in Delhi'. *PoLAR: Political and Legal Anthropology Review*, 35 (2), 206-222.

Weber, M. (1991). *From Max Weber: Essays in Sociology*, London: Routledge.

Weibing, X. (2010) 'China's Limited Push Model of FOI Legislation'. *Government Information Quarterly*, 27 (4): 346–351.

Welch, E. W. (2012) 'The Relationship between Transparent and Participative Government: A Study of Local Governments in the United States'. *International Review of Administrative Sciences*, 78 (1): 93–115.

White, N. (2007) *Free and Frank: Making the Official Information Act Work Better*. Wellington: Institute of Policy Studies.

White House (2009) *Memorandum for the Heads of Executive Departments and Agencies: Subject: Freedom of Information Act.* https://www.whitehouse.gov/the_press_office/FreedomofInformationAct (last accessed 2 November 2015).

Whiteley, P., Clarke, H. D., Sanders, D., and Stewart, M. (2015) 'Why Do Voters Lose Trust in Governments? Public Perceptions of Government Honesty and Trustworthiness in Britain 2000–2013'. *The British Journal of Politics & International Relations*. doi: 10.1111/1467-856X.12073.

Whitlam, G. (1972) 'It's Time: Whitlam's 1972 Election Policy Speech'. http://whitlam dismissal.com/1972/11/13/whitlam-1972-election-policy-speech.html (last accessed 7 September 2015).

Wilkinson, D. (1998) 'Open Government: The Development of Policy in the UK in the 1990s', in A. J. McDonald and G. Terrill (eds) *Open Government: Freedom of Information and Privacy*, London: Macmillan, pp. 13–25.

Willman, J. (1994) 'The Civil Service', in D. Kavanagh and A. Seldon (eds) *The Major Effect*. London: Macmillan, pp. 64–83.

Wilson, C. (2015) 'In the Beginning was the Request: A Street-Level Perspective on the FOIA Process'. Doctoral dissertation, Emory State University.

Wilson, D. (1984) *The Secrets File: The Case for Freedom of Information in Britain Today*. London: Heinemann Educational.

Wilson, D. (2011) *Memoirs of a Minor Public Figure*. London: Quartet Books.

Wood, A. K. (2012) 'Exposing Malfeasance: Government Transparency in the Fifty States'. Doctoral dissertation, University of California, Berkeley.

World Justice Project (2015) *WJP Rule of Law Index 2015*. http://worldjusticeproject.org/rule-of-law-index (last accessed 28 June 2015).

Worthy, B. (2007) *The Development of Freedom of Information in Britain*, PhD thesis, University of Manchester.

Worthy, B. (2010) 'More Open but No More Trusted? The Impact of FOI on British Central Government'. *Governance*, 23 (4): 561–582.

Worthy, B. (2013) '"Some are More Open than Others": Comparing the Impact of the Freedom of Information Act 2000 on Local and Central Government in the UK'. *Journal of Comparative Policy Analysis: Research and Practice*, 15 (5): 395–414.

Worthy, B. (2014a) 'Freedom of Information and the MPs' Expenses Scandal', in J. Hudson (ed.) *At the Public's Expense? The Political Consequences of the 2009 British MPs' Expenses Scandal*. London: Oxford University Press, pp. 27–43.

Worthy, B. (2014b) 'A Powerful Weapon in the Right Hands? How Members of Parliament have Used Freedom of Information in the UK'. *Parliamentary Affairs*, 67 (4): 783–803.

Worthy, B. (2015a) 'The Impact of Open Data in the UK: Complex, Unpredictable and Political'. *Public Administration*, 93 (3): 788–805.

Worthy, B. (2015b) *UK IRM Second National Action Plan Progress Report*. www.opengov partnership.org/country/united-kingdom/progress-report/2014-2015-progress-report (last accessed 13 May 2016).

Worthy, B., and Hazell, R. (2016) 'Disruptive, Dynamic and Democratic? Ten Years of Freedom of Information in the UK'. *Parliamentary Affairs*. doi:10.1093/pa/gsv069.

Wraith, R. E. (1979) 'United Kingdom', in D. C. Rowat (ed.) *Administrative Secrecy in Developed Countries*. New York: Colombia University Press, 1979, pp. 183–216.

Wright, T. (2015) 'Recalling MPs: Accountable to Whom?' *The Political Quarterly*, 86 (2): 289–296.

Wright, A., and De Filippi, P. (2015) 'Decentralized Blockchain Technology and the Rise of Lex Cryptographia'. http://ssrn.com/abstract=2580664 (last accessed 5 May 2016).

Yasseri, T., Hale, S. A., and Margetts, H. (2013) 'Modeling the Rise in Internet-Based Petitions'. http://arxiv.org/pdf/1308.0239.pdf (last accessed 12 March 2016).

YouGov (8/4/2016) 'Cameron's Ratings Now Lower than Corbyn's'. https://yougov.co.uk/news/2016/04/08/camerons-ratings-now-lower-corbyns/ (last accessed 12 May 2016).

Yu, H., and Robinson, D. G. (2012) 'The New Ambiguity of "Open Government"'. *UCLA Law Review Discourse*, 59: 178-208. http://ssrn.com/abstract=201248 (last accessed 12 January 2016).

## Interviews

Patrick Birkinshaw (2005).
David Clark (2015).
James Cornford (2005).
Mark Fisher MP (2005).
Maurice Frankel (2005).
Lord Goodhart (2005).
David Hencke (2005).
Jack Straw (2015).

# Index

EU authorised representative for GPSR:
Easy Access System Europe, Mustamäe tee 50,
10621 Tallinn, Estonia
gpsr.requests@easproject.com